No Going Home

Also by Toni Maguire

Don't Tell Mummy
When Daddy Comes Home
Helpless
Nobody Came
Don't You Love Your Daddy?
Can't Anyone Help Me?
Pretty Maids All In A Row
They Stole My Innocence
Did You Ever Love Me?
Daddy's Little Girl
Silent Child
Please Protect Us

No Going Home

A true story of childhood
secrets and escape

TONI
MAGUIRE

with Daisy Jones

JB

First published in the UK by John Blake Publishing
An imprint of Bonnier Books UK
4th Floor, Victoria House
Bloomsbury Square
London WC1B 4DA
England

Owned by Bonnier Books
Sveavägen 56, Stockholm, Sweden

www.facebook.com/johnblakebooks
twitter.com/jblakebooks

Paperback: 978-1-789-465-19-8
eBook: 978-1-789-465-20-4
Audiobook: 978-1-789-465-66-2

A CIP catalogue of this book is available from the British Library.

Design by www.envydesign.co.uk
Printed and bound in Great Britain by Clays Ltd, Elcograf S.p.A.

1 3 5 7 9 10 8 6 4 2

This book is a work of non-fiction, based on the life, experiences and
recollections of Daisy Jones. Certain details in this story, including
names and locations, have been changed to protect the identity and
privacy of the authors, their family and those mentioned.

John Blake Publishing is an imprint of Bonnier Books UK
www.bonnierbooks.co.uk

To my children, who grew up with me

Contents

Author's Note
from Toni Maguire

When I first received a message on my laptop from Daisy, it only took a few seconds for me to be gripped by her story. Unlike other lives I have written about, her early years were happy ones. Which, in a way, proves that the quote from Aristotle, 'Give me a child until he is seven and I will show you the man,' or in this case, 'a bright and well-adjusted young woman', has a lot of truth to it.

In Part One of Daisy's story, I show her happy years in the UK and how important they were. It was that time that gave her the strength to overcome the years that were far from the safe and secure ones of her early life. The second part of her story shows her touching relationship with her older disabled brother Tommy, a boy who was unable to either speak or walk, yet had an incredible amount of courage. As Daisy says, he refused to allow his disabilities to define him. I found their bond extremely moving, for when Daisy was a tiny child she was able to communicate with him using the sign language that he had invented.

I so enjoyed Daisy telling me some of the stories her mother told her about her teenage years. The music festivals in huge fields she and Daisy's dad went to, where up-and-coming rock singers entertained thousands of teenagers who turned up. Carefree teenagers who came to see their favourite bands while they danced until the early hours – it took me back to when I was one!

It is in Part Three, titled 'The Step-Father', that Daisy's life changes, and not for the better. Yet, to begin with, when she is barely nine, she manages to cope with extraordinary calmness. It is her brother she worries about much more than her own life.

As for the rest of her story, I don't want to spoil it by giving away too much.

In books that I write, I do try and cover certain themes and make certain points. In *No Going Home*, telling Daisy's story, I wanted to show to readers who are parents the long-time harm that watching porn does to children. It's a central part of Daisy's story and the experiences she is forced to participate in, and it's accessible on nearly all devices. You will see in this book how it has affected people, and I strongly believe that more needs to be done to block these sites for children.

I hope you enjoy reading about Daisy's story as much as I enjoyed writing it.

Toni Maguire, January 2022

There is another story linked to the one I'm going to tell you. It's about 'the boy'. I call him that for it was the name his stepfather gave him. He, I have also given no name to. I might have heard it, but I've erased it from my mind. For he doesn't deserve to have one. And even if he once had parents who gave him a name, in my wildest imagination I cannot picture him being christened in a church so I shall just call him 'the man'.

The boy cannot remember what life was like before his mother moved into the building the man owned. Miles away from the nearest town, with only a long, rutted path just wide enough for a truck to drive on, to connect them to the main road. With the thick undergrowth and woods on either side of it, few passers-by would have thought anyone lived there. Nor would they have been able to see the sweeping fields behind the building. In some, grazing cattle munched comfortably away, while others were planted with the man's crops. It was not corn or wheat that he grew, but leafy green marijuana plants. The boy was not to know what made his father's crop different from the other farmers', a mile or so away. But then when he was still little, he had no way of understanding that the house, infested with mice and spiders, was one that even the poorest families would not have agreed to live in. Outside the back door was a small hut that housed nothing more than an old, battered tin bath. It was there that the boy and his two younger siblings had their weekly bath. Without running water in the hut, it took a good many buckets, which had to be carried from the house, to fill it. Not that there was a proper kitchen inside; just several rooms, where in one a tap gave water and a camping stove was used to cook on.

The first sounds that stayed in the boy's head were not birdsong, nor the doleful echo of the cows mooing when they were led into the truck, but the screams of the woman he knew was his mother.

The one who cuddled him when the man was not around.

The one who told him to hide when the man returned home.

The one he loved.

I'm sure that once, before he came to live in the man's house, the boy must have had a few good memories of being tucked up in bed and sitting on his mother's knee for a cuddle. But once they moved in with the man, those memories were replaced with ones that only belong to our nightmares. The boy's first memory, the one he has never managed to erase, is the picture of the florid-faced man towering over his mother, bellowing drunkenly with rage. That night the boy had done what she had told him to do: hidden under the table as soon as he heard the truck's engine and stayed there until she knew just what his mood was. For the boy was only four, far too small to have the man's meaty fists connect with his small, vulnerable body. His young bones could break, while hers were stronger.

There were times when the man returned with good humour written on his face, a brace of bloodied rabbits he had shot slung over his shoulder and a bottle of whiskey held aloft for him and his wife to drink. Then the boy knew it was safe to crawl out of his hiding place and wait for the man to ruffle his hair and call him 'my boy'. On those nights, which his mother must surely have prayed for each day, his two siblings – one a toddler, the other still a baby – were allowed to sleep peaceably.

His mother's job was to skin and gut the rabbits, light up the camping stove and prepare vegetables and herbs to be added to the pot. The moment the scent of cooking meat filled the room, she would join her husband in sipping a shot of the whiskey.

The boy's mouth would water at the thought of the meal he was going to be given before he went to bed. For there could be days when the man was away and the only food in the house was the vegetables his mother grew in the dark soil at the back of the house. He had heard her asking the man to allow her to keep chickens for then there would be eggs for the children. His response was to laugh in her face before telling her that any chickens would be killed by the foxes living in the woods even before an egg was laid.

It was those times, when the man returned with money in his pocket and fresh food he had caught, that were the good ones. But on the night engraved in the boy's mind, within seconds of the door being opened and slammed shut, he heard the bellows of rage and knew the man was looking for any excuse to hit his wife. Cowering in the darkness under the table, he tried to close his eyes. He did not want to see the man's huge fists smashing into the woman he called Mum.

The only word coming out of the man's mouth he could understand was 'dirty'. The boy could not stop himself from seeing his mother being dragged by her hair from the room, hands raised to her head to try and protect it.

Just before that door too was closed the man turned. 'I can

see you,' he said, looking towards the table. 'Now you know what happens if you don't obey me.'

The boy stayed where he was, hands over his ears, head between hunched-up knees, trying to shut out the screams and sobs ricocheting off the walls of the ramshackle house.

That was the day when an unwelcome guest named Fear climbed up into the boy's head.

It was not an easy guest to evict.

That took a long time.

Part One

My Happy Years

1

My name is Daisy. This is my story. Though our personal stories are not ours alone, are they? For small children have no say in the direction their lives take. Even before they have learnt to walk and talk, they are trained to obey the demands of those charged with their care. For most of us, those demands are necessary ones as they help us grow and learn, establishing boundaries along the way. But for others, it takes the years between babyhood and becoming a teenager to realise just how wrong those demands have been. As it was for me, my early years where I had a wonderful family were happy ones. I felt loved and secure, I never thought all that was going to change; that there would be two big upheavals in my life that would rip away both my feelings of security and my happiness. But there are acts of fate that no one can foresee ... such as a mother wishing to move to the other side of the world.

'Better jobs and better weather,' she kept telling her husband, a man who did not wish to leave his family or his friends.

Had he not been so in love with Mum, we would never have left everything so familiar and dear to us. And then my mother would not have met the man calling himself The Bushwacker.

Which is why I say this is not just my story.

Part of it is Mum's, who with her long brown hair, large eyes of a deeper shade of brown and her petite figure, was what most men would describe as 'stunning'. Floating around in her boho-style brightly coloured clothes, she appeared to drift through life without a care. Whatever problems came her way, she always found an adoring male to look after her and protect her.

Five years before I came into the world, Mum gave birth to my wonderful, mischievous, plucky brother. He is someone I want to introduce you to. His name is Tommy and as you will come to see, he was an exceptional person.

Tommy's father, my mother used to tell us, took off the moment she told him she was pregnant. 'He wasn't very nice' was about all she said about him. Maybe that's how she felt then, for when for reasons I will explain later, she did have some contact with him, she told me just the opposite. But then that's Mum; her stories change with her moods. I'm still not sure what really happened.

I still don't know where she was when my older brother was born. All I've ever been told was that when Tommy was barely more than a few days old, he contracted Meningococcal disease, an infection of the protective membranes surrounding the brain and spinal cord. Watching him fight for his tiny life through the glass partitioning of ICU would have been traumatic for our mother, though maybe not as traumatic as when she was told that the inflammation on the brain could leave permanent mental or physical damage, maybe even both. I should think she just about went to pieces then and the waiting must have been terrible; watching for signs that would support her worst nightmares. These nightmares were confirmed eighteen months later when the doctors finally diagnosed Meningococcal disease induced Rett syndrome. Now not only would Tommy be unable to walk, several months later, they told our mother that he would never be able to communicate orally. The best he would be able to do was express his needs with a few grunting sounds.

I don't know exactly when it was arranged for him to learn to use what he and I called his 'talking machine'. To begin with it sounded really weird, but after a while I became used to it as did all Dad's family. My brother was so excited the first time he managed to crack a joke and we all laughed.

For Tommy, his condition was always going to be something that he refused to let define him. He also made up his own sign language, which I learnt to understand from my earliest days. I think I mastered his language of grunts and signs long before I spoke English and having this secret language made us even closer than most siblings. And when my brother was older, he fell in love with computers. They too became a way for him to communicate. Amazing with only one working arm, just how fast he could get his feelings and thoughts down on that screen.

So, as I tell my story and repeat some of our conversations here, there were many ways we had invented to have them. To me, Tommy spoke with clarity and depth, which is why he does within these pages. But for our mother, being a single parent with a disabled child, life was even harder. Her mother and sisters, wanting a life in the sun, had moved to Australia. Doubtless she would have followed them had she not been pregnant. When she received letters from her siblings telling her of the numerous job opportunities that offered twice the amount she would receive in the UK, the glorious climate where the sun shone nearly all year round, she came to believe that life was just great out there. Photographs accompanied the letters showing white beaches under a blue sky, as did pictures of her sun-kissed sisters, partying in the beach bars with bronzed surfer boys. 'You would love it here,' was the message on each one.

I'm sure well before she became pregnant with me, Mum simply yearned to join her family there but, much as she missed them, she cared for her son's wellbeing more. He needed his regular hospital visits, which helped with his special care. So, what did she decide to do? When Tommy was little more than a toddler, she looked up an old boyfriend from her teenage years. They had been a couple as far back as when they were in the same senior school.

Mum loved telling all about those times when she and Dad were together. According to her, they had been deeply in love right up until when she decided to leave the town they had grown up in. Not that she has ever given me an explanation as to what went wrong between them. Maybe it was simply because she just felt too young to settle down. I guess the wider world's promise of excitement once she entered it was just too seductive for her to ignore. Maybe she asked Dad to go with her to Australia and being content to stay where he was, he refused. Whatever the reason, it's never been a question I felt I could ask.

I do know that Tommy was still very young when our parents met up again. He can't remember much about that time, but he did have a few memories of the wedding. For it hadn't taken Dad long not only to propose, but also to state that he wanted to adopt Tommy and help bring him up as though he was his own son. A promise, which as my brother said, he has more than kept to. Dad loved both of us, we never had any doubt about that.

'I was so happy,' Tommy told me, 'when they both sat down with me and explained that they were getting married and that Dad was really going to be my father. I might have been little then, but I already loved him. All I could think of was that Mum and I were going to stay with him. And,' he added with a grin, 'there was a bit of a bonus – he was strong enough to carry me up the stairs and in and out of the bath. I had got too big for Mum to do that easily.'

'And what was the wedding like?'

'Full of people with big smiles, Mum looking pretty, and Dad? Well, he never stopped beaming.'

'So what happened then?' I asked, for what little girl doesn't want to hear about a wedding?

'Well, there was a party after the minister had said they were man and wife. Loads of speeches, really good cake and then music for them to dance to. Everyone made a fuss of me as usual. There I was, hardly taller than Dad's knee, dragging myself along on that little walker I had then – made it easy for them to pat my head.

'Nan and Grandad took me back to their house so that Mum and Dad could have a couple of days of holiday together. It was after the wedding that Dad told me he was now legally my father. And then what happened just when we were having a good time? Why, you came along! All cries and snivels. And let's not talk about nappy changing! That was really ugly. I asked them to send you back, you know?'

'You didn't?!'

'No, all right, I didn't. I thought you were the cutest little thing. So, are you satisfied now?'

'Oh, I knew that already,' I told him nonchalantly.

When I look back and try to picture the pair of us then, I can see Tommy's wide smile and hear him cracking jokes. He worked on his small frame to make the upper part of his body stronger, determined to keep up with us when we left the house.

'You don't need to slow down for me,' he kept saying as he swung himself along on his walker.

'Don't need good running legs to be top of my class,' was another one of his sayings when he was brought back from school. He might not have been able to play games but nothing stopped him from watching from the sidelines and cheering his friends on.

Yes, that was my brother, all right.

2

I found it hard to believe everything Mum told us about how wild their teenage years were. According to Mum that is, I never heard Dad say much about that time. Only the music he had liked, some of the bands such as The Rolling Stones that he had seen and of course how he had been over the moon when Mum agreed to go out with him again.

Mum, on the other hand, took a delight in reminiscing about their youth. She had photos she had kept of when they were teenagers (and had dated at school) and she loved telling us little stories about those times. Both of them looked so carefree back then, Mum in a miniskirt and a frilly, low-cut blouse and Dad in his bell-bottom jeans.

'I was a bit of a wild child then,' Mum told us when she fished out another photo from that straw bag of hers that always appeared to have bottomless memories. There she was in the picture with her hands held up to her face, showing both her silver painted nails and her lashes loaded with thick black mascara. 'The teachers were hardly pleased with me,' she said with a grin, 'not that they ever were really. I was certainly never going to be a teacher's pet. I was told to go to the loo and wash off my make-up. I think the teachers didn't like it that I only had to change my hairstyle or roll my skirt up to make it even shorter for all the other girls to want to copy me. I was definitely the trendsetter in our school, that's for sure.'

I knew that Mum simply loved reminiscing about those times. A whimsical smile would settle on her face when she described them, those worry lines that had appeared since then simply slipped away, leaving her looking more like the carefree girl in the photos.

Another photo she enjoyed showing my brother and me was the one of Dad astride a scooter – 'Your dad was part of a scooter gang back then. They got up to all sorts of mischief. All the girls fancied him, said he was cool.'

Looking at the picture of my father wearing an unbuttoned leather jacket with the collar turned up, his floppy hair and the devilish grin on his face, I could see why the girls had spotted that special something in him.

'Anyhow, I thought he was the best-looking boy in the school. All the girls wanted to date him. Hard to believe now that they thought he was a bit of a bad boy as well, isn't it?' she added with a tiny frown.

Not that I worked it out then. It took a few years for me to understand that the boy she had once been in love with did not really exist any longer. Once he might have raced around in a gang, gone to music festivals, smoked dope and knocked back beers when he was underage. But that was the boy he had been, not the man he had grown into.

Dad worked hard, he had a great group of friends who like

him had steady work and young children. Often we were all invited as a family over to their houses, especially during the summer months, for then there was enough space for all of us children to play outside while the adults cooked on the barbecue. Or rather the men did.

'The only time they ever do,' Mum said laughingly.

Tommy and I enjoyed those days when we met up with other children who I had known since I was born and my brother since he first lived at Dad's.

Yes, Dad was a man who liked routine, something I completely understand. Once a week it was the husbands' night out, most of them being his work colleagues. They all met in the local pub, played darts, had a few drinks and came home in, as Mum told me, a much better state than when they were younger.

The dads would also offer to look after the children if their wives fancied a night out as well. More often than not, Mum made an excuse not to go. From what I overheard, she told Dad that nice as the other women were, she just didn't have much in common with them. Anyhow, she liked staying home with all of us. A comment that pleased Dad. Though Mum enjoyed female company as much as she did being with the men. Not that she ever made an excuse when once a month the babysitter arrived. A restaurant had been booked, as had a taxi, for Dad would never drive if he had more than one drink. Mum's glossy hair would be freshly washed and I would smell her perfume which reminded me of spring flowers as she came to say goodnight and admire her floating pastel-coloured dress when she twirled around to show it off. 'Doesn't she look wonderful?'

Dad would enthuse and I could hear the pride in his voice as he whisked her off for what they called their 'date night'. On those nights she practically glowed, for she told me a long time later, those were the times when she could still glimpse the boy she had once fallen in love with.

'But it was only on those nights,' she added sadly.

Mum told me most of her stories when I was pretty young. Not that I can remember the order she put them in, mainly because she had a knack of repeating them with various embellishments added. As a small child, my eyes would open wide when I heard them. When I was a little older I came to realise she was using them to express how much she missed the boy Dad had once been and being young, wild and free herself – 'Oh, those were such exciting times!' she so often told me. 'There's nothing like those music festivals, where we camped out in the fields in a tent so small, we could hardly turn over. We cooked food on small paraffin stoves and didn't have to leave the site.'

To be fair, she did wait until I was entering my teens before she told me about the scent of dope perfuming the air at the festivals. 'We only had to sniff the air to get high,' she said with a giggle. 'And the bands were wonderful. They were up on that stage with the huge speakers blaring their music. Your whole body throbbed with the sound vibrations. We might have begun by sitting on the ground but it wasn't long before the music pulled us up onto our feet. Why, the whole area was full of our generation dancing away until dawn was breaking, it was all simply magical! Wish I had more photos of that time. I'd like you to have seen all of us, barefoot, in shorts or brightly coloured miniskirts. Some of our group had spent their gap year in India or Thailand and brought back some really amazing stuff. Bright floating skirts and embroidered Afghan waistcoats. Made me wish I could take off and visit those places as well.'

And as she spoke, I would see the dreamy look on her face which told me that it was a part of her life now missing that she would always hanker after. I sometimes wondered if Mum's life before Tommy and me had really been so carefree and perfect, or had those years simply been airbrushed with a golden hue? Oh, I knew she loved me, but I was never sure how much she loved the life that went with the responsibilities of being a parent whereas Dad seemed just as happy, although in a slightly different way than I had seen in the photos. I knew that Mum felt those were the best days of her life and she so wanted them back, while he was content with the life he had.

It was when she reached a part in our lives where she had some explaining to do that she told me about the parties, the cocktails they drank, the clubs they went to, the clothes they wore … in fact, just about everything except, thankfully, the sex they had.

There's only so much information a child wants to hear about their parents.

From what Tommy told me, when he first met Dad, our parents appeared happy together but then maybe it took her a while to get to know the man he had grown into. On the other hand, she had hardly changed, which I know was why his old love for her swiftly returned. Maybe because Dad was so happy to have her back in his life, he didn't realise she was still the same girl who had once walked into the wide world with scarcely a backwards glance.

Had he done so, he might have realised that one day she would seek out another adventure.

Because that was who my mother was.

Mum's family had clearly not given up hope that she would join them in Australia. They certainly tried every trick in the book to gain Tommy's and my interest, as well as hers.

To begin with, their letters came in packages stuffed full of alluring photographs of the family Tommy and I had never met. Judging by them, it appeared that winter did not exist on the other side of the world. No matter what part of the year those letters arrived, the photos were either of them sunbathing on a creamy white beach under a clear blue sky or taking part in a barbecue. One or two of the photos showed the glint of sun on their swimming pool, which caught Tommy's attention. As no doubt they were meant to, for swimming was one of the exercises he needed to strengthen his upper body.

'That's so cool,' he said, stabbing a finger where the edge of the pool was showing on the photo. 'Just imagine having that in our garden, Mum.'

'One day perhaps we will,' was all that she said but I could tell Mum was pleased by his remark. I understand now that she wanted her children to back her up when the time came for her to try and persuade Dad to take us there.

The photos that I was drawn to were of my three cousins in the wildlife parks. They were standing close to animals I had only ever seen in books. After a while Mum's family enclosed with their letters the Situations Vacant pages from the local papers. Large red circles were drawn around the ads they thought were suitable for both Mum and Dad.

If all that wasn't enough to keep Mum's desire to go to Australia foremost in her mind, it had certainly made Tommy and me eager to visit. I wonder which one of our family had thought about trying to get Mum's two children on their side. Then there were photos of the cousins we had never met, tanned faces smiling away into the camera as if they were saying to Tommy and me, 'Come on, you, we want to meet you!' They all looked such fun, we thought. And smiling back at their images, we in turn decided we both felt we would like nothing better than to join them on those miles of white beaches. Every time Tommy saw those fat letters with the Australian stamps and postmark arriving, he asked when we were going there to meet them all. Not that we understood that it was not just a visit Mum had in mind, but something far more permanent for the family.

Even when we heard her talking to Dad about the jobs they could both get there, Tommy and I thought that we would still stay with our grandparents at weekends and play with our cousins and Dad's friends' children. Neither of us understood what 'the other side of the world' meant in terms of distance. OK, we knew the only way to get there was by plane or boat but that meant little to us. Plus, Mum was careful not to say anything that would tell us that once we went there, it would be goodbye to everything that was familiar.

Once there, it was unlikely we would ever return. There would be no more staying at our grandparents' home, which Dad, Tommy and I loved going to. No more walks with Grandad, when he taught us all about nature. Even now when I look back to that time, I can remember how happy my brother and I were then. Dad's family was always so pleased to see us. They had given Tommy and me our own rooms too. Mine was decorated in pink and white and Tommy's had a Spider-Man bedspread. Some of our toys were left there, waiting for our return – as it seemed did Fred, their ginger and white cat that I loved playing with. The moment we entered the house, there he was, tail up in the air, purring away as he rubbed against our legs. All of that made us feel my grandparents' house was really our second home. For Dad of course, it was. On most Saturdays when we were there, his younger brother David would arrive with his two sons, Ricky and Daniel. Ricky was the quiet one who would chat away to Tommy, whereas Daniel, who was born just two days before me, was the one who enjoyed getting up to mischief. And didn't he enjoy teasing me because, as he kept saying, I was the younger one. His fingers would poke me in the ribs until we fell about giggling before a stern look from Mum sent us all out into the garden.

I have other memories of being there that I have managed to keep tucked away safely in my mind. There was the Sunday roast that Nan spent all morning preparing. Dad and Mum would help carry in all the items, such as her homemade horseradish sauce, and place them on the table. Grandad would pick up that special long carving knife of his, sharpen it on his steel and run the blade across his thumb to check the edge. Dad always said he got it so sharp, he could have shaved with it. The ritual over, Nan would place the carving dish in front of him and he would start carving the roast beef. Mountains of roast potatoes, Yorkshire puddings and an assortment of vegetables were waiting in serving dishes from which we could help ourselves. Often David and his pleasant, round-faced wife and family would be there as well and then the room just hummed with chatter and laughter.

Those were such happy times.

5

I don't think Dad was aware of just how much time Mum had spent showing my brother and me all the photos of her family's life in Australia. I suspect she was waiting for the right time to try again and encourage him to agree to go. I don't know if Tommy was as aware as I was that only one of our parents wanted to get on that plane that would take us to the other side of the world. What I do know is that my dad really liked his life in the UK. He felt settled there, he had a good job and a group of friends and a family he adored.

I overheard some of the conversations they had. Mum trying to tell him that we would have a better life over there and then there would be his voice giving her his reasons for not wanting to leave: 'I don't want to leave my life here. Look, I know I was a bit of a wild teenager and we had great fun all those years ago, but that's not who we are now, is it? We're adults now with two children to care for, one of whom needs the services the NHS provides.'

Trouble was, I don't think he got it – Mum was none too keen on being an adult.

The other argument I overheard one day made me feel really sad. I was at the top of the stairs, a good place for a small child to be, if eavesdropping is their aim. Dad was standing and Mum was looking up at him.

'Anyway, Liza, what about my mum and dad? You know how much they love both of our children. They'll be heartbroken if they're not able to see them. And what about me? Those aren't my relatives over there, are they? And I don't have any friends there but here I've some really good ones, lifelong friends that really matter to me. Ones that I've known practically since we were all in kindergarten. And you've also known some of them from when we were at school as well.'

Mum's answer to that was that she barely knew them because they weren't part of her group. 'Too busy studying,' she added with a light laugh, which contained more mockery than amusement.

'Oh, come on, Liza! They've all made you and Tommy really welcome, haven't they?'

'I suppose.'

Now you might have thought that after her days of being a bit of a wild child and then a single mother, Mum would have felt content just being with Dad. He had given her stability and his family had more than welcomed her into theirs. And I think for a while she was happy – that's until she felt that safety and comfort were just not enough for her.

More letters arrived. I'm sure that Dad wanted to toss them all on the fire, but being Dad, he simply handed them to Mum. More discussions bordering on arguments took place until gradually Dad looked as though he might be relenting. Not that

I knew then what I know now: that there was a reason he began to change his mind. In the early nineties there was a recession in the UK and although my dad was a skilled carpenter, work was tightening up as the building industry faltered.

It was then that Mum handed him the newspaper cuttings her family were still sending.

'Look, Peter, they're short of skilled workmen over there. Loads of jobs for craftsmen and look what the wages are. We'd be much better off, you know we would. And it's not like it was years ago either. When those early immigrants travelled out by boat, OK, they were unlikely to come back. But people travel everywhere now so we could too.'

'And Tommy's treatment?'

'They have wonderful medical care there – all the family say so.'

So in the end, we went.

When the man was away from the house there were times when the boy's mother read him stories from the books she had hidden away. He had been told never to tell the man about them, that they were their secret. The boy looked forward to those times when he sat as close to his mother as it was possible to get, feeling the warmth from her body pressed against his. She would hold the book between the two of them to show him the pictures inside its covers. It was the ones of trains, cars and animals that he kept asking to see over and over again. He asked her to read these stories so many times that he suspected she recited them without having to read the book. He had not known before that there were people who had pets in their homes and gave them saucers of milk to drink – he thought these creatures were only on earth to be eaten.

The pictures in the books were much nicer than the ones covering the walls of the house from top to bottom. The boy knew it was the man and not his mother who liked them. He had seen him paste them onto the walls. He asked his mother why those ones, which were in all the rooms, even the lavatory, were there.

'They're just wallpaper,' was the answer she gave him.

He wished he could ask the man why he did not bring home other pictures, like the ones he saw in his mother's books. He didn't though – he understood it would cause trouble.

And trouble meant the next morning his mother's face would be bruised.

He wondered where the stories that went with the pictures were. For except for a few big letters, there was no writing on the walls. It was when he looked at the pictures under those letters that he thought those naked men and women were playing some peculiar games. Some looked as though they were tied to chairs and beds, others looked even stranger, for they were lying on top of each other. He knew his mother did not like him looking at them, but when she was busy he would sit on the floor beside them and trace their outlines with his fingers until they took root inside his head.

As he grew a little older, he decided that the people in those pictures were ugly but that did not stop him having tingling feelings when he peered at them.

It took until he reached his fifth birthday for him to become the target of the man's rage. He was sitting on the settee next to his mother, holding the book she had been reading to him, when she heard the truck's engine and sprang up.

'Quick,' she said, holding out her hand, 'give it to me.'

Not understanding the importance of his mother taking the book from him, the boy clutched it tightly to his chest. It belonged to him, not her. For it was his birthday and hadn't she just given it to him? He heard the door swinging open and the second he looked up at the man, he knew he had made a mistake. He wished he had obeyed his mother, but it was already too late and the book was snatched from his hand.

The man turned a couple of pages then stabbed his finger on a picture of fluffy kittens.

'You turning that boy into a poofter,' he shouted before bending down so his face was on the same level as the boy's. 'A right little Mummy's boy you are, aren't you?' he snarled before straightening up as he lifted the boy up by the scruff of the neck and dumped him back down on the floor. 'You want to grow up to be a man, boy?' he shouted and laughed when he heard the frightened child's whispered 'Yes.' 'Mm, I don't think you do,' and drawing back his hand, he slapped him hard across his head.

The boy had seen his mother being beaten, but this was the first time the man's fist had connected with him. He could not stop the wail of protest from leaving his mouth nor hold back the tears that formed in his eyes and trickled down his cheeks.

It only took a second to realise that this was his second mistake.

'Stop your goddam snivelling,' the man shouted.

The boy lifted his hand to his face, brushed away the tears and tried to stand up.

A large hand descended on his back. 'Let's see what you're really made of then,' the voice above him grunted as he was pushed towards a door at the back of the room, one that was not much higher than the boy.

He heard his mother screaming at the man, telling him not to do it.

'It's your fault, woman. I'm not having any poofters growing up in my house,' he snapped. 'Take a look at your mother, boy, it's her fault you're going in there,' and, opening the door, the man pushed the boy through it.

The boy saw only darkness within before the man pushed

him inside. He heard the sound of the door slamming behind him, then his mother's voice pleading and more bellows from the man. Then there was silence.

He kept telling himself that the man would open the door and let him out. It was his birthday, he kept reminding himself.

He was hungry.

His stomach hurt and he wanted to pee so badly.

He managed to squat, pull his little willy out and released a stream of liquid.

Now the man would be even angrier with him.

Then he heard scuttling noises and knew that the mice were in there with him. He bit down on his lip and tried not to scream when one ran over his leg.

When was he going to be let out? He kept asking himself that question.

More tears came, until tiredness fell over him, his eyes drooped and then closed, and a restless sleep took over.

It was his mother who opened the door, letting harsh sunlight bring blindness to his eyes.

Reaching out her hand to him, she told him the man had gone.

This time he didn't want her to pick him up and cuddle him for hadn't the man told him that it was her fault he had been locked in that dark cupboard?

6

Once it was decided that we were going to move, Mum was like a small whirlwind, ordering big crates that were needed for shipping our possessions, sorting out what needed to go in them and what could be left behind and given away or taken to the tip. Tommy and I were given the task of deciding which toys and games we wanted to take with us. My brother chose Lego, which helped his arm movements, while I chose Snakes and Ladders because we liked playing that together; there were a few picture books and my fair-haired doll Belinda too.

Mum also put aside most of our winter clothes: 'We won't be needing that many coats and thick jumpers in the future,' she told us gleefully as she placed almost all of them in bags for the charity shops.

As soon as Dad told Mum that our tickets were booked and paid for, there were a few long-distance calls to and from her family, which made her simply glow with excitement. She kept telling Tommy and me how much everyone was looking forward to meeting us.

'You two are going to have such a great time, your cousins

have got loads of things planned for you,' she kept saying, 'and my sisters have for us as well, darling,' she added, beaming up at Dad.

'I'm sure from what I've been hearing about them, they will have,' he replied, although I felt that his response lacked some of Mum's excitement. He seemed more preoccupied with our last trip to his parents. For he and Mum had arranged for all of us to spend our last week with his family. As we were going to the airport from there, he had arranged for all our boxes to be collected the morning we set off to stay with them. As they were being shipped, they would arrive quite some time after we had. Mum kept reminding us that what went in the suitcases would have to do us until the freight arrived, reminding us that the seasons would be reversed so we would arrive in Australian summer, leaving behind England's grey winter skies and the sleet, snow and rain.

In the meantime, Dad's friends had busied themselves with arranging a farewell party for him and Mum. A large room in a nearby hotel had been booked so that, as they said, the whole crowd could be there.

Babysitters were arranged for Tommy and me. This was a grown-up do, we were told when Tommy protested.

'Don't you remember you had all your little friends over and I even baked a cake for you all? And didn't you promise to write to them and send pictures of what it's like in Australia?' Mum said to him.

'Yes.'

'And you had fun, didn't you? So, you kids, it's our turn now.'

Apart from Tommy complaining about the word 'babysitter' because even if I was still one, he wasn't, that was the end of that conversation.

*   *   *

The following morning, Mum came into my room to help me dress and while I went to the bathroom, she started packing a case of clothes to take with us to our grandparents and then on to Australia. Meanwhile Dad sorted Tommy out and carried him down to the kitchen.

She chattered a little about the evening before, while Dad remained ominously silent. He was, I guess now, realising just how much he was going to miss everyone. He would have known that their lives would carry on and the gap his departure made would be covered in time. I'm sure he was asking himself would the same apply to him.

That last day in the house was a blur. I only have a vague memory of all those boxes and some of the furniture being carried out into a big truck. Tommy told me later that he thought Dad looked totally miserable while Mum seemed really happy when she said goodbye to the house which had been her home for over five years.

The next thing I remember is arriving at Nan and Grandad's house and the warm welcome we received as they ushered us in. Outside the house was a white landscape and Tommy and I just wanted to go outside and scoop the snow up. Not that I knew it then, but this was to be the last time I was to feel cold for over ten years.

Uncle David was already there with his sons, so outside the four of us went and made a huge snowman. Later, carrying a bag of carrots less one for the snowman's nose, my uncle took us all down to feed the horses in a nearby paddock. The owners were friends of Nan and Grandad's and they were happy to let us feed them some treats.

I loved the way their velvety mouths gently nuzzled them from my fingers. The other happy memories I still have of that time were going to the shops with Grandad and spending time with Nan as she baked and cooked for our journey. She always loved spoiling me because although she loved her sons dearly, she would have liked a daughter as well.

'And now I have a lovely grandaughter, which is just as good,' she sighed, giving me a hug.

I also have a picture in my head of her cooking one of her lovely traditional English roasts. The whole family were there, which included my great grandmother as well. And finally, I still have the memory of feeling tearful when we all hugged each other goodbye.

'We'll be coming to visit you, don't you fret now, Daisy,' Nan told me.

Uncle David had kept Dad's car and was going to sell it for him. After endless goodbyes and hugs and a few tears we climbed into the large taxi and then we were on our way to the airport. Sitting in the back, I got onto my knees on the seat and waved away until we turned the corner and they were gone from my sight.

7

As my memory of the journey to Australia is rather sketchy I asked Mum what it had been like. When it came to her replies, I almost wished I hadn't! 'You were a little nightmare,' she told me. 'You wouldn't sit still for more than a few minutes. I don't know how many times you managed to unlock your seat belt. You just wanted to walk around everywhere and annoy everyone. The stewardess kept complaining as you wanted to wake everyone and chatter.'

So that's her memory, while mine is of sleeping most of the time. Though I do have one of us being in the airport before we left, where Tommy was placed in a wheelchair. Dad carried him onto the plane and made him as comfortable as he was able. The other memory is of the feel of the plane's noise as it went shooting up into the sky and Dad's knuckles turning white because he had gripped the chair arms so hard. When I turned my head towards him I thought he looked sad and I put my small hand over his for I had seen the same expression appear fleetingly on his face when he said goodbye to his parents. Oh, everyone was trying to stay smiling, making promises to visit when we were settled, and his brother was saying how wonderful it all sounded, but underneath they seemed sad. All his friends had told him they expected long letters showing them what life was like 'Down Under' as they called Australia. I might have been very young then, but I still knew that the only person who was truly happy about us leaving was Mum.

Whatever Mum says, I'm sure I did sleep a lot on that plane for the only other picture that I can find in my mind is the one of being in a big space where everyone looked different from us. There were hordes of small pretty people with black hair and dark eyes that slanted slightly, speaking a language that I couldn't understand a word of. Of course now they don't look strange to me at all, but then to a small child who had never seen them before, they did.

As I know now that flights from the UK to Australia often stopped in the Middle East and then Singapore, I asked Mum about that stopover. She told me it was Singapore. We wished we could have stayed there and explored the country a little, she told me. Not that we could have because Tommy was already very tired. We had to wait at least a couple of hours but got some really tasty snacks to eat, explored the huge airport a bit and freshened up. I wish I could recall some more about all of that! Not that I can recall the final changing of planes when we arrived in Australia either, though I woke up all right when Mum whispered in my ear that we were on our way to Byron Bay, where her family lived.

Tommy's eyes were shut: 'Don't wake him,' Mum said, 'he's very tired.'

*   *   *

If I can't visualise much of that journey, I can certainly remember meeting Mum's sisters, Gerry and Jenny, and my Australian grandmother – Gran – for the first time. I had seen photos of them so I just about recognised the group waiting for us, although if I hadn't, their shouts of 'Here you are!' as they rushed towards us would have told me they were Mum's sisters. Like my mother, they were both small and dainty, while Gerry, the youngest out of the three sisters, looked even more like Mum then I could have expected. Then there was Gran, who with her short blonde hair and brightly coloured clothes, hardly looked old enough to be called that.

There were certainly lots of hugs and exclamations about how much like Mum's family I looked, while Tommy was told how much they had looked forward to meeting him and that he was better-looking than his photos and how much he was going to love being there. And then Gran telling Dad that she could still recognise him from when he and Mum had been dating, back when they were still at school.

'You hardly look a day older, Peter,' she told him.

'Nor do you,' was his smiling response, which earned him yet another hug.

'God, you two look like twins!' he told Gerry and my mother when they stood next to each other.

Gerry laughed at that. 'So everyone says when I show them the photos of all of you. But wait till Liza gets some sun on her, then we'll look even more like twins. Now everyone's going to tell you're a group of Limeys! You're all so pale.'

'Plenty of relaxing on our beaches will do you all the world of good,' Gran added as she smiled at Tommy. 'You'll be just as brown as your cousins then. Anyhow,' she said, turning to Mum and Dad, 'let's get you all over to our house. I expect you're dying to get something to eat and get some rest.' And I knew from the concerned look she gave Mum that it was clear she thought Tommy needed it more than any of us. 'But give it a week and you won't recognise yourselves. Come on now, let's get you home, you must have had enough of airports.'

Our luggage was piled into their cars, then us, and off we went. Tired and flushed as he was, Tommy managed to smile when he stared out of the window. To think just over a day ago we had left a white England, where icicles hung on Nan's trees and bushes, and now we found ourselves under a blazing sun.

If everything was seeming unreal to me, it became even more so when we reached the edge of the rainforest where Gran, Grampy and Mum's sisters lived. I could hardly believe my eyes. There, almost in the lush green rainforest, as I was told it was called, was this weird-looking house that I thought at first was four different bungalows joined together. But no, it was one big house. Except instead of being able to walk from one room to another, we had to step outside, where the forest was only a few feet away, to reach them. When Tommy and I eventually lay down that night there was a chorus of the tree frogs filling the warm air with their chirpy croaks, lulling us to sleep. Tommy and I agreed that everything was simply awesome.

It was as though we had stepped into another world called Byron Bay.

8

I think we all had a wonderful time on those ten days we spent stepping in and out of a forest and sunning ourselves on the beach. I heard that some of the trips the family wanted to take us on had to be cancelled because Tommy was hardly up to moving far. It took him quite a few days to get back to being his normal perky self. The first few days, within a short time of being up, his eyes were drooping even though he did his best to keep them open. Even so, we really enjoyed ourselves.

The first night when he was put to bed, I wondered when he was ever going to wake up. I knew Gran was concerned for him by the amount of times she tiptoed into our room to check on him. Mum and Dad slept for hours as well. When it was explained to me that it's because we had lost ten hours and that everyone gets tired on that journey, I found that really hard to understand.

'Where have they gone?' I kept asking, no doubt leaving Gran wishing she hadn't bothered explaining anything to me. Not that I was tired when the sun's rays came into our room to tell me it was morning. I woke up full of energy so maybe my memory of the journey is the right one. Outside my window I could see green fronds brushing the windows and for a moment as I glanced around at a room I hardly recognised, I wondered where I was. As soon as I realised that I was in Gran's house, I swung my legs out of bed, trotted through the sliding door and went in search of everyone.

'Seems like small children don't get jet lag,' exclaimed Gerry when she saw me still in my pyjamas, wandering in.

'You hungry then?' Gran asked and in no time at all a bowl of fresh fruit and a crunchy cereal was placed in front of me.

It was Jenny, the middle sister, who told me that the house would not be quiet for long as my cousins were due back the following morning: 'They're looking forward to meeting all of you too,' I was assured.

There were three of them, red-headed twins, Jo and Sam, and a blonde-haired one who was around Tommy's age. I found out a bit later that they were staying at friends' houses so that we could all have a relaxing couple of days.

It was Gerry who found me a swimsuit and took me to the beach that morning. All I could see was what looked like miles of white sand and a sea so much bluer than the one in England. And the water was much warmer too, I found, when I went paddling with my water wings on my arms.

In fact, the journey had completely exhausted Tommy. All the trips that had been arranged were put off for a while. He was clearly not up to them and he could not stop sleeping. Instead of the trips, after just about every inch of our bodies had been covered with sun cream, we picnicked on the beach. Even Dad was looking cheerful when he raced Mum and her sisters into the water.

9

A lot of my memories of Byron Bay are from all the times I have visited my family there so I'm not sure which were from when we first went there or if they are an accumulation of ones I have stored in my head over the years. I'm sure the one thing my younger self would have loved more than anything was seeing those cute koala bears close up; cuddly little creatures that I had only ever seen pictures of. And I know I liked the beach and spending time with all my cousins. I also know that I loved Mum's family straight away. The sisters were such fun, and as for Gran, she was so kind and thoughtful, as was my grandfather, or 'Grampy' as he told me to call him.

What I didn't know then was that Gran was an artist, who did both sculptures and paintings. I was pretty amazed when she took us all to a gallery and pointed out which ones were hers. Everyone we met seemed to know her as they came over to say hello and make more comments about how much we all looked alike.

When Mum and Dad were well rested and Tommy was up and about without sleeping all the time, Mum sat us down and explained that as soon as our holiday with her family was over, we were travelling back on the last plane we had been on: to Melbourne.

'Oh, we'll be coming back here for more holidays,' she told us when she saw our faces drop. For what child wouldn't have wanted to stay in a forest on the edge of a beach? 'But you will like Melbourne as well, it's a beautiful city. And your gran's found us a house in a really nice area.'

What Mum didn't say then was that it was one that had been designed for families where a family member was disabled.

'And,' she added, 'the school you will be going to is only a few minutes from it. Couldn't be better.'

Mum didn't tell us the other reason for going there. Nor did she say how much she would have liked to have stayed with her family. But both she and Dad needed to get work and they already had a few interviews lined up. Even more importantly, they were moving close to an excellent hospital specialising in children's disabilities, which was needed for Tommy.

So about ten days after we had left England, we were back on the plane again.

Only this time it didn't take more than an hour.

Mum's family all came to the airport again but this time to say goodbye, but with lots of promises made to see each other soon. And Gran told me that she would be up in Melbourne for a visit as soon as we were settled.

I managed to choke back tears when we went through the barrier, for I felt that once again I was saying goodbye to a family I already loved.

When the man that the boy grew into closes his eyes, those sounds of his mother screaming and the man bellowing come flooding back to haunt him. As do the memories of his punishments, the pain his body felt afterwards and how frightened he was every time he was locked in that dark cupboard. Nor can he forget the day when he first heard derisory mutters and unfriendly looks on his new peers' faces.

It was the boy's first day at school. His trousers and shirt were patched and clean for his mother had made sure of that. But nothing she could do made them look anything else but threadbare and old.

The day began with the man shouting at his mother: she wanted to go with him to the school.

'There you go, trying to mollycoddle him again. He can find his own way. He's only got to get on a bus and get off it. Told you I didn't want no Mummy's boy in the house, didn't I?'

'Yes.'

The man instructed the boy to walk to the end of the rutted drive. There he would see the bus stop, he told him, handing over some money – 'That's your fare and ask the driver to call out when you've reached the school. Got that?'

'Yes.'

'Good, off you go then.'

The boy did exactly what the man had told him. What he hadn't known was that his journey was going to take him two hours. All he knew was that it had been a long one. He saw other children walking beside their mothers. They must be going to the school, he thought, and so he followed them. Once he reached the gates he was aware that he was the only small child without an adult accompanying him. He forced himself to draw his shoulders back and looked straight ahead as he made his way to the teacher, who was greeting all the new arrivals.

'Your mum not here?' he was asked. On replying 'No', the teacher frowned and paused to look over his clipboard as he asked for his name. The boy noticed that the teacher's face froze slightly when he heard what it was. Not that he understood why, not then anyway. Without being asked any more questions, he was then led into a classroom full of small, shabby desks and wooden chairs. He was told that would be where his lessons took place and to stay there until all the other children arrived. He heard the comments about how he was dressed from those already in the room. Most of the other children had stiff shirts with folding creases on the front and smart grey shorts and shiny new black shoes.

When he first started school, they called him 'The Bum' and other such words he knew were insulting. He knew the other children kept glancing over at him, but he just ignored them. Over the first few weeks he heard them sniggering about how he was dressed. 'Hi Bum,' some of the older boys would say as they pushed him, nearly knocking him off balance. More than once he had fallen but no one came to his aid. He was mocked when he had to go to the lavatories. That all stopped when they were told by their parents who the boy's stepfather was. Then, *throughout his years at school, they heeded their parents' warnings and stayed clear of him.*

When winter came, the house was icy cold, and shivering, the boy would wash in the tin hut then dress before daylight broke. He did not have a jacket or a school blazer, just a thick woollen jumper his mother had found for him. Far too big for his slight frame, it came down nearly to his knees and however much he tucked his sleeves up, they crawled down his arms to cover his hands. He might have been the only boy at school without a coat, but at least he was warm, he kept telling himself. Not that anyone mentioned his lack of regulation attire; the teachers must also have noticed his bruises and the occasional black eye and made no comments.

They too knew who the man was.

In the boy's mind there was only one thing that made going to school worthwhile. That was, even though the man never gave him money to pay for them, he was given his lunch every day so at least he wasn't hungry when he returned home, as his growing tribe of younger siblings often were.

When I grow up, he told himself every night as he got into bed, I will never go hungry or wear patched-up clothes. I will have smart suits and drive a big car. Not that he had yet made plans as to how he was going to do that.

They would be made over ten years later.

10

By the time the plane landed in Melbourne I was back to being cheerful again. Mum had told us a little about the school and the house – both of which, she promised us, we were going to love.

'Will we have our own bedrooms?' Tommy asked.

'Yes, you will.'

By the smug look on his face that answer clearly pleased him. Mum also reassured us that the tearful goodbye to her family was not going to be a long-lasting one.

'You've seen how quickly we can get on these small planes that fly from one airport to another, haven't you? Why, it's hardly going to take us much longer than it did when we drove down to Nan and Grandad's so of course we'll be seeing lots of my family and Dad will arrange for us to visit them as well. Now does that make you both feel better?'

A question she received two positive responses to.

I realised she was right about how short the journey was for she had hardly stopped talking when we heard the announcement to put on our seat belts because the plane was preparing to land. Dad had arranged for a hire car to be at the airport and as soon as we collected our luggage, we went to pick it up. He pushed the trolley piled with luggage, while Mum was in charge of the wheelchair the airport had arranged for Tommy. Not that he was in the least bit grateful. The moment he saw it being brought towards him, out came the indignant protests assuring us that he could manage on his walker.

'You only have to stay on it until we get to the car pick-up place,' Dad told him. 'It means we'll get there faster and you want that, don't you?'

'Oh, all right then.'

I must say I was pleased to crawl into the back of the car while my parents packed the luggage into it. I felt a little tremble of excitement when, with Mum holding a map in her hand, we drove off for the next chapter of our adventure. I wondered what our new home was going to look like, but hadn't she told us that we were going to love the house and the area we were going to live in?

The drive from the airport to Bendigo, a southern suburb of Melbourne, is another memory that has stayed in my mind. To children who had only been in that country for a short time, every new thing we saw was tremendously exciting. Having only seen cows, sheep and a few horses in England's fields, it was pretty amazing to see whole families of kangaroos hopping along on the side of the road we were driving on. Of course Tommy and I asked Dad to stop so we could get a closer look.

'Not a good idea. Remember they're wild animals, not docile

pets,' he told us, but at least he humoured us a bit by slowing down before continuing to drive along the road that seemed to stretch ahead as far as the eye could see.

We were certainly in luck that day for no sooner had we passed the kangaroos than Mum suddenly said, 'Oh, just look up there! Can you see all those parrots?'

Tommy and I just gasped when we looked up and saw a flock of red and green birds, their vivid coloured wings stretched wide, flying above us.

'Wow, they're so beautiful!' Tommy exclaimed, while I was so enchanted by them that I could hardly get a word out.

'Not often we would be so lucky to see so much in one day,' Mum said.

Not that this stopped us from pressing our noses to the car windows, hoping to see more. Tommy was the first one to spot the houses built on sticks.

'Just look at those weird houses, Mum. Why are they built like that?' he asked, pointing to them.

Mum went a bit silent then, no doubt groping for the right answer. 'I suppose some people like them built that way,' she replied, leaving out the fact that in some areas it was necessary to prevent poisonous snakes from slithering in through doors and windows.

His next question was 'Ours won't be like that, will it?' And I could tell he was worried about how he would get up from the ground into the house.

'No, there's nothing like that in the area we're going to as far as I know and ours is a lovely single-storey,' Mum replied quickly while she consulted the map again – 'Ah, we're nearly there!' I heard her tell Dad to turn left. 'Pull up, Peter, it's just down here,' she said, a few minutes later.

I gave a gasp of pleasure when we drove down the drive to the house which, with its sloping tiled roof and large sliding glass doors, looked much bigger than the one we had moved from. When Mum and Dad took us inside we almost forgot how wonderful Byron Bay was when we saw the size of the yard, as we had learnt Australians called it. Though in England, Nan would probably have said it was a really lovely big patio; either way, it certainly had plenty of space for a family. There was the built-in barbecue, a whole set of outside chairs and a large table for outside eating.

'Sun loungers are already in that little shed,' Mum told us, reading from her set of instructions. 'So you two can spend all your time outside.'

Inside, it got even better. It looked as though it had just been decorated for it smelt and looked so clean, the walls were a rich cream, the floors a pale wood and in the sitting room was a pile of boxes that Gran had organised to be waiting for us. Inside them were all the household necessities – towels and bedding, pots and pans, cutlery and crockery. Everything we needed to keep us going until our own boxes arrived. It had some furniture – a light oak table and a deep blue settee – but when ours arrived, we could return any of it to the charity that offered this sort of rental accommodation for families with a disabled child.

It only took a couple of days for Tommy and me to be enrolled in the local school and not much longer than that for both Mum and Dad to find jobs. Mum found one with an estate agent, while Dad had been taken on as a carpenter. He seemed a lot more content then for with both of them working, money would not be so scarce as it had been for several months before we left.

The school we were to go to was only a few minutes' walk away. Though Mum said she would take us and either she or Dad would pick us up in the afternoon until we were confident about in going ourselves.

Our first day came, with Mum walking us there and introducing us to the Head. Tommy and I both, to his surprise, really enjoyed our first day. Not only were the teachers friendly, but so too were all the other pupils. There were no comments about the fact that Tommy needed a walker, nor any questions about why he did. Instead on our breaks, they plied us with lots of questions about what we thought of Australia and what life had been like in the UK.

Some of the children had relatives there who came over to see them and a few in Tommy's class had visited the UK for holidays. And like us, their grandparents had settled in Australia well before they were born, while others could trace back their ancestry to people who had settled much longer ago.

What I can remember most about those first few weeks was that apart from learning letters and counting up to ten, I spent a lot of time turning playdough into different shapes and learning to play with hula hoops. Our teacher told us that she had arranged for all of the younger ones that were really good at swirling the hoops around their waists and hips to put on a show at the shopping centre. To my surprise I was one of the children who was chosen. Good thing Mum was handy with a needle as she spent a couple of evenings making me a shiny blue skirt with a big frill at the bottom especially for the occasion – which of course I absolutely loved. Dad took lots of photos to send to all the relatives.

Mum's family visited us more than once and each time, I found myself growing closer to Gran. At the weekends when we were free from school, they took us all out sightseeing – Gran always tried to organise something that we would all enjoy. It was the nature parks I loved the most, being close to animals I had never seen before. There were fluffy koala bears, another small creature I learnt was a wombat and behind them, several kangaroos. Not that I can remember much more of those days, just that back then, we seemed to be a normal and happy family.

Part Two

My Brother and I

11

Tommy had to go to the hospital fairly soon after we arrived – the doctors there wanted to do a complete appraisal of his medical condition.

'Oh, it's just a routine check-up,' Mum replied airily when I asked about it.

So I forgot all about it for well over a year. It was when I began to notice that Tommy was finding using his walker even more difficult that I asked Mum if he was all right.

'Of course he is, Daisy, why do you ask?'

'Don't know,' I mumbled.

Tommy, though, was far more clued-up than me. He had other examinations that I hadn't been told about – I suppose I was considered far too small to understand and they didn't want me worrying.

'Daisy, I've known since that first time I went to the hospital here that I was going to need an operation one day. And it looks as though that day's just about arrived. The doctors have explained everything to me, so don't worry, Sis,' he told me.

I didn't ask him what it was they were going to do, I thought it was better to wait until he wanted to talk about it. But it was explained to me by Mum when I asked her that the leg muscles were tightening, which was why he could seldom place his feet down flat. She said that if the procedure wasn't done very soon, then Tommy's muscles would tighten even more.

'So, when is he having it?'

'He's being admitted in a week's time.'

'How long will he be in there?'

Mum gave me a slightly exasperated look. 'That's something we won't know until after the operation.'

'But ...'

'No more questions now, Daisy, and don't pester your brother with them either.'

I was sure by the way her eyes slid away from mine that there was something she wasn't telling me and I became even more certain when over the next few days I could see that, however hard they tried to hide it, both Mum and Dad were anxious and distracted.

*   *   *

'Come on in,' Tommy said, patting the edge of his bed when I put my head round his door.

Taking no notice of Mum's remark about pestering him, I asked him what it was the doctors were really going to do. One of his puckish grins came my way: 'Took you long enough to ask! I'm going to have the operation and then a plaster cast will be put on, going from my hips to my toes. Guess they're going to make me look like an Egyptian mummy. Better gets loads of signatures on the cast though. Your job is to tell all my friends they'd best start practising drawing funny pictures that they can decorate that cast with.'

Once he saw I was more relaxed, he explained patiently what the doctors had discussed with him: 'They were a bit secretive at first, those doctors, they wanted me to leave the room when they talked to Mum and Dad, but I soon sorted them out. I told them it was my body and I might only be eleven, but living in my world makes you pretty mature so if I was old enough for the op then I was old enough to hear it all and be able to understand them. Then they agreed and talked me through everything, like what they would have to do and what the results might be. So I know that I'm going to need strong painkillers and that it will take a bit of time to get over the op. Means I'll miss some school as well. But what do I care if I'm able to walk after it?'

Before I could think of an answer to that he smiled again and I could see the hope shining in his eyes that his biggest wish in life might just come true.

'Daisy, just imagine what it would be like for me if I could dump my walker? Come on, say something. It would be great, wouldn't it?'

'Yes,' I answered, for what else could I say? I swallowed hard for I had a lump in my throat. He might want to cling to that belief but I was pretty sure our parents didn't believe the op was going to do as much as Tommy dreamed of.

'And Daisy, when I say walk, I mean properly, not just mincing around on my toes and bending my knees. I mean, move about like everyone else. Well, almost – they say whatever happens, I will still have an arm that refuses to work.'

What he didn't tell me was that some of those problems were caused by the misalignment of his bones as well as the tightening of his muscles. Nor did he say that he knew the operation was a risky one. He had, not that I knew then, been told by the doctors what the result was most likely to be, as had Mum and Dad. There really hadn't been any choice for without the operation, Tommy's already limited mobility would have deteriorated rapidly.

I'm sure that it wasn't easy for the doctors to explain all of that to an eleven-year-old boy. When I think about it now, I question if all of that should have been explained to him. Was he really mature enough to understand all the implications? Those were the questions Mum and Dad asked each other in the privacy of their room.

Dad asked me my thoughts about his maturity when I was much older. And my reply? Yes, he was. My brother was not only mature for his age, he was also really brave. He had been told very clearly that there was less than a 5 per cent chance of him being able to walk again. The doctors asked him twice if he fully understood this. His answer, he told me later, was 'You'd better go ahead then, hadn't you? Doesn't sound as though I have much to lose.'

For the whole of that week while waiting to be admitted, Tommy focused on thinking what his life would be like if he was one of that elusive 5 per cent. However small a chance he had of walking, he wanted that operation to be done. My brother was certainly a boy who believed in positive thinking.

Mum told me later that he was barely more than a toddler when he demonstrated that he was not going to let his disabilities control his life.

While he talked, Tommy's hand crept up to me and I felt his fingers curl around mine. 'Don't think of the operation,' he said, 'think instead of the fun we could have afterwards. Me running on the beach with you and diving into the sea. Why, one day, Daisy, I might even play football. Now wouldn't that be great?' That was the first time I understood that more than anything, he wanted to escape the life he was trapped in.

'Yes, it would,' was all I managed to say.

That day, I felt so close to him. For I knew then that however brave he was trying to sound, he was scared.

And so was I.

12

'What will happen if it makes him worse?' was the question I heard Dad asking Mum when they thought no one would hear them. But her reply was the same as Tommy's.

'Peter, he's got very little to lose really, hasn't he? Just how much worse can it be?'

Tommy appeared more concerned about missing school than he did about going to hospital – I guess that was another act of bravado. He and the teachers had talked about his absence and he was anxious for schoolwork to be sent over to him.

'You won't have much of a problem catching up anyhow, Tommy, you are an extremely good student,' they told him reassuringly.

At home Mum seemed focused on making him eat as much healthy food as he could manage right up until the morning he was going into hospital. I was to be taken to be school by Dad that day, even though we normally walked. I stood near the dining table at a complete loss for words. It was my brother who said, 'Hey, wish me luck, won't you?' I did and gave him a quick hug and somehow managed to say 'Bye and see you soon.'

'Come on, let's get you to school,' said Dad, trying his best to appear cheerful. Perhaps he realised I was close to tears and wanted to avoid me breaking down in front of Tommy. It seemed strange walking into school without him by my side. Each day after as I walked that route, I felt as if part of me was missing.

When school finished, it was Dad who was waiting for me. When I got out of the car, he opened the boot to take out Tommy's walker.

'He insisted on using it, right up until they got him into bed,' he told me with a wry smile.

He got me something to eat, not that I can remember what it was – I was far too busy thinking about my brother. I knew that the operation wasn't happening until the following morning but that didn't stop me from worrying about how he was.

Mum was still at the hospital with him and Dad was going to visit Tommy and pick her up.

'We'll not stay long,' he told me. 'Will you be all right on your own? The neighbours will be watching out for you from their yard. Any problem, just give them a shout. You can watch television till we get back.'

'I'll be OK,' I answered and, giving me a kiss on the top of my head, he hurried out. The walker was where Dad had left it, in a corner of the room. Glancing at it, I wondered if Tommy would ever need it again. OK, there were times when we'd squabbled like all siblings do, times when I wished he would be quiet, times when I wanted Mum to pay me attention instead of him, but that didn't stop me from missing him acutely.

Over the following days Mum hardly left the hospital. She

came home for a few hours when he was in the operating theatre. The ward sister promised to phone the moment he was out
and starting to come round. Not that she seemed able to relax
for one minute.

Dad told her to put her feet up for a while and if she had
dozed off, he would waken her – 'I can't stand not to know
how it went,' was her answer.

The call came late afternoon. This time, not knowing how
long they were going to be at the hospital, Mum arranged for
one of her friends to come in and stay with me. Which did not
stop me from fretting. I wanted to know how Tommy was too
– I so hoped the operation would be a success. But my heart
sank when Mum and Dad finally returned home and I could
tell immediately that she had been crying and Dad looked totally washed out. The questions I wanted to ask dried up in
my throat for if it had been good news, they would have been
bursting to tell me. I had prayed that he might be granted his
wish of being able to walk but Mum and Dad's faces told me it
wasn't going to happen.

* * *

It was around a week later that Mum took me to visit Tommy:
'He wants to see you,' she told me. 'Now, you can't stay with
him too long and you mustn't get him excited. He's still got to
take it easy for quite a while,' she warned. 'He might ask you
if you've heard anything about his results, but I've told him it's
too early for them to judge.'

I still wanted to ask her more about the operation but I

couldn't bring myself to. I felt nervous as, holding onto Mum's hand tightly, I walked into the hospital. We took a lift up to the floor where he was – Mum had given me some fruit that I could give to him.

'Here we are,' she said as we reached the room where he was. 'You can go in and chat to him and I'll go and get a coffee.'

Somewhat apprehensively, I entered, calling out 'Hi Tommy' as I walked over to his bed. My first thought was how very pale he was – all his Australian summer tan seemed to have gone in a matter of a week. I perched on the chair beside his bed and he pulled himself up a little and did his best to smile.

'You were right, you do look rather mummified,' I told him, peering at where his legs should be. On one side there was white plaster all the way from his hip to his toe, on the other from his thigh down. In-between his legs there was something that looked like a thick metal bar where his knees were, holding them rigidly apart.

'What's that?' I asked.

'It's there to stop my legs moving and to make sure that they won't take it upon themselves to close together when I'm asleep,' he explained, trying to make a joke of it. His hand covered mine as he added, 'but if I can walk, then all this will have been worth it.'

I gulped for what could I say? So, no one had told him anything. I then understood the reason Mum had told me it was too soon to tell what the results of the operation were. And that must have been what she had said to Tommy as well.

'Mind if have a look at these?' I asked, changing the subject quickly as I pointed to all the get-well cards that Mum had decorated the room with. There were some lovely ones from our Australian family and some really nice cards from the UK family and friends too. Most of the others were from his new school friends and quite a few from his teachers, which didn't surprise me – he was so bright, and even though it was a different syllabus, he was just about first in every subject. I knew his teachers thought a lot of him and his classmates also really admired him. He was one of the most popular children at school almost as soon as he had started there.

We chattered a little more before Mum put her head round the door and said it was time for me to go.

'I'll be back a little later, you get some rest now, son,' she told him before whisking me away.

'He's not going to walk, is he?' I blurted out as soon as we got into the car. And even before she could answer, my anger bubbled up and I found myself almost shouting, 'It's not fair! He still thinks he is going to and no one has told him the truth. He's not a baby, you know!'

For a moment there was stunned silence in the car. Shouting at Mum was not something I had ever done before.

'Listen Daisy, there are reasons and I'll explain later,' she told me after a pause. 'All right? I need to concentrate on driving us home safely.'

'OK,' I muttered, thinking at least she hadn't tried to lie to me.

And she kept her word. As soon as we were back home, Mum sat me down and explained the results of the operation. Not only had it not given Tommy the ability to walk like any other boy, now he would not be able to walk at all.

'Not even to use the walker?'

'No, he will have to be in a wheelchair,' Mum told me.

I could see she was close to tears.

'Why hasn't he been told, Mum?'

'The doctors thought it would be best if he was a little better before they tell him. Which they are going to do tomorrow morning. I'll be there with him of course, as will Dad.'

I wasn't sitting next to Tommy when the news was broken to him so I didn't actually witness any hope of his living a normal life drain away. I just sat in class looking at the clock until the hands told me that by eleven o'clock he would have been told.

Did he cry?

I know I did.

13

Mum's friend came to collect me from school and left discreetly when their car pulled into the drive. Dad's face was chalky when they came inside.

He told me years later that he felt so guilty for allowing Tommy to have all that false hope. Even though he knew there had not been a choice, my brother had to have that operation. I tried to tell him that even if Tommy's body had not needed the op, he would still have fought to have a glimmer of hope. For if there had only been a 1 per cent chance that he might walk, he would have taken it.

'Dad, he knew what his future was. He might have been very young when Google became available on our computers. But you know how he was a real whizz on them? He did loads of searches and of course he learnt all about Rett syndrome and all the different treatments for it.'

I can still picture him now, lying in that hospital bed, his lower body plastered and his legs held apart, after the day his doctors had explained the results of his operation. It was as though my brother, that spunky boy who cracked jokes, loved computer games and pounding music, had just disappeared, leaving a wan, silent boy in his place.

Nearly every time I sat with him, his eyes turned away from me towards the window. All I could do was hold his hand and try and talk when he wanted to. Eventually they removed the plaster and he had physio each day. It seemed to take forever before he was home but when he did come back, it was an ambulance that brought him. A couple of medics wheeled him in on a hospital bed. Seeing him like that was really heartbreaking. I was aware that he was often in pain and that Mum and Dad were really stressed out. It was not a happy time for any of us, and certainly not for Tommy, who, despite being fiercely independent, could hardly manage to do anything for himself.

I did my best to try and get him interested in just about anything I could think of. I told him about school and the different animals I had seen when I had been in the car a couple of times with Dad, but nothing that any of us did could put the sparkle back into his eyes. I don't know how long he had been back home before he suddenly smiled at me. Instead of silence I was greeted with a 'Morning, Daisy,' when I walked into the living room which acted as his temporary bedroom. An answering smile spread across my face, even if he hadn't yet given me his old cheeky grin that I so longed to see, but it was at least a start.

'Have to get my muscles working, don't I? The physio coming is one thing, but I need to make an effort too,' was the next thing he said. 'I'm going to ask Dad to get me some weights so I can work out a bit more. I know only one arm works, but that needs to be really strong, doesn't it? I'm going to need it for my wheelchair, aren't I?'

That was the first time the word 'wheelchair' had left his mouth.

Mum, with a beaming smile on her face, bounced into the room the moment she overheard us talking.

'Hey, Mum, we were just talking about my new chair. Now, I want you to know I don't want a dreary old black one,' he told her.

'Well, what colour would you like?' she asked as calmly as she could.

'A bright blue shiny one. Then the other kids are going to be so jealous of me because I'll be able to move faster than them then, won't I? And that will make me look so cool.'

And I saw Mum swallow hard before she managed to say, 'Yes, you will.'

*　　*　　*

I remember the day that wheelchair took up its residence in the house. It was what he had asked for, a bright blue one. Dad helped him onto it and showed him how easy it was to operate.

'Now, I want to go out for a test drive,' he told us once he had shown us all that he had grasped how the controls worked. 'I can manage it down to the shops and we can go to the café where they have ice cream and cakes.'

Of course this suggestion was agreed to immediately for no one refused Tommy anything then. So off we all went with

Tommy confidently taking charge of what he called his new 'speed machine'.

'I'll be able to go back to school now,' he told Mum later that day.

'You deserve a little holiday first,' she insisted, making his face look even brighter.

'What, all of us?'

'No, just us two.'

'So, where are we going to?'

'Here,' and without telling him anything more, she handed him a brightly coloured brochure. 'It's all about a camp site and I think it looks really amazing. Loads of things to do there.'

'It's for disabled kids who can't walk, isn't it?' he said after flicking through the brochure.

'It's for young people who are determined to enjoy life whether they can walk or not,' she insisted.

I waited for an outburst but instead, to my surprise, he sat up a little bit straighter in his chair.

'You're right, Mum. I was told what could happen when I had the op. And it has. So now I have to stop moping and make the best of it, don't I?'

'Yes, Tommy,' was the only answer Mum managed to give – for there wasn't another one, was there?

What none of us knew, when Tommy and Mum set off, was that their holiday would result in all our lives changing once again.

The boy was aged somewhere between eight and nine when the man taught him to shoot. Though when he was asked how old he had been his answer was always, 'When I was big enough to carry a gun.'

The day the man decided to teach him how to survive out there in the bush was when the boy told his mother he was not hungry. He had seen how little food there was on the table and felt that his younger siblings were hungrier than him. After all, he had already eaten at school.

'You only get one meal there, don't you? That's not enough for a growing boy,' his mother argued.

'I don't believe you're telling the truth, I think you want some food,' the man said, giving a smile that the boy had learnt was treacherous. 'So, I'm going to sort that out for you.'

Before the boy could think of anything to say, the man opened up the large leather bag he always carried with him. For a moment the boy thought it was a chunk of meat or a rabbit that the man was going to take out and felt almost dizzy with relief. Soon it would be in his mother's hands and in no time at all the room would be perfumed with the heady scent of simmering meat. Instead, the man took out a small brass key and walked over to a locked cupboard. The boy knew what was inside – those scary metal and wood things called guns.

The man unlocked it and removed two of them.

'Here's yours,' he said as he handed the smaller one to the boy. 'You can carry it. It's food we're looking for.'

The boy heard his mother protesting – he was too small and too young to manage it.

A plea that the man took no notice of.

Together they left the farm, the man taking long strides, the boy stumbling behind him trying his best to keep the heavy gun up against his shoulder.

The man finally came to a stop. After looking up at the sky where the pigeons and black currawongs (a lot like ravens) were flying, he lifted his gun and fired.

'Pick it up,' he told the boy, who hated the sight of the blood on the feathers. 'Now I'll show you ...' and taking hold of the boy's arm which was holding the gun, he raised the gun into position against the boy's bony shoulder and pointed it up towards the sky. 'You point and pull that trigger, but quick before they fly off' was just about all the advice he was given.

Instead of a bird landing near his feet, the shot missed its target. The unexpected recoil of the rifle flung the boy to the dusty ground. And it was too late to try for another. He could hear the birds cawing to each other as with wings flapping, they gradually disappeared out of sight.

The boy's face reddened with embarrassment, he just hadn't been fast enough. Getting up, he brushed the dust from his clothes and got back in the firing position again. It was he who saw the squirrel perched on a branch of a tree and pointed to it. With his gun resting on his shoulder the man moved closer, a shot rang out and the small creature came tumbling to the ground.

'There's your supper,' he was told, as the squirrel and the bird were placed in the leather bag.

'Now this is what real men do,' the man told him as they walked through the bush back towards the farm. 'That's how they get the food for their families. So if you want to be someone I can be proud of, then you'll learn to shoot.' The boy knew then that he wanted to be like the man, to be able to stride through that bush with his gun placed on his shoulder, killing those small animals and bringing them home to his mother.

'I want to learn to shoot like you,' he murmured and this won him a pat on the shoulder.

Once back at the farm the boy watched his mother deftly skinning the small fluffy creature and plucking the other, before placing them in a pan of boiling water with a few handfuls of vegetables.

'Right, boy! Saturday, you learn to shoot and also strip down and clean a gun,' the man told him.

When dawn was breaking, causing slivers of sunlight to come through the windows, his mother woke him. 'He's waiting for you,' was all she needed to say for the boy to scurry out of bed, pull on some clothes and rush to the kitchen. The man handed him a slice of bread before taking him outside.

'Now what do you see?' he was asked.

'Bottles,' he replied, for there was a selection of beer bottles placed on bricks and stones of different heights. He was told to shoot them down and if he did, he would get a good breakfast as a reward. He tried, but the gun was heavy and his hand kept shaking, causing him to miss every one.

The man told him to try again but to first make sure his eye as well as the gun was aimed at his target. So, the boy did as the man had told him and several bottles fell from the bricks, leaving shards of glass scattered over the yard. Now the boy was blushing, but this time with pride.

After reloading the gun for him, the man replaced the missing bottles in the line. The boy fixed his eye on the target and one by one the bottles fell until there were none left on the bricks.

That morning, the breakfast was bread dipped in meat juices.

By the time the boy was about nine, he had perfect aim.

He was also able to strip down and load his own gun.

14

A couple of nights before Tommy and Mum left for the holiday camp, Gran, carrying a large bag packed full with appetising food as well as a large suitcase, arrived from Byron Bay – 'Got some shopping to do while I'm here,' she told me, 'so I will need your help, my darling.' But I wasn't fooled by that, I knew she had come to make sure I had company while the others were away and Dad was out at work. And just to confirm my suspicion, she added, 'You and I can do a few fun things while I'm here as well,' and she gave me a mischievous smile.

The morning Mum and Tommy departed we were all up early to say goodbye. I hugged my brother tightly and he gave me his cheeky smile and told me not to miss him too much. The bus that picked them up was specially designed for people in wheelchairs and as soon as he was on board, I could see him chatting to the other children who were already seated. We all waved as the bus reversed down the drive and Gran reminded me it was time to leave for school.

Even though my school was only a few minutes' walk away, she nevertheless insisted on going with me. 'A bit of exercise is good for me,' was her excuse. In fact, although I tried to be independent, walking there on my own without Tommy by my side still seemed quite strange. When school ended, she was waiting for me again, carrying more shopping.

'Had to get a few nice tasty snacks for our tea,' she said when she saw me looking at the bulging shopping bag. Back home, she fished out some fresh juice and a sugary pastry for me before disappearing into the kitchen to prepare our evening meal. Certainly, Dad looked grateful when he walked in from work to be greeted by the aromas of herbs and spices that had escaped from the kitchen.

'God that smells good! I'm hungry already.'

'Well, you'll have to wait, Peter. We're having my one-pot chicken casserole in case you were wondering. Have a beer while it's cooking and take the weight off your feet for a bit.'

I must say, Gran was a really good cook and she produced delicious meals for us every night.

True to her word, at the weekend she took me shopping with her although it seemed she was more interested in what I wanted than what she did. She bought me a couple of really pretty dresses, as well as a pair of trendy cut-offs, a few bright coloured tops and new sandals. And then to celebrate our purchases, as she put it, she took me to her favourite café, where we had the Australian version of afternoon tea. While I was tucking into a huge pink meringue covered in fresh cream and strawberries, Gran and I tried to picture what Tommy might be doing. I had seen in the brochure some of the activities that were planned for those, who like my brother, could not walk and the wheelchair treasure hunt had looked like his sort of thing.

'I expect he'll have loads to tell us when they get back, Gran.'
'I'm sure he will, love. Now, how about another meringue?'
Well, I could hardly refuse, could I?

*   *   *

The following day, when Dad was also free, Gran made up a picnic as she had arranged for us to spend at the day at Daisy Hill, a nearby nature reserve. It was hard to believe that it was so near to the city, it was just so tranquil there. Naturally, its very name made me want to visit it! Once there, we visited the cute little koalas and I was allowed to hold one and stroke it. Dad snapped lots of photos for us to send to Nan and Grandad, back in the UK, and to show to Tommy and Mum and then we all walked to the lake, where we laid out a blanket and had our picnic.

'It makes us feel so close to nature, doesn't it?' said Gran. 'I think that's such an important part of life – it certainly is in Australia.'

Dad, I noticed, was looking really content as they chatted together while I took a walk near the lake – I suspected he was now starting to believe that the move from England had been the right decision after all.

I think that was probably one of the best days I ever had in Melbourne.

Part Three

The Stepfather

15

I might have been wondering what Tommy was up to, but I hadn't given much thought to what Mum might be doing too. I was looking forward to their return, although I would definitely be sorry to see Gran go. Dad, I guess, must have been feeling the same. It was not until they'd been back for a few weeks that we had an inkling that their stay in the camp heralded the beginning of all our lives changing irrevocably. And at the time there was no one, save Mum, who thought it was for the best.

It took me a while to piece everything together for Tommy kept quiet initially about what Mum had been up to at the camp. It turned out that there had been good camp counsellors there so that the parents were also able to take a break and naturally, Mum being Mum, she was only too happy to take full advantage. A group of other mothers she had become friendly with had told her about a nearby bar with live music: 'We're going,' they said, 'we need a bit of fun. And they've booked a really good singer there tonight so why don't you come along?'

'Yes, you go, Mum,' Tommy insisted. 'You deserve some time away from me! Anyhow, we have a computer games night tonight in the community hall.'

I'm sure had he known just what the consequences were going to be, he would have kept quiet.

'Are you sure, love?'

'Oh, come on, Mum! I can see you really want to go so just go and enjoy yourself, you can tell me all about it when you get back.'

'Not that she told me everything,' Tommy observed wryly a few weeks later. 'I wish now I'd done the selfish bit and told her I wasn't feeling well and then she would have stayed. I wish I'd said I was unhappy with being left that night.'

What I gathered from Tommy was that Mum, being Mum, had packed a pretty dress as well as a bag full of make-up: 'She certainly looked happy when that group she hung around with asked her to join them. A night out was just what she wanted. She spent all afternoon getting ready, washing her hair and getting all dolled up with full make-up and jewellery. Have to say, Daisy, she looked really great.'

He went on to tell me that he was back in their room when she eventually returned. Of course he asked about the evening, wanting to know if she had enjoyed herself. To which she had replied yes, she had and her group had been great company. He noticed that she was a bit flushed but had put it down to having a few too many glasses of wine, not that she had met someone she fancied. Even so, my brother had always had sharp ears and an enquiring mind. Listening to the group's chatter after breakfast the next day, while he pretended to be engrossed in a book, he was able to hear enough to work out their version of Mum's evening out.

A trio were on the stage when Mum and her friends walked in. They had quickly bagged a table, ordered their drinks and were beginning to relax. A little later when the trio played their last song and left the stage to a round of polite applause, the MC climbed onto it. Taking hold of the mic, he told the audience in a loud voice that bounced off the walls to please give a warm welcome to the star of the night that they had all been waiting for: The Bushwacker. Applause and welcoming shouts and whistles boomed out as the singer took to the stage.

His arrival caused gasps among Mum's circle of new friends. He was around six feet tall, with a great tanned body, every muscle showing through his tight T-shirt and long dark hair that he lifted a hand to sweep back from his face as he glanced around at his audience. His first song – 'Ned Kelly' – was one made famous by the legendary Johnny Cash. It was about the infamous Ned Kelly, a man who considered himself a freedom fighter but the police regarded as a bandit, who had been hung for murder at the Old Melbourne Gaol over a hundred years earlier.

It was as he sang the last note that Mum caught his eye. Dark sultry eyes were looking straight at her and a smile crossed his face as he picked up the mic. His gaze remained on her as he broke into his second song – 'Pretty Woman' – followed by a wink when he sang the words, 'the kind I'd like to meet.' It was a voice, Mum told me a long time later, that sent goose bumps all over her body.

'A bit too much information for me,' I told her.

And if I hadn't wanted to listen to Mum reminiscing on how she met The Bushwacker, I hardly relished hearing his version either.

'I could barely take my eyes off her,' he told me.

Well, at least he stuck to her eyes, I thought with some relief.

'You know, Daisy, when I saw her, that petite woman with her long glossy hair and those smouldering eyes of hers, I just wanted to get to know her.'

Didn't notice the wedding ring then?

Tommy had heard the ribald jokes from the group about their lead singer's rendition of 'Pretty Woman' and how on his break he had made his way straight over to the women's table. He told them his real name was Ned and asked if he could buy them a round of drinks, knowing full well who he wanted to sit near. With a few chuckles, they all said yes. They might have been married women, but a little flirtation wouldn't do any harm. After all, they felt the need to escape a little from the stresses and strains of caring for their children; all of whom had various types of disability.

From what Tommy told me, he had a shrewd idea Mum was spending more than the odd evening with Ned but as far as he was concerned, it was just a holiday flirtation. He never thought she would carry on seeing him once they left the camp.

When they eventually arrived back, both Mum and Tommy looked amazing well. No stress lines on Mum's face and even on his first day home, I could see that my brother was far more confident. Any bitterness about ending up in a wheelchair seemed to have completely disappeared. He chattered away about how great a place it was, the people he had met there and the games he had played with other children in wheelchairs.

'I didn't know there were so many others like me,' he told us. 'Also, I've got an idea of what sort of career I could start working towards.'

'What's that, son?' asked Dad.

'Well, I spent some time playing computer games with some of the older guys there. They also help run the programme where you look at possible careers. They were all studying to get into university to get a BSc in Computer Science. It's worth having, they told me, even though there are companies who will take school leavers on if they see real aptitude. And they told me they thought I was somebody they would be interested in. That they would most probably offer me a job, with some training of course, as soon as I got my exam results. That sounds great, doesn't it? And those guys were good, but they told me it wouldn't take long before I was better than them. And by the way, when I wasn't looking at computers, I let that blue machine of mine know who was boss. Really got it under control now.'

Tommy never used the word 'wheelchair' and had christened it instead 'my blue machine'. I could see he'd mastered it when we went out – he seemed to think he'd progressed to being a racing driver.

'Slow down!' Mum kept telling him.

Obeying her, he gave his old cheeky grin: 'Sorry, Mum, I keep forgetting I'm faster than you mere mortals.' It was when the pair of us were in his room that he kept asking questions about school. 'Can't wait to get back,' he told me with one of his beaming smiles. 'Loads to tell my classmates when I get there.'

'Good, you're going next Monday,' Mum told him when he repeated that conversation to her. 'And all right, before you ask, you can both take yourselves there. But you're to behave yourself on that wheelchair, understood?'

* * *

On the Monday morning, armed with a packet of photos he wanted to show his friends, Tommy and I left together. It felt good to have him alongside me again.

'What on earth!' he exclaimed when we had nearly reached the school gates.

'Reckon your friends are waiting for you,' I said, grinning down at him.

We had both spotted a large group of not just his classmates but most of the school, hanging out near the gates, while a smaller group were holding a long banner with the words 'Welcome Back Tommy,' written in enormous letters.

'Did you know about that?'

Before I could say no and tell him that they had kept it a secret, my voice was drowned out by the cheers he received as he drove his wheelchair through the gates. My brother's face was pink and for a moment I thought he was going to burst into tears, he was so moved.

It took only a couple of days before he managed to get ticked off from a teacher. Which told everyone that the old Tommy was back. I could see the teacher didn't find it easy, but as he said, it had to be done.

What happened was a couple of girls were teasing me and Tommy, my ever-protective brother, sped his wheelchair towards them, leaving putting on the brake until he was only a couple of inches away from them. I tried hard not to laugh when they both jumped out of his path emitting screams of fake terror.

'You leave my sister alone,' he told them menacingly, 'or next time my brakes just might not work.'

I couldn't help letting a giggle escape me then, causing the girls to cast dirty looks in my direction.

'That's not funny,' one said and I shrugged.

Overhearing the confrontation, one of the teachers came over. He obviously didn't think it funny either, or if he did then he hid it well.

'Look, Tommy, I know you've only been back a couple of days and I understand that you want to be treated like everyone else, don't you? Then you'd better act the same. And don't use your wheelchair as a weapon, all right?'

It might have been on the tip of Tommy's tongue to argue, but he took the sensible route and made an apology.

'Accepted, isn't it, girls?' asked the teacher.

'Ah yes, sir,' the two replied before scuttling off.

I think the teacher understood why Tommy was so fiercely protective of me. He still wanted to act the part of a big brother and look after his little sister and that was the only way he could. 'You've certainly adjusted well to your machine, just don't race it around the playground or use it as a weapon,' he told him and after giving him a reassuring pat on the shoulder, he walked away.

If Tommy was determined to make the most of the chair, life with it in tow turned out to have other uses, not just for him but for me as well. Shopping could be placed on to it, which helped Mum and even better, I could ride on it as well. That was something we practised in the yard. Tommy wanted to make sure I knew what I was doing: 'You place your feet on that step bit between the wheels,' he told me the first time. 'Then hold on tightly and I'll give you a lift.'

The two of us would take off, giggling away.

When Mum saw what we were doing, she told Tommy not to go too fast once we took the wheelchair outside the house: 'Don't want her landing on her head now, do we?'

'I suppose not.'

My brother's new wheelchair certainly made shopping easier: not only could bags be stashed on it, I could perch on the battery while we walked around the shops in the centre of town. Much better than walking beside Mum, I decided, although things did go wrong once or twice. One day, we were outside in what I had finally learnt to call the yard, as opposed to the patio, throwing a ball back and forth. Then Tommy hit on the bright idea of getting me to stand on the back of his chair while he practised spinning it around in circles. Faster and faster it went, with me screaming with excitement. Well, that was until it fell sideways, throwing both of us out and pinning me down under the chair and the still-rotating wheels.

We must have screamed pretty loudly for both Mum and Dad came rushing out to rescue us. The wheelchair was pulled up and I crawled out from underneath it.

'Are you OK, Daisy?' asked Mum, checking me for obvious damage.

'Yeah, I think so.'

And taking my word for it, she moved over to where Dad was checking Tommy.

I felt a bit left out then as neither of them seemed too worried about my bruises, they were too busy checking my brother's legs and torso.

Oh well, I told myself, *life's back to normal, isn't it?*

I got that one wrong.

The boy was now nine – old enough to hunt on his own, wasn't he? He wanted to prove to the man that he no longer needed his help. For wasn't the man waiting for him to show him that? What else could be the reason for letting him see where the key to the gun cupboard was kept? So before his mother had a chance to argue he unlocked the cupboard, took out his gun and quickly loaded it. After calling out, 'I'm going to get us a good supper tonight,' he left the house. Already he had become well practised in listening to the sounds of the bush animals. He was aware that they could hear him more clearly then he could them so he lay under some foliage waiting patiently for his quarry to emerge.

He could hardly believe his luck when instead of one of the many rabbits out there, a young deer appeared. Feeling his fingers tremble slightly, he lifted his gun and lined up the small creature. With one shot, he felled it to the ground.

That should impress the man, he thought, for wasn't his trophy bigger than the couple of rabbits that the man had brought home the day before? For a brief moment he wondered just how he was going to carry both the deer and his gun. It was sheer determination that gave him the strength to do so. With the gun on his shoulder and the deer looped over his other arm, step by slow step, he made his way laboriously back to the house. The first thing he saw was the man's truck outside, which for once pleased him.

Good, he told himself, he's back and now he'll see what I've done without him.

But the man sat at the table and scarcely lifted his gaze when the deer was handed over.

'Well done, boy' was all he said but even that small bit of praise caused his son's chest to puff up a little.

The following evening, the boy went out again, only this time he did not take his gun – with the daytime heat, meat could go off fast and now there was plenty of it in the house. What he was looking for now were wild birds' nests. It was the right time of the year for them to be laying eggs. They might be much smaller than the ones from chickens but they had a delicate taste which his mother liked.

His ears picked up a sound that told him to go on full alert, that there was some sort of creature nearby, one much bigger than him. Holding his breath as much as he could, he stood completely still while trying to place where it was. He understood that bush animals could smell the scent of humans and were frightened by this. The only ones he knew that could be dangerous were the feral pigs – he had been told to avoid them. How he wished he had his gun – those razor-sharp horns could rip human limbs to shreds.

It was when he heard twigs snapping not far from where he stood that he realised it was not an animal but a human. His senses warned him that it could also be a dangerous one. Both the man and his mother had told him that it was not only pigs that were feral. The only men who came near the house were the ones the man invited over. The boy never learnt who they were, he just knew the man had been doing business with them as he had witnessed money changing hands. So far strangers had not risked attempting to hunt on their land. But why then *were there guns in the house? And why had the man finally taught his mother to handle one? Those were the questions that shot into his head. It could only be so she could protect the pair of them when the man was away.*

The boy's eyes focused harder on the undergrowth and even though the moon's rays hardly penetrated the thick foliage, he saw just a few metres away from him a bulky body crouching in the shadows. Without thinking, the boy called out, 'Who are you?' No reply came as the bulky outline turned into a bearded, long-haired man who came rushing towards him. He knew he had made a terrible mistake in letting the man see him. Why, oh why, had he not done the sensible thing and wriggled on his belly snake-like through the undergrowth? He was small enough to cause hardly a ripple in the long grass.

It was fear that for a few moments paralysed his limbs until the man was so close that he could smell the rankness of stale sweat and see the layers of grime and dirt that even the darkness could not hide. It was then that fear released its hold on his limbs, telling him to run away as fast as he could. Quickly turning, he sprinted off.

It took less than a minute for him to be caught.

To be thrown face down onto the ground.

He tried his hardest to escape, only to receive a blow to the head.

Rough hands tore the bottom half of his clothes from his body. The boy knew then that something bad was about to happen. Raising his head to spit the dirt from his mouth, he tried to shout as loudly as he could.

The foul-smelling stranger clenched his fist and landed

another blow, much harder this time. Mercifully the boy was unconscious when violently raped. He only understood what had happened when he later regained consciousness and felt the pain of being violated spring up. It took him some time before he was able to stand and pull his trousers back on, though first he placed a hand on the part of him that was throbbing. His fingers touched something damp and as he held up a hand to his face, he saw that it was streaked with blood.

Now he knew what the man had done to him. His natural urge was to lie down again, to curl up in the foetal position and fall asleep, but he knew that he must return to the safety of the house. Weak and dizzy, he stumbled through the bush, pain shooting waves around his head and his lower back; every small rustle he heard causing him to shudder with fright.

Seeing the light shining from the windows of the house, he breathed a sigh of relief. The creature from the bush would not have dared to follow him there. With shaking legs, he made his way to the door, pushed it open and took only one step inside before he collapsed on the floor.

Through a haze he dimly felt himself being lifted and carried to the couch. Heard his mother's voice harsh with fury when she saw the blood and the scratches those rough nails had left on him. Neither the man nor the woman waited until he could tell them what had happened. They both knew – his bleeding and those scratches had spelt it out for them. The only question the man asked was what part of the bush had he been in. The boy whispered the direction before his eyes closed again.

The man instructed the woman to warm some milk and put a few drops of brandy in it.

'It's good for shock,' he told her before picking up his gun and striding out of the house.

The woman must have listened for the sound of gunshot while she sat with her son.

She heard none.

Whoever had been in the woods had disappeared.

The man said nothing to the boy about what had happened.

'Heard there are bums around this area,' he announced the following day. 'Nasty feral creatures they are, wanting to steal our livestock. Bringing some fellas over to rid the area of them. Got to protect ourselves. So you stay in until I say so.'

The boy just nodded his head. Later, he would remember that was the man's first act of kindness towards him.

Over the weeks that followed the fear he had felt became smothered by a rage that was beginning to boil inside him. Once told that there was no sign of any human vermin in the bush he decided not just to shoot small animals but to lay traps for them as well. Killing them with a bullet might have been more merciful, but that no longer interested him. When after a day he looked to see what the trap had caught, he would sit beside it miserably, staring at the snared rabbit with its broken leg and terrified eyes.

After a while he would pick up a stone and bring it down hard on its furry head.

He could have told himself that it was only kind to put it out of its misery. But then why had he needed to bludgeon so firmly what little of the head the first blow had left?

16

Several weeks after Mum and Tommy's return, the atmosphere in the house began to feel disconcerting. It started with Mum staying at work later and later, returning when it was our bedtime, or even after it. As he got on with cooking supper, Dad kept telling us that she was doing well at the estate agents and busy showing clients around properties. An excuse that became increasingly regular, though for a while he acted as though he believed her.

But then, don't we often believe what we want to?

It was when Mum began to use a mixture of excuses to explain why she was now going out for the odd evening that I felt the atmosphere chill between them. The first time, when having returned from work at a reasonable time, she made the excuse that she was meeting up with work colleagues again later.

'It's to celebrate some of our recent sales,' she told us.

I watched the welcoming smile that had appeared on Dad's face when she came in carrying a large carrier bag slide off.

'Oh no, Peter, I don't want anything to eat,' she told him when asked, 'it's a dinner we're going to.'

One which clearly did not include an invitation for partners. I think that must have been the night he stopped believing her excuses. There was no mistaking that Mum had been shopping for a lot of new clothes recently.

'Not another new outfit, Liza?' I overheard Dad say when she had changed and her reply: 'Oh, come on, Peter, I need them for work! Have to look the part now, don't I? You want me to be successful, don't you?'

I didn't hear him mention it again, though I could see she'd been treating herself to quite a collection of fancy clothes. I certainly hadn't seen the one she was wearing that evening before and by the expression on Dad's face, neither had he. Black with tiny silver straps, it hugged her figure and showed off her tan. And those shoes – really high heels and very strappy – they must have been new too.

'Talk about dressed to the nines,' Tommy observed later. 'She looks great, doesn't she? But I know Dad doesn't believe it's a work do. Not that he would say anything in front of us.'

A waft of a perfume I didn't recognise floated above our heads as Mum kissed Tommy and me goodbye and then she was off in the waiting taxi. From the tight-lipped expression on Dad's face, I knew something was bothering him.

'Most probably Dad thinks she's having a fling with her boss or someone at work,' Tommy told me when he and I were chatting in his room later. 'No wonder he's looking far from happy most of the time. He's wrong though, it's not someone from her work she's interested in.'

'Well, who is it then?'

'It's some guy she met at camp, he was singing in a bar she

went to. I just thought she was having a bit of fun and I think that's all it was then but I know he's been emailing her. Anyhow, has she said anything to you?'

'Are you talking about the guy with tight jeans and long hair?'

'Yes, that's the one! I only saw him once though when he picked her up at the camp. So you've met him, have you?'

'Yes, but I thought he was just a friend. That's what she told me. I mean, he's nothing like Dad, is he? They picked me up from school and took me for an ice cream. It was when Dad had to take you for your therapy,' I told him.

'Oh, when I was strengthening my muscles, you mean? Not that that guy needs to do that. He's all muscles, that one. So, what did Mum tell you about him?'

'Just that she met him at the camp and he had come up to Melbourne on business and had asked her to meet up, that's all. Maybe she wanted me to be with her because she didn't want to meet him on her own. But now when I think about it, I can see what you mean – he kept smiling at her a lot.'

'And what did you think of him?'

'I don't know. He seemed nice enough, but he's a bit different from Mum and Dad's other friends, isn't he?'

'He certainly is! Let's just hope she tires of him sending her emails.'

But she didn't. It's a shame that Mum didn't realise that emails only show the person they want the receiver to believe exists. Around six months after she had taken Tommy to the camp, she told us that she and Dad were separating. I was around nine at the time. She told me that he had found those emails on her computer and tackled her about them.

'We're going to stay friends,' she insisted. Somehow having felt the atmosphere in the house growing icier each day, I doubted that. There were children in my class whose parents were going through a divorce and I knew that they felt torn – I just hoped we were not going to be like that. Seeing I was close to tears, Mum quickly added, 'You'll still be seeing a lot of your dad so don't worry about that. He's going to have you every second weekend.'

'So where's he going to live?' asked Tommy, thinking it would be Dad who would be leaving the home.

'He'll stay here for a while.'

'You mean it's us who will be leaving?'

'Well, yes,' she said and as she began to try and explain why that was, Tommy cut across her.

'So where will we be living then?'

'Are we going back to Byron Bay?' I asked.

'No, but it's somewhere you'll love,' she told us.

The man the boy grew into still remembers the day when his mother took flight from the house. Another row had gone on all night. He had lain in bed listening to the uncouth bellows of the man telling her she was useless, that she hadn't cleaned the house properly. He heard the shouts and then the sound of the man's fists landing on the woman's body. The screams that followed, a mixture of pain and anger, sank into his ears.

'I'm sick of feeding your kids!' he was yelling.

The boy grimaced at that accusation for wasn't it he and his brothers who brought in the food? Rabbits, birds and occasionally bigger animals, which were all turned into meals that the man ate as well. He waited for the woman to point that out, but knowing better than to stand up for her boys, she kept silent.

It was when the man disappeared again that the woman he knew was his mother told them she was leaving and that one day, she would come back for them. The boy did not believe she would – he felt that the reason she had asked them to help with the cooking was so they could fend for themselves – which in her absence, he knew he had to.

The boy made himself stop laying traps for small animals – he did not like the part of him that wanted to watch small creatures die in agony when he took the rage that had grown inside him out on them. He got his brother to help him get rid of the traps and fill in the pits they had dug to capture larger animals. Though tempted to have a much larger one with spikes at the bottom of it made for trespassers, he decided not to, for it was more likely to be a deer that would fall into it.

The man did not return for two days and when he did, the boy heard his roars of rage when he found the woman gone. He questioned the boys, threatened to thrash them if they lied. Then when he eventually believed that they did not know where she had gone, he left.

They were big enough to look after themselves was his parting remark.

He was not missed for without him in the house they all had more freedom to do as they wished. Taking his gun and the eldest of his two brothers, the boy went out hunting every day when he returned from school. He might have stopped using snares but a bullet shot properly gave his prey no time to suffer, he decided.

Although he was able to ensure there was food in the house that he managed to cook, what they really needed was money. That was when he discovered that those green leaves could be ground into something that he had seen his father smoke and easily be sold to the senior boys in school. Some threatened to take those small packets he had placed in his pockets off him. And one boy who was older than him laughed in his face as he did so.

That was something that he told himself he had to put a stop to: he needed to be bigger and stronger; build up his muscles until he could walk with a swagger like the man then no one would be able to take advantage of him again. He decided to begin with pushups – he had learnt at school that they strength-ened the body – he just needed to work harder at them than his classmates. And so he worked on them every night until he could do a hundred easily enough.

The next exercise he thought of was boxing – with one punch, he would be able to floor anyone who attacked him. He found a sack, filled it with soil and then hung it outside. The first time he hit it so hard, it bruised his knuckles but the pain did not make him cease. He was concentrating so hard that he was unaware that the man had returned – he had been crafty enough to leave his truck at the bottom of the rutted lane so no one would be alerted to his arrival.

The man stood silently watching before he decided to show him a few more moves. 'What are you doing, boy?' he eventually asked, though for once there was a good-natured smile on his face.

'Learning to be strong like you' was the answer. The man smiled for he had never thought that he would become the boy's role model. And the boy saw that his answer was the right one.

'You mean, you refuse to put up with any nonsense or take shit from anyone?'

'That's right.'

'Well, boxing is not always the best way to get your opponent on the ground. You've got to learn a few more moves, how to headbutt, where the vulnerable parts of the body are. A punch to the kidneys is always a good one and even better, a blow to the windpipe – that really finishes them off. You have to be careful with that one – unconscious is all right, dead can get you in trouble.' With that thought, he burst out laughing. 'Still, you need to grow a little first and then I'll teach you headbutting as well – that's always unexpected.'

The boy might have been skinny and wiry, but then after a few months he began to fill out. Exercise made both him and the man hungry so out to the woods he went to make sure there was always plenty to eat at home.

It was the boy who skinned and cleaned the rabbits, he who made sure the vegetables growing outside were looked after and he who placed netting around the ones the rabbits preferred eating – he had come to enjoy living off the land. Their breakfast eggs came from birds' nests and he had his lunch at school, as did his brother who began school a year earlier.

As the months and then the years passed, the man knew the woman was not coming back. Over time the boy had stubble growing on his chin and soon he had reached six feet. Once skinny, his body was now lean and muscular. At the same time his voice broke. To his dismay it wavered between gravelly and a high-pitched squeak. He knew that this was not unusual for boys of his age – several of his classmates had the same problem. Still, it made him unhappy for men did not have a voice like that and he was impatient to be one.

To him it seemed to take a long time before his voice developed into a rich deep one. It was then that girls who had been told to steer clear of him disregarded their parents' advice and made every excuse to get close to him. It did not take him long to lose his virginity – by the time he was sixteen, it barely took much time to lose. Once he had his way with a girl who had been so lovesick, he discarded her and moved swiftly on to the next and the next.

When he left school, he continued to work on the farm while his brothers disappeared off the land to seek adventures in the city. The man told him that he had become too old to farm; that the boy could stay there – 'If you do well, you can buy it from me,' he said.

It took a long time but eventually the man who had been the boy did just that.

17

I felt sick to the core at the thought of us leaving Dad and going to, exactly where? Tommy just stared disbelievingly at Mum. She, on the other hand, was flushed with excitement and her voice kept rising as she described what was to her a fulfilment of her own dream, a dream she wanted us to be a part of.

'It's a farm,' she told us, 'something I've always wanted. There's so much space there, so much tranquillity. And it's not a small one either – there's 300 acres of land and some really lovely walks in the bush and the woods there.'

Tommy took little notice of that last remark, which made me cringe. Wheelchairs were not good on rough terrain, had she really forgotten that? Instead he asked what crops were grown on those many acres.

She paused then and I saw an amused smile cross his face. He had a pretty shrewd idea that Mum knew very little about farming or crops. Eventually, she said, 'There's a lot of grass that feeds the herd of cows, around forty of them there already. Then there are some horses and we want to add more animals. Now before you ask about the house, it's old and has been neglected for quite a while. Needs some work doing on it.'

'It's got electricity and running water, hasn't it?' Tommy wanted to know.

'Of course it has. It's just that the man who owned it lived alone there for some time and let it run down a bit. It needs some modernising anyway. We've already made plans to renovate it. It'll be fantastic then, glorious views as well.'

'You've said "we" twice now, Mum, and you've just told us that you and Dad are separating so if he's not the other half of that "we", who is? And while we're on the subject, just why are you leaving Dad anyway?'

'Because we've not been happy for a while ...' She paused and then added, 'Well, *I* haven't. And now I've met someone else who I feel wants the same sort of life as I do.'

'You mean that long-haired singer you met at the bar when we were at the camp, don't you?'

I saw Mum blush a deep pink as she replied, 'Yes, Tommy, that's him. How did you know?'

'Oh, please! It was hardly difficult. Anyway, what about school, how are we going to get there if we move? I mean, where exactly is this farm? It's certainly not five minutes from here, is it?' he persisted.

Mum was still trying to appear enthusiastic but was beginning to look more and more uncomfortable. Surely she hadn't thought we would jump for joy when she broke the news? She managed to tell us it was just about a hundred miles from Melbourne: 'Right in the middle of wonderful countryside. We'll be so in touch with nature. I know how much you love it, Daisy, and it will be so good for you and Tommy. All that fresh air will be so healthy for us.'

It was not often that I saw my brother becoming angry and certainly not with Mum, but I could tell that he was seething.

'You mean deep in the bush, where there's no shops or no towns, cafés or cinemas? No nature parks and no nice smooth pavements for me and my wheelchair. Like all the things we appreciate and enjoy about Australia. That's where you've decided to take us, isn't it? And why haven't you discussed this with us before? You don't care what's good for us.'

But before she could think of an answer to defend herself with, Tommy gestured with his one arm that worked for her not to: 'After all, it's you who are leaving him and taking us away as well, isn't it? Taking us from Dad and everything we've just got used to. So why exactly can't Daisy and I stay here with him?'

I heard Mum say that wouldn't work, not with the hours Dad had to work. They had already discussed that possibility but thought it would be best for us to live with Mum. I said nothing, just waited for the two of them to finish arguing. But I felt that Tommy was right. The trouble was that he and I loved both our parents and didn't want to see either of them unhappy.

'So, what about school, Mum, seeing as you don't want us staying here? What are your plans for getting us there each day, or are you thinking of home schooling now?'

There was certainly a long pause after that as she tried to think of an answer that would satisfy my brother. I could see that with every question he fired at her, she was looking more and more uneasy. It was somewhat obvious that she hadn't succeeded in making her dream become ours too.

Before she could answer Tommy's question, I managed to

get the next one out: 'And how about Nan's visit? She and Grandpa are coming over from the UK and I want to see them!'

'Well yes, Daisy, you will. They will stay with your dad. They're coming in the school holidays and you two can spend time with them then as well. And to answer your questions, Tommy, of course you will both be going to school and there's a town quite near the farm, a very nice one too. There are plenty of shops that stock just about everything we will need so no worries about that either, though we intend to live off the land and become self-sufficient as much as possible.'

As pizzas were one of Tommy's and my favourite foods, the thought of living off the land was hardly an exciting one for either of us. But taking little note that we were looking far from happy, Mum continued talking about the area and how beautiful it was.

'And school, Mum?' Tommy cut in. 'You've not told us how you're going to manage that. Do you know how hard it is for the teachers and the kids to learn how to communicate with me?'

'There's a really good one in the town. I've checked it out and they say you'll get on fine. And there's a school bus that will take you. Well, take Daisy, that is, but they have a special one that will pick you up right from the door.'

She omitted to tell me that although Tommy's journey would only take forty minutes, mine with all its numerous stops and diversions to pick up from all the farms along the way, would take the best part of two hours.

My brother's face brightened a little then. He had been perfectly aware that he and I would not be able to go to the same school once we moved. Anyway, he was due to change to a senior school. The one Mum told us she had checked out and enrolled Tommy in also catered for children with disabilities.

'And the hospital?' I asked, knowing that he had regular appointments. 'Is there a good one near us?'

'We'll still take him to the same one here. It's not as though he has to go that often, he's recovered from the operation now.' And turning slightly to Tommy, she told him that the doctors only wanted to see him for check-ups three times a year.

'And Dad?' I asked hopefully, biting my lip to stop the tears forming in my eyes.

'He'll drive down every other weekend and pick you up. And you'll be able to see your friends here then. Now, Daisy, do you remember how many times you've told me that you'd like a dog?'

'Yes,' I replied sullenly, 'and you said there was not enough space for one and who would look after it anyhow.'

'Well, that won't be a problem where we're going to, will it? There's plenty of space where it can run around and I'll be there to look after it when you're at school.'

'You've given up your job then?' my brother asked.

'Yes, Tommy.'

I'm sure she noticed me sitting up a little straighter when I heard the word 'dog'. A smile returned to her face as she leapt in with 'Ned has told me there's a farmer nearby whose dog produced a litter of pups just a few weeks ago. He'll take you there once we've settled in and you can see if you'd like one. How does that sound?'

Being too young to understand the word 'bribe', I managed to smile back at her and say, 'That sounds good.'

18

Mum and Dad must have arranged for them to talk to us separately. For after Mum had busied herself trying to paint a glowing picture of our future lives, one that neither Tommy nor I were impressed with, she told us that Dad was taking us out for supper.

'Pizza place, is it?' Tommy asked.

'Yes, I'm pretty sure that's what he would have chosen for you two. He'll be back from work soon, so you'd better get ready.'

Accepting our conversation had come to an end, I scurried off to change.

I must say that Dad put on a really brave face that evening – it must have taken all his willpower to do so. Of course I didn't think about what he was going through then. I hadn't reached the age where I thought about adults' problems, even if Tommy did. Now I can guess that once Dad had accepted that Mum was leaving him, he must have wanted to jump on a plane and return to the UK. His parents and brother would have loved to have him back in the fold, as would all those friends he left behind. They would have supported him as well and now I understand just how much he would have needed that for he must have felt completely devastated when Mum told him that their marriage was over. After all, she was the one who had persuaded him to travel to the other side of the world where she would meet up with her family again, while he was leaving his behind.

There was only one reason that made him stay after accepting he was going to be unbearably lonely: he could not bring himself to say goodbye to us. And I think there was another one as well: something must have told him there would come a day when we would really need him. He wanted the evening to be pleasant for us, which it wouldn't be if we realised just how broken-hearted he was.

Until every last crumb of pizza had been consumed, Dad kept the conversation as light as possible. When our plates were taken away and fresh soft drinks were poured, he started with 'I know your mum's explained everything that's happening now.' To which Tommy immediately replied that she had, but that he was not very happy about it.

'I'm not either,' I told him. 'I like it here, Dad.'

Meaning I didn't want any more changes to my life.

'Oh, I don't think it sounds too bad,' he replied, 'the farm does sound wonderful and you will be staying with me quite a lot of the time, won't you? So, think about it. You're going to have both a country home and a city one. Now not many people can say they have that, can they?'

'Well no, I suppose not,' answered Tommy, with the beginnings of a smile crossing his face.

'And you, Daisy, Mum's told me that as she won't be working, you'll be able to have the dog you've always wanted, won't you?'

'Can I bring it with me when I stay with you, Dad?'

'Of course you can, once you get it house-trained, that is! Not that it should take long. There's plenty of places we can take a dog to.'

'And Mum said we could see our friends when we come back to Melbourne.'

'You both can, Daisy. It's good you want to keep in touch with them. Of course I'll be only too happy for them to come over. Get the barbecue out, if you like. I'm a dab hand at it now, you know.'

He carried on telling us about some outings he had planned for all of us, the nature park we had gone to with Gran was on his list. Then he chatted about when his mother and father were coming over and how they were looking forward to seeing us.

'Do they know about you and Mum?' Tommy asked and for a second, a sad expression hovered fleetingly on Dad's face before he quickly managed to replace it with a smile.

'Yes, they're sorry, of course. But people do, you know – split up, I mean. I seem to remember you telling me that a few of your schoolmates' parents have divorced.'

Tommy just nodded at that, while I felt like saying that I didn't think the average mum ran off with a muscle-bound singer she had met in a bar. But I kept that thought to myself, as did my brother.

Dad tried his hardest to reassure us that he and Mum had our best interests at heart, that we would never be caught up in having to take sides like some of my classmates had, but nothing he could say could stop there being some tension to that part of the conversation.

A strain that increased even more when he drove us home and we realised that he was not coming in the house with us.

'It's for the best,' he told us. 'I'm staying with a friend for a few days. But I'll see you before you leave and you'll be coming back to spend a weekend with me very soon.'

Hugs were given just before Mum opened the door to let us in.

However much Dad had tried to cheer us up, the moment he drove off, the stark reality of what was happening struck me. Without saying a word to Mum, I rushed into my room, threw myself on the bed and howled. I wanted us to all stay together. I'd said goodbye to the family in the UK and now everything was changing again and I hated the thought. I wanted to be able to see Dad every day, not just every other weekend.

It was Tommy not Mum who came into my room.

'Don't let what Mum's doing upset you so much,' he told me gently. 'Dad's told us he'll always be there for us, hasn't he? And you know he will be, don't you, Daisy?'

'Yes, I suppose so,' I muttered.

'Well then, we've got each other too so let's just make the most of it.'

I sat up then and tried to mop some of those tears up.

Leaning forward from his chair, Tommy squeezed my shoulders. 'Now come on, wipe those tears away and blow your nose, then come and say goodnight to Mum, will you?' He reached down with his good hand and took hold of mine. 'Or me and the chair will pull you up.'

Miraculously, the last of my tears dried up and I giggled.

'OK,' I said and swinging my legs onto the floor, I did as he asked.

If Dad could put on a cheerful face, then so too could I was what I told myself as I followed my brother out of my bedroom.

19

Not being totally satisfied with Mum's description of the farm, I kept asking her questions. Not that it did me much good, she kept giving me the same sparse answers: that it was really peaceful, there were cows and horses and admittedly it needed a little work done.

'It just needs a woman's touch,' she kept saying happily.

Tommy and I began to wonder if Ned had even taken her there, or was she merely repeating what he had told her? I must say her face dropped a bit when I asked her if it was similar to Nan's friends' house in England.

'No, that was an old Georgian farmhouse and there's not many like that over here,' was her answer.

'So what's it like then, Mum?' asked Tommy yet again.

She was uprooting us once more, taking us away from Dad, but she couldn't paint a picture of where she was moving us to.

'You'll both just have to wait and see. Ned has lots of plans for it. Been in the family for years, but his father got sick and let it go a bit. Anyhow, now it belongs to Ned and he'll be busy modernising it.'

The only other thing she mentioned about the house was that we would all have to muck in a bit to get it tidier once we got there.

We had to tell our friends that we were moving and they too asked all sorts of questions we were unable to answer. We promised to meet up with them on the weekends we were spending at Dad's when we stayed with him.

Over the next few days while we went to school, Mum was busy packing. A couple of boxes were loaded up with her favourite cooking pots and whatever else she thought was essential. She told us to leave some of our clothes, games and books for when we were with Dad – 'You'll still have your rooms here,' was the reason she gave, 'so you only need things for the next couple of weeks. We've got to have the house sorted a bit before we bring everything down.'

An understatement if ever there was one, I found out later. My memory of those early years might be a bit skewed, but there's no way I can forget the first time I set eyes on that farm. If I had any illusions still that it might look just a teensy bit like Nan's friends' house, then I was in for a huge disappointment.

Tommy and I had been in that truck for hours, driving along long roads where with every mile, it seemed houses and buildings grew more and more sparse. So we were relieved when we heard the words 'Here we are' as Ned pulled up in front of a metal gate and jumped out of the truck to open it.

'Oh, it's just so wonderful out here, isn't it?' I heard Mum saying as I peered out of the window. Instead of the beauty she saw, I was looking at a long, deeply rutted track that was far from attractive. Not only was it ugly, but one glance was enough to tell me it would be difficult for an ordinary car to drive along, far less a motorised wheelchair. On either side of it there were none of the wild flowers Mum had enthused over, just tall, sun-scorched grass. As we drew closer to the house, I couldn't see either a garden or a yard, just flattened clumps of grass.

So how on earth was Tommy going to manage? I asked myself.

And then there was the house itself. Made of part wood and cracked peeling grey plaster, it was topped with a rusty tin roof – not remotely similar to Nan's friends'. Catching Tommy's eye, I grimaced while he gave me a pretty sardonic smile in return. I got the impression that he had expected something like this.

If all that looked pretty desolate from the outside, the rooms we walked into were even worse. I heard Tommy gasp as he wheeled his chair over to the wall to see just what sort of wall-paper had been used.

The man who had grown up there, the one his father called 'the boy', smiled contentedly on the day he finally brought Liza and her children to the farm. Hadn't he always wanted to be part of a family?

Well, now he had one of his own.

He could see the girl's look of dismay when she saw the house but he had worked out how to get round her. She would come to like being there – he knew how to win her round. And the boy? His speech only a mix of grunts, signing, typing and his voice machine, his legs might not work and only one arm did, but his brain certainly did. He was the one he would have to be careful with. Tommy had courage though and that was something the man admired.

The girl's mother had told him the about the boy's passion for computers. He had already made sure they were connected to the Net. That would keep him quiet. While the girl, who he thought as pretty as her mother but still innocent, would be easier to control. Her mum had told him she wanted a dog – and a dog she was going to get. That would make her grateful and put a smile on her face, though he felt some amusement when she walked over to the wall to see what the boy was looking at. She had a lot to learn but then he had plenty of time. If she thought those pictures were shocking, what would she think of all the videos he had hidden away? He almost burst out laughing at that thought.

Still, one step at a time for her was the best approach.

20

When I stood beside Tommy, I saw why he had sounded shocked: it wasn't wallpaper he was looking at, but horrid pictures torn out of goodness knows what type of magazines. Every single one had a naked woman in it and with some there were men as well. Feeling my cheeks turning red, I turned away from them.

Ned was looking over at us with some amusement and I forced myself not to say a word, casting my eyes on the furniture instead. I have to say I almost wished I hadn't. It looked as though both the settee and the one and only armchair had sat there for years without anyone thinking to beat the dust from its stained dirty cushions. *Now what was the kitchen going to be like?* I wondered, thinking of piles of dirty dishes and a floor in urgent need of scrubbing.

The quick answer to that was that there wasn't one – just a type of stove on a wooden block and a sink at one end of the room. *Where was the fridge?* I wanted to ask – with the heat of Australia, one was really essential.

Mum must have read my mind because she quickly told us

she had ordered one and it would be arriving in the next couple of days.

'So where are we going to sleep?' Tommy asked as he wheeled his chair around.

'Well, you and Daisy will have to share a room for a few weeks. We'll be sorting out making a separate room for you later.'

I followed Tommy into the one we were told was ours. At least that was clean and I could tell by the state of the walls that Ned must have stripped those grotty pictures off. Mum must have arranged for new beds to be in there as well.

'Come on, Daisy, let's pay a visit to the bathroom next. After that journey I need to find it, expect you do too. Wonder what horrors that's got inside it?' my brother said.

When we asked where it was, Mum looked awkward – 'Er, it's outside,' she told us. 'That's going to need some work too.'

'*Work?* It needs pulling down,' Tommy exclaimed when we saw the tin shed.

Once inside, it took us a couple of moments to get our breath back for the walls there were completely covered with those horrid pictures. Ones, I learnt from Tommy, were called porn.

'What sort of place has Mum brought us to?' he asked through gritted teeth. 'Those pictures should all have been taken down before you came, anyway. And look at the bath, that old tin thing, who'll want to wash in that? And I can't believe it, there's no taps anyway!'

There was a loo, a surprisingly clean one, and to my relief at least that had a chain.

'We have to carry the water out,' Ned explained when we asked, before showing us a rod that heated the water: 'Of course you two won't be able to manage that, but don't worry, I'll be the one carrying and filling your baths.'

A wry smile lifted the corners of my brother's mouth at that thought.

'There's no light either,' I told him, 'means if I need to go in the night, I'll have to go outside in the dark.'

'You'll have a torch, so will Tommy,' he told me and I could hear a tinge of impatience in his voice.

Now I did say early on in my story that I'm a bit like Dad in as much as I like routine and everything around me to be tidy and while Mum might have seen an adventure in living on a farm and I'll admit that the trees and fields around it did look worth exploring, I was still standing in the House from Hell.

21

'I know the place is a mess,' Ned said once I'd stopped asking questions and I watched a mocking smile form on Tommy's face.

We had decided not to mention the porn, 'Because he'll be expecting us to.' Tommy had signalled to me and I just cast my eyes down.

The thought going through my head constantly was what was Mum thinking? However determined Tommy was not to show any weakness, we all knew he was not just disabled; he was fragile and what was a minor bug for other children could make him ill for days. So, had Mum forgotten how often she had to call in the doctor?

I thought of the clean house we had just left, where everything was put away in its right place, and wished we were still there. Mum might have had a fantasy that we were all close to nature now, I just saw a filthy place that I wanted to walk out of. And as for those nasty pictures, the sooner we got rid of them, the better – certainly before Dad came to collect us.

'My dad was a bit odd,' was all Ned had said, nodding his head at what he persistently called 'the wallpaper'. I guessed he must have seen the mixture of embarrassment and disgust on our faces but he made no excuses as to why he had left it there: 'It's not been lived in for ages. My father left it like this when he went away and I bought it off him.'

That was all the information he gave us then. It was a long time later when he confided in me what his life had been like when he was a boy growing up in that house. I can remember so clearly looking into that dark place where he had been locked up so often. It made me shudder then and it makes me shudder again now as I write this. The question I had when he showed it to me and still have now, although it was never answered, is why did he ever want to return there? He added that he was going to work flat out, turning it into a house that would be good for us all to live in.

'And it won't take long for the place to start looking more like a home ...' Ned continued.

'Like I said, it needs a woman's touch,' Mum chimed in, flashing him a twinkling smile. 'Now you two, just try and imagine we've gone on a camping trip.'

We all heard Tommy's snort of pure derision at that idea of Mum's – one she managed to ignore.

'Campsites are a lot cleaner than this,' Tommy observed with a twitch of his eyebrows when she was out of earshot. His face was contorted with anger and frustration.

'Now, Daisy, why don't you sit down for a moment and I'll get us some drinks?' Mum suggested.

'Sit where? Mum, have you not seen those bugs on the sofa? Horrible wriggling yellow ones. I'm not going to sit anywhere near them, I'll sit on the wheelchair battery.'

'Oh, don't make a fuss, love. I know it's a little primitive, but we'll have fun fixing it up now, won't we?'

Personally, I thought it would take all the guts I had to brave using that lavatory again.

'Ned's already laid down planking to make it easier for Tommy to move around outside and he's putting some more down. He knows the priority is to make everything easier for the wheelchair. Now after we've had some lunch, you can give me a hand scraping those walls down. I'll start in here and you two can work on the walls in the bathroom. Now give me a hand with these ...' She pointed to the hampers full of food she had brought with us in the truck. Already she had thrown some rugs on the ground outside so we could, as she said, 'picnic in the fresh air', which somehow made the farm seem better. Mum did look so happy and relaxed, as did Ned.

I just wished Dad was with us. Already, I missed him terribly.

In the distance I could see the herd of cows and wondered what other animals Mum was thinking of keeping.

Once we had finished eating, it was 'stripping the walls' time. Tommy and I took our scrapers and a bucket of warm water to the tin hut, which the sun had already rendered unbearably hot, so we wedged the door open to get some air in and began our task.

'What sort of person would paper the walls with these?' I asked.

'A nasty old pervert,' Tommy replied, not that I knew what that meant.

'Wicked, aren't they?' he observed when he stopped scraping to look at some of the pictures. 'I mean, what great bodies these girls have.'

'Shut up, Tommy,' was my response as I carried on scraping the parts of the walls that he couldn't manage. I was almost shaking with annoyance at his flippant remarks.

* * *

It took two full days of scrubbing, scraping and throwing out old rotten furniture before the rooms were almost bare, but at least the house looked and smelt a lot fresher. The settees had been shaken and scrubbed with shampoo, all the mouse droppings were swept up and the spiders' webs were gone. It might have looked basic, but at least it was now clean.

'You three have done a great job,' Ned told us. 'This evening, we'll have a really nice meal to celebrate and relax.' He patted my shoulder then. 'You've worked really hard, turning into a country girl! Now you and I are going for a short drive, Daisy, so clean clothes and a quick wash and we'll be off. OK?'

I felt a tingle of excitement at those words and had hardly managed to answer him with an OK before I was rushing to the bedroom. There could only be one reason he was asking me to go on a drive with him, I told myself: I was going to see the puppies. I don't think I had ever cleaned my face and hands, brushed my hair and pulled on clean clothes as fast as I did that day.

'Where are we going?' I asked as soon as I climbed into the truck.

'You'll see when we get there, Daisy,' he told me.

And off we went, bouncing up and down over every pothole in that lane.

Ned kept looking at me, a smile lighting up his face, and I found myself smiling back at him.

'Goodness, you're a pretty little thing,' he said, 'going to be a real wow when you're a bit older.'

I felt myself blush a little at that, but what nine-year-old girl doesn't like being told she's pretty?

'Here,' and his hand brushed a lock of hair from my face as he stroked my cheek. 'Your skin is like velvet,' he told me, 'I bet your whole body feels like that too.'

This time I squirmed with embarrassment. I didn't like the words 'whole body'. I had already entered the shy stage about any part of me normally covered with clothes being seen. The days of Mum soaping my back and washing my hair in the bath were already behind me. Sensing my embarrassment, he changed the subject and rattled on about the farm and what he wanted to do there.

'We're thinking of building a couple of holiday cottages on the land at the back of the house – people love staying on farms. That's after I've done the house up a bit more and got an inside bathroom.' He glanced over at me again. 'I think you're already liking being in the country.'

As I had spent most of the time since we arrived scraping porn off walls in the baking-hot tin hut, I wasn't too sure about that. Still wanting to please him, I mumbled a yes. I might have loved going to the nature parks in Melbourne and visiting Byron Bay, but I was also used to the bustle of towns.

'Now, Daisy, I know you and Tommy haven't said a word about it, but you can tell me, what did you think of my dad's wallpaper?'

'Didn't like it! It was horrid,' I answered vehemently, wishing my face wasn't turning bright pink again.

He laughed. 'Thought as much. Can tell you're not a country girl yet! All normal stuff that, though he shouldn't have put it in every room. You know, when I was around your age I used to watch my father putting them up. Afterwards, when he wasn't around, I would just sit looking at them but I preferred the pictures in my mother's story books. Dad didn't like them being in the house though, so she had to hide them.'

'Why?' I asked.

'Told you he was odd. Still, we've got it all off now so that's another memory of my younger days thrown in the bin.'

That was my first glimpse of Ned's childhood.

*   *   *

'Almost there,' he told me and I felt that tingle of excitement again as he pulled into a well-maintained driveway leading up to a house that looked in much better repair than Ned's. The farmer's wife, who was about the same age as Mum, came out to greet us.

'So, you're Daisy, I've heard so much about you,' she said with a friendly smile. 'I'm Joyce. Ned here has told me you want a puppy. My two kids are out today but you should bring Daisy down to meet them another day, Ned. Now let's go into the barn. My bitch had a really big litter this time so you've plenty of choice.'

The moment she swung the barn's door open and I stepped in, I could smell the warm puppy smell. There on a mattress was a wriggling mass of cute little pups running around their much larger mother.

'We're keeping that one,' the woman said, pointing to a feisty little dark brown one. But straight away, my eyes had fixed on a squirming body of a lighter shade. Bright brown eyes met mine and when I squatted on my heels to stroke him, he rolled over onto his back with his legs wriggling around in the air.

'I think he's chosen you,' the woman said with a chuckle. 'They say animals do that, you know.'

'What are you going to call him or haven't you thought of a name yet?'

'Eddie,' I told her and after picking him up, I held his warm sweet-smelling body against my shoulder as his rough pink tongue licked my ears.

'He's ready to go,' Joyce told me.

'You mean I can take him now?' I asked, looking from her to Ned. 'What should I give him to eat?'

'Ned knows. Basically, they eat what we do, don't believe in all the fancy tinned food stuff. Now don't forget, Ned, bring her and her brother down to us when you are all a bit more settled. As they are all going to the same school when their half-term holiday finishes, it'll be good for them all to know each other.'

'Right, Joyce, will do.'

*   *   *

The journey back to the farm should only take a few minutes, I thought. I was impatient to get Eddie back there and show Mum and Tommy. After that, we could play a little then show him where he was going to sleep.

We had turned into that rutted lane leading up to the farm when Ned braked and stopped. His arm was halfway out of the window and, leaning back, he observed me.

'You happy with your present, Daisy?' he asked.

'Oh yes!' I exclaimed as I uttered a whole load of thank yous, one after the other.

'Then don't you think I deserve a kiss?'

'I suppose so,' I said with a grin and leant forward, expecting him to offer me his cheek. Instead, he pulled me forward and planted a damp one right on my mouth. I wanted to wipe it away with the back of my hand, but stopped myself and bent down to stroke the puppy curled up under my feet instead.

I think that was the beginning of me feeling uncomfortable around Ned. Though not all the time; he could be charming, no doubt about that, as well as kind. Mum, I could see, was completely besotted with him, but over the next few months there were too many times when I looked in his direction only to find his eyes already studying me.

22

Oh, Ned could be charming and he was actually good company a lot of the time. He could also be kind, as well as generous. The day after we collected Eddie, he disappeared into town for a while and then returned holding a very large brown paper bag: 'For Eddie,' he told me as he dumped it in my lap.

Inside my hands went and the first two things they pulled out were a couple of metal feeding bowls with the word 'Eddie' engraved on them. Next came a bright red collar and a tiny red harness, 'Safer for small puppies, the man at the pet shop told me,' and a matching lead, 'Good for training him to walk at heel, even out here on the farm.' At the bottom of the bag I found packets of dog treats, 'Good for rewarding him when he does as he's been told,' and a rawhide bone, 'Stops him chewing up shoes and keeps his teeth clean,' and finally my fingers pulled out the last object, a bright yellow ball, for us to play with him: 'We can try training him to bring it back,' Ned enthused.

'And then he gets a treat?'

'You're catching on already, Daisy.'

I just beamed at him, as did Mum. I thanked him about five

times, before suggesting we went outside with my new puppy. Although he did not need the harness then, Ned slipped it on him – 'He has to get used to it, Daisy.' Eddie, with tail wagging away, just looked up at us trustingly. He stood still and made no fuss at all until the last strap was tightened.

'Good boy,' I said, giving him a flurry of strokes. Then Ned and I went outside, with the excited puppy prancing around our feet.

'Always wanted a pet when I was a kid,' Ned told me. 'But my dad was against them.'

After we had played chase the ball for a while and even got it returned a few times, Ned suggested that we went up to see the horses and get Eddie used to them: 'Best to start getting him used to the animals, Daisy. Dogs that worry the livestock are not good on farms. Put his lead on and hold it tight, we don't want him rushing into the field,' he told me before we walked to where the horses were. The glossy dark brown creatures came trotting up to him when he whistled. I was desperate to stroke them as they rubbed their muzzles against his neck.

'Best wait until they know you before you put your hand near their mouths,' he told me as he fished in his jean pockets for some carrots, which the horses gently removed from his fingers.

The next stop was the field where the cows were. Some of them had their baby calves nuzzling away on their udders as they filled themselves with her milk, while the other larger calves appeared a little more adventurous. Standing in a field on his own was the bull.

'He's got a right harem here, hasn't he? No wonder he looks contented!'

'What do you mean?'

'Why, he's the father of all those calves, you see, and a few of the cows as well. He doesn't believe in monogamy, that's for sure. Not that many men do either.'

I almost asked him what that word meant; I knew he wanted me to, but a sixth sense told me by the teasing glint in his eyes that the answer he would give was not one I wanted to hear.

Ned showed me a few paths that he said would be good to take Eddie walking on: 'Just don't go too far, don't want you getting lost,' he told me. His arm went round my shoulders and he gave me an affectionate squeeze.

I smiled happily up at him. It was such a lovely day, a puppy I had wanted for so long was near my feet, the sun was warm against my face and Ned had been so generous with his puppy presents that those feelings of being uncomfortable around him had slipped to the back of my mind, but it did not take long for them to return.

My feelings for him became mixed although Mum, I could see, was completely besotted with him. In fact, I had seldom seen her looking so happy and he seemed equally keen on her. He bought her different large pots of flowers, some that could brighten up the house and others where she could begin turning part of the unkempt plot just outside the house into a garden.

'My mother used to grow vegetables there, but they have all gone now,' was all he said when he pointed to it, 'so if cabbages could grow well there, so can flowers.'

Another little piece of his childhood about when he lived there was revealed; not that I asked him questions about it, for something told me not to talk about it. However nice he was being during those early months, there were too many times when I had looked in his direction only to find his eyes already on me. I did try and tell myself that I was imagining how often they seemed to be fixed on me. After all, with my childhood, which had, up until then, been a secure happy one, I would hardly have understood the reason for his interest in me. Nor would I be able to put into words why I was beginning to feel nervous at being alone with him.

Maybe sometimes children can see what adults can't, because within less than a few weeks of being there, I sensed there was another side to Ned. Both Tommy and I had seen that he drank a lot of beer and brandy and one drink too many could make him snappy. I knew Mum was not entirely happy about it.

'And it's not just tobacco he's smoking either,' my brother said and I could tell that worried him a little.

'How can you tell?' I asked.

'By the smell and his eyes too. Have you not seen how large his pupils grow some evenings? Still, from what I've read, it might be better for all of us, including him, if he's stoned rather than drunk. Evidently smoking weed, as it's called, makes you quite mellow – there's something inside Ned that's angry.'

I watched him one morning when he didn't know I was there. There was a tension to his jaw and in the knuckles of his clenched fists as he gazed into the distance at the woods. It was as though he could see someone he wanted to punch and punch. But there was no one there, just me.

When he turned and saw I was standing with Eddie at my side, his face relaxed and a smile crossed it as he loped over in my direction. 'Ah, you caught me doing my exercises,' he told me, linking his arm through mine. 'Let's go in and get some breakfast.'

But that image of him stayed with me. I told Tommy what I had seen because it had unnerved me a little.

'I said there's something he's hiding, haven't I? He might keep it under control, but there's something very dark inside him. Don't you feel it, Daisy?' my brother said.

Truth was, I did. Whatever it was that was bugging Ned, he was careful to keep it under control. Now I'm able to understand that it was his demons that were tormenting him and spurring on his inner rage. I felt guilty when I agreed with Tommy, felt we shouldn't be talking about him behind his back, but I no longer feel that way. Nor do I now ask myself why he chose to live alongside the ghosts of his childhood that lingered on for him at the farm. For a long time I've thought that the anger coiled up inside him made him want to control the past instead of the present. Of course when I lived there with him, I had little understanding of all the complex emotions that drove him. Instead I felt guilty about allowing bad thoughts about him to creep into my mind. He went out of his way to be nice to Tommy and me. When we started school, he drove us there.

'You'll have to catch the bus once you've settled in school, but then you'll get to know some of the kids,' he told me. 'When I can, I'll pick you up. Though it's not too bad for you, Tommy, you get a door-to-door service. But remember, Daisy, you'll be on it for a long time. Take something to read with you.'

And then he told us that when he was a boy he had travelled the same route as us.

'Did your dad never take you?'

'No,' was his terse reply and a shadow seemed to fall over his face as he thought about that long-gone time.

That first day at the new school was hard for us both, but all Tommy's usual confidence had disappeared and I could tell that he was really nervous. How long would it be before the kids in his class and the teachers could understand his communication? What he didn't know was that at assembly the day before, the Head had explained to the entire school what he knew about his medical condition.

The Head explained that he had talked to our previous school and learnt about the way Tommy communicated. He told them it would take a little time to become attuned to him, but they should all make an effort – he was one of the brightest pupils his previous school had ever had: 'Remember, he might not be able to speak, but he can hear everything you say.'

The Head finished up by telling them that he wanted both Tommy and me to feel welcome at the school.

That speech worked wonders: we were greeted with really friendly hellos, 'My name is...', 'Join us in the break, won't you?', 'Sit with us at lunch' and 'Any chance of a ride on the back of that machine of yours, Tommy?'

I could see all the worry drain from my brother's face and I just wanted to hug everyone, I was so relieved.

23

Then came the weekend that Dad was picking us up. He had told me on the phone that he was so looking forward to us coming and Tommy and I were thrilled to be seeing him too. Although so much had happened in those two weeks, because we had missed him, it all seemed a long time. Hardly a night had gone by without me wishing we were all together still. I might have begun to like Ned, but he was not Dad and never would be.

That morning, I was up early. Eddie needed his pee walk and I wanted to pack everything I needed to take with me.

'I'll pick you both up from school,' Ned told us, 'that will give you more time with your dad, won't it? He's told Mum that's he's finishing work early and will drive straight down for you this evening. As you've told him that Eddie is house-trained, best make sure he's taken out for his early morning pee walk and his bedtime one too.'

'Be easier for him to pick you up by the gate tonight,' Mum told me when she saw I was ready. 'His car might not like that lane to drive up, Ned will drive you down.'

'I can manage,' Tommy protested, only to hear, 'It's not good for your wheelchair.'

As soon as we were by the gate, Ned managed to turn the truck and head back to the house. Guess they don't want him to meet Dad, which I suppose was pretty understandable and besides, we wanted Dad's time to be pleasant right from the start. Tommy and I both thought it was more because Dad did not want to see Mum and with Ned too. I'm sure she was none too keen for Dad to see the house either. OK, the porn was gone but it still looked a mess from the outside and pretty ramshackle too. The timing was pretty good though and the dust that Ned had stirred up on the track had barely settled when Dad, driving slowly so as not to miss the turning, pulled in next to us. The moment he opened his door, I was wrapped around him and we hugged tightly.

'Missed you,' I told him as Eddie jumped up and down with excitement, wanting to join in with the cuddles.

'And I've missed both of you more than you can imagine,' he said in return and I think there were tears in his eyes as he busied himself helping Tommy into the car and putting the wheelchair in the back of the car.

Dad must have left very early in the afternoon to pick us up so soon. *He really must have been wanting to see us*, I thought. The journey back to the house went quite quickly as he was all smiles as he chatted about what he had planned for the weekend. He told us that he had contacted some of our friends and invited them over for a barbecue.

'Their parents are coming as well, so it will be a busy afternoon on Saturday and tonight, I'm going to take us out for a pizza.'

There was a cheer from Tommy because not only was pizza his favourite but he didn't have to struggle with cutlery and could just hold the slice in his hand and eat it.

'As Eddie has had her injections, we could take her out for a walk in the morning and stop for coffee and cakes in the shopping arcade too?' Dad knew Tommy and I loved that coffee shop – they made the best cakes ever.

'Not been near any shops for ages,' Tommy chipped in because his special bus gave him no time in town at all.

* * *

Our rooms were just how we had left them. Everything was neat and tidy in the house – well, it would be with Dad in control. There was nothing of Mum's lying around as before, no scarf hung over a back of a chair, no shoes kicked off in the hall – all the little things that always told of her presence.

Although he didn't say anything about Mum, I noticed his lips tighten when Tommy or I mentioned her. He might not want either of us to know he was angry with her, but we both could tell. Neither of us blamed him for not wanting to talk about her, or ask how we were all getting on at the farm. He must have had to bite his lip a lot not to come out with what he really felt. Let's face it, she had persuaded him to move to a country he hadn't wanted to move to, where he had to leave behind the life he was really happy with. He missed his friends and his family – and now he missed Tommy and me. For not only had Mum left him, but she had moved out to the bush where we were so far away, not just from him, but from the hospitals as well. I think he realised more than we did that Tommy's condition could become critical and proximity to emergency care was important; it just fuelled his anger at Mum.

We were just grateful that neither of them had asked us to take sides. Though, much as we loved Mum, we could hardly say that Dad deserved what he got.

*   *   *

That weekend, everything went as planned. Pizza that first evening. And the BBQ, or as we were now learning to say, the 'Barbie', the next. Both Tommy and I were so pleased to see our friends and we had so much to tell them.

I heard a couple of the parents saying Dad must come over for dinner one night.

'The wife's a good cook,' the husband said, 'and you and I can have a few beers outside.'

So, at least Dad has a few friends now, Tommy and I agreed later.

Tommy told me he had been worried that Dad might be lonely and miss his friends in the UK even more but he had joined a social club and teamed up with a couple of guys who loved football as much as he did.

'So that's good, isn't it?'

It was.

I felt a little relief at that: it was as though by living with Mum, we had taken her side. But Dad reassured me this was not the case because after the last guests had said their goodbyes, I blurted that niggling worry out.

'Look, we might have fallen out,' he said with typical under-statement, 'but both of us have you and Tommy's best interests at heart. And that's all you have to think about, Daisy. I don't want you worrying about your mum and me – we both love you and Tommy to bits. You know that, don't you?'

I tried to say yes, of course I did, but instead I burst into tears. His arm immediately went round me and he pulled me onto his knee.

'I miss you so much, Dad!' I blurted out, without telling him how, on those first few nights in that horrible place, I had cried into my pillow. It was getting Eddie that had put a stop to my tears. His furry little body was in a basket next to my bed and just reaching down and stroking his head made me feel better. Even so, wild fields and doggy love failed to make the farm a place I ever wanted to call home.

The last thing Dad said to us when he drove us back to the farm was if we ever had a problem, I was to ring him. Young as I was, I sensed his sadness. Only a few weeks earlier, if there had been something I wanted to tell him, I would have sat next to him to say it.

* * *

Naturally, Mum asked if we had a good time with Dad, to which both of us said yes. What neither of us told her was that it hadn't been that easy. Being with Dad even for what was a relatively short time just made us both wish even more that nothing had changed.

It was not that I was angry with Mum – after all, I loved her

– but that did not stop me resenting her making us move from a modern house with all the mod cons, such as a proper bathroom, an inside lavatory and a kitchen with hot water coming out of the taps. And I could not help resenting Ned. If it wasn't for him, we would not have to wave goodbye to Dad when he drove off – at least that was how I saw it. Ned didn't get out of the truck when Dad stopped at the turnoff. He waited until Dad had pulled off before helping Tommy into the truck. And yet all the way back to the house the question that kept coming into my mind: how could my mother prefer a six-foot-tall, dope-smoking, heavy-drinking man like him?

All right, I had come to like him a little. He could be fun and I had to admit that he had been really thoughtful on more than one occasion, but he wasn't Dad.

Dad was practical and caring, and the last thing he had said to us was to get me to promise to call him if ever we had a problem whereas having a problem or a worry was not really part of Ned's vocabulary.

24

The first time I got a glimpse of the other side of Ned, I had every right to be frightened. It happened on the day the school rang Mum to ask if someone could collect me. The Head explained that I was really not well and it looked as though I had caught a nasty bug that was doing the rounds and it would be better if I went home as soon as possible.

I can still remember that day very clearly. It's one of those memories that just refuses to go away. Our teacher had taken us to the swimming baths. I was fine in the water for a few minutes until I suddenly felt dizzy. I just had to get out and reaching the steps, I hauled myself over the side. My legs were really wobbly, black dots floating in front of my eyes and I felt waves of nausea overwhelming me. My teacher came rushing up when she saw me. One look at my face, which I'm guessing had turned a pasty hue of green, and she quickly took my arm and led me to the changing room.

She had to support me even more for the last few steps as I was swaying all over the place. Once there, she quickly rubbed me down with a thick towel before helping me to pull on my clothes.

'I'm all right,' I kept saying, but I wasn't.

Getting dressed turned out to be a mistake. No sooner were my clothes back on than I threw up all down them. Which was the reason the Head, when she made that call, also told Mum she had better bring me some clean ones and some fresh underwear – 'She's had a little accident,' was how she tactfully put the fact that I'd wet myself when I couldn't stop throwing up.

My teacher was able to make the phone call to the school to call Mum and then returned, carrying a large T-shirt for me to wear: 'Wrap yourself in that until your mum gets here.' I stripped off all the vomit-covered clothes and put the top on; luckily it came to below my knees.

Once we were back at the school, she popped me in a small sickroom with a daybed and instructed me to lie there until Mum came. 'Just try and doze a bit,' she told me as she put a blanket over me to stop my shivering. A cool hand touched my forehead. 'Mmm, you're a little hot but don't worry, you'll be home soon.' My forehead was hot and clammy when I touched it, but at least the nausea had gone.

When I heard my teacher's voice outside the door saying 'She's in there, resting,' instead of seeing Mum when the door opened, it was Ned who entered.

'You do look a sickly little thing, Daisy,' he said, 'best get you home fast.' Turning to the teacher with his winning smile, he added, 'And don't you worry, I'll look after her so you can get back to your class.' She of course was charmed by this tall good-looking man with his tight T-shirt showing off a lithe body and blushed a deep pink.

'Right, here's your clothes, Daisy,' he said.

I waited for him to turn his back or better still, go outside the door and stand in the corridor so I could shrug off the large T-shirt that was the only thing covering me and get myself dressed. But no, he stood there watching me, while I just about squirmed with embarrassment. He had my panties in his hand and holding the shirt in front of me, I put out my hand to take them.

'Oh, don't be so modest, Daisy,' he snapped as his hand shot out, grabbing hold of the shirt and tossing it onto the daybed.

I could feel his eyes running up and down my body and glancing up, I saw his gaze was fixed on that part of me between the tops of my legs, what I know now is called my vagina. I stepped into my knickers as fast as I could before my T-shirt went over my head and my clean shorts were pulled up. I might not have been old enough to understand what his behaviour could mean but I was definitely old enough to know it was not right. Dad had never come into my room when I was dressing and never kissed me on my mouth, only on my cheeks or on the top of my head. So why was Ned acting so differently?

I didn't speak to him when we walked out of the school, just said goodbye to the Head. 'Hope your daughter gets better soon,' she told Ned, making me want to scream out that he wasn't my father. Once outside, he tried to take my arm and I shook it off without saying a word to him. He offered to help me climb into the truck, I ignored him and once seated, turned my face to the window.

I could feel him glancing at me while I waited for him to turn on the ignition. I just wanted to get home and curl up on my bed and go to sleep. I was also scared that I might be sick again. He broke the silence by asking me to turn round and look at him.

'Daisy, look, I'm sorry if I embarrassed you there. It's just we're a bit different over here than in England.'

'What do you mean?' I asked stiffly as I turned towards him slightly.

'When I was your age I had a sister and when it was hot, we ran around with hardly any clothes on. Did that when we were older too. And we went swimming without any. My brothers did as well. None of us thought anything of trying to hide our bodies. That's country people for you. And maybe we do show our affection to each other more physically than you're used to, most probably because we're not so good with words. And I didn't correct your head teacher because I didn't want to embarrass her either. You know I don't want to upset you.'

The answer to that was no, but I didn't say anything, just waited to hear what he was going to come up with next.

'Look, Daisy, I know you love your dad so don't think I'm trying to take his place. Couldn't even if I wanted to, could I?'

The answer to that was also no, which was all I said. What else was he going to come up with?

'What I would really like is for you and Tommy to see me as a friend, one you can ask questions of and chat to. How does that sound to you? I know you've not found the last few weeks easy.'

I found myself relaxing a little at those words and looking up at him, I saw an understanding smile on his face. Then his hand wrapped around mine.

'So what do you think, Daisy, can we be friends now?'

'Yes,' I replied and smiled a little at him.

'Shake on it?'

Beginning to giggle at his earnestness, I let him shake my small hand gently. He turned on the ignition then, mumbling something about me looking as though I needed to get into my bed, and then he promised to walk Eddie, who would be pleased to see me back so early.

We drove on in silence. A little later, he said, 'I've come up with another idea. Seeing you and I are friends now, how would you like to come to one of my gigs? A bit of an evening out, you and your mum. It's not for a week so you should be better by then – you've already got some colour in your face.'

'What about Tommy?' I said.

'The place our next gig is in is no good for wheelchairs. I'll get him some company. Evidently, Joyce's son Bertie is into computers and the same age, so I can arrange for him to come over. So, what do you think, would you like me to set that up?'

'Oh yes,' I answered, feeling a little excited at the thought of going to a grown-up event.

'Your mum says you've a good voice, you must have got it from her so I think I might get you up on the stage as well. You can sing with your mum and me. What would you think of that?'

I think I must have blushed a little at the thought, but I couldn't say I didn't like the idea. Later, when they thought I was asleep, I heard Ned telling Mum he thought it would be great for me to join them at his gig.

'But we'll be out really late, she's not used to that.'

'It's a Saturday night, she can sleep in late on Sunday,' he insisted.

'I'm not happy about that. She's always been sheltered. What happens when we're on the stage? Can't have her out there alone. You know there are a few rough guys who go there and they're hardly careful with their language. I mean, we'll be all right, but she's only a child,' Mum persisted.

'I've got a couple of friends coming, they can look after her. Don't look so worried, Liza, they're a married couple with grown-up children. They'll look after her all right. And you'll meet them when we go, so you can see for yourself. How does that sound?'

'If you're sure they'll be there then I suppose it's all right. But if there's a problem, you'll be singing on your own. God knows what her dad would say, though.'

I breathed a sigh of relief and patted Eddie on the head.

A gig was something to look forward to, I decided, as I drifted back to sleep.

25

On the afternoon of Ned's evening gig, he must have spent hours carrying buckets of hot water through to the tin hut. We all decided we wanted a bath, including Tommy. He never did like being left out, but getting my brother into the bath was another task that Ned was thoughtful about. He was the one now who had to lift him in and out of it, which he always turned into a bit of a joke, making Tommy laugh along with him.

When we were getting ready for school, Mum just brought bowls of warm water into our room and helped Tommy wash. She had chosen a mid-length cream dress for the evening and when I came back from the hut she went through my clothes to find me something pretty to wear as well. 'No shorts for you tonight,' she told me as she pulled out a couple of dresses and held them against me. 'This one, I think,' she said, holding up against me a pale blue one with a square neckline that Gran had bought me on her last trip. Then she sat me down and blow-dried my hair so it fell neatly to my shoulders.

Before we left, Joyce's son arrived and to Mum and Ned's amusement, both boys were already deeply engrossed on the computer before we even left the house.

The bar was tucked away in a small village and judging by the amount of trucks parked in the field behind it, people must have come from all over the place to listen to Ned and Mum. Once we reached the bar and went in, I understood why it was not suitable for wheelchairs. I could also see why Mum had been none too happy about me coming with them: the place was jam-packed, the noise level was high, the crowd were rowdy and the air full of swirling smoke. There were loads of wolf whistles coming in Mum's direction as we entered, which I could see made her feel a little uneasy. There was no way that it was the kind of place that she would have been taken to by Dad but Ned was too busy looking around for his friends to take much notice.

'Ah, there they are,' he said and I saw an arm waving from one of the tables not too far from the stage. 'Come on, you two,' he added and we managed to wriggle through the crowd to where a couple were sitting. 'Saved you the seats,' said the sandy-haired man who told us his name was Mick. 'And mine's Jenny,' his blonde-haired wife piped up, as patting the seat next to her, she added, 'and you must be Daisy.'

Drinks were ordered; beer for everyone except Mum, who had a white wine and a cola for me. Jenny chatted away, trying to make Mum and me feel more comfortable. 'We'll look after her, Liza, no sweat,' she told Mum more than once. She must have been aware that being out in the evening in a place like this was completely new to me. After all, there were no other children there that I could see. And I doubt she thought it was the type of place Mum was used to either.

'Have to go and check the mics,' Ned announced after draining the last drop of his beer. 'So, you'll be alright now, Daisy?'

'She will,' Jenny answered for me, 'go and have fun, Liza. And don't worry, Daisy and I are waiting to enjoy the show.'

Both Mick and Jenny were really nice and even if I found their rather broad accent a little difficult to understand, I was enjoying their company. They too liked dogs, it seemed, and had a grandaughter just a little younger than me. As with Gran, it was somewhat hard to think of Jenny being a grandmother. Not with her wearing the shortest, tightest skirt and a clinging top; I had never seen someone of her age dressed like this before. Still, she had twinkling blue eyes and after talking about Eddie to her, she asked me how I enjoyed being in Australia. The backing tracks started before I could answer that, for I could hardly tell her that I had liked Melbourne and Byron Bay but I didn't like this part of Australia at all. Luckily, as both their heads were now turned towards the stage, I knew that conversation was over. I too turned my chair and watched as Ned, holding the mic up close to his mouth, let out the first lines of the lyrics of 'Pretty Woman'.

Mum was right: he did have a good voice and I saw her smiling at him with an adoring look on her face. Apart from a few cat calls when Mum started swaying to the music, the bar went surprisingly quiet while he sang.

The next number was a duet. More whistles when Mum sang and thunderous applause as they reached the end of their first

set. People were congratulating them and asking Ned to introduce them to Mum as they made their way back to the table.

Mum was pretty flushed when finally she was able to grab a
seat and a sip of her wine, which Mick had ordered along with
some beers and another soft drink for me. When they had consumed a couple of drinks each, it was time for them to get back
on the stage. As he stood, Ned told us, 'Only this time you're
coming up with us, Daisy,' and he grabbed hold of my hand.
Back towards the stage we went, then Ned turned around and
said with a wink to me, 'Your turn now.'

A mic was placed in my hand and I sang a few bars along
with Mum and Ned. I wish I could remember what song it was,
but what happened a few minutes later washed it out of my
mind. I remember there was a big round of applause and then
Ned helped me down from the stage and told me to make my
way back to the table.

Even though it was not far from the stage, I still had to wriggle through groups of people to get there. I was so tiny for my
age, Mick and Jenny told me later that they could hardly see
the top of my head, but then Mick spotted the man who approached me: 'Nice voice, girlie,' he said, 'so what's your name
then?' he added, laying a hand on my arm and standing in front
of me. He managed to block my way through the crowd.

Not thinking that the rule of not talking to strangers ap-
plied where Mum and Ned were singing, I told him, even
though there was a shifty air about him that made me want
to get back to our table as fast as I could. But between his
unpleasant-smelling body and the crowd, I couldn't move. I
heard him ask me where I lived and then I heard another voice

raised in anger: Mick was there saying, 'Take your hand off her and stand back.'

'Let's get you back to the table,' he said to me and in one movement he bent down, swung me onto his shoulders and took me to my seat.

'He's not a nice man,' was all I was told even though Ned seemed to know him. I spotted them talking together at the bar as soon as the set ended. Not that they appeared friendly. I thought then from the bit of body language I could see that Ned appeared angry with him – I think now that he was warning him off for I never saw him again at any other gig.

It was years later when I saw his face again in the newspaper. Odd in a way that I was able to recognise it. But I did – maybe because both Ned and Mick looked angry at him approaching me, that face had etched into my memory.

It was a fairly long article and under his name it told me that he was a dealer in illegal porn, which meant it must have been of underage children. If that wasn't bad enough, the next piece I read made my skin crawl: he had abused and murdered two little girls. The worst part of it though was that it was a historical crime – the date of those murders was around the time I had seen him in the bar. I could only give thanks that Ned's friend Mick was so quick in catching on and stopping him talking to me, otherwise I might have naively told him where I lived.

Part Four

Tommy

26

Ned brought Mum up to the house where Tommy and I were staying for the weekend. They had decided that because of what I was about to be told, it would be better coming from both of them – they knew how upset I was going to be.

Tommy was visiting one of his friends who was another computer geek, a visit no doubt orchestrated by Dad. They had wanted to be together when they broke the news that after Tommy's latest check-up, the hospital decided that he needed another operation and it was to be very soon.

'Why?' I asked.

'It's his spine,' Mum explained and as she uttered those few words I could see that the specialist's diagnosis had devastated her. Normally she would have brushed it off as routine but seeing her high level of anxiety was enough to cause me to feel the chill of despair. I wanted to ask how long it would it take. I was aware that for someone like Tommy, who could hardly have weighed more than six stone, being kept under with large doses of anaesthetics could be as life-threatening as the operation.

Maybe Mum didn't know I had learnt how to use Google.

Tommy was my personal technology coach and there was not much I hadn't learnt about Rett syndrome . And if I knew, then he must as well. Not that he ever mentioned it – he was so stoic.

I could tell that Dad, who was usually quite good at hiding his feelings, was equally concerned as Mum. Well, she would have not been made to feel welcome and given cups of tea, had he not been – it was only when they shared concerns about us that a truce was called between them.

When it came to Tommy and me, we were always put first, not Dad's feelings about Mum having left him. She knew that and I had heard her on the phone, asking him to go to the hospital with her. And no doubt they would have gone for a coffee afterwards and discussed just what the operation could mean and planned how they were going to approach telling me.

Hearing the crack in Mum's voice, Dad squeezed her hand and took over: 'Daisy, have you noticed your brother's back getting rounder? And that he's no longer able to sit up straight even when strapped in his chair?'

'Yes, but I thought it was because he was bent over the computer a lot. Oh …' I felt the tears prickling behind my eyes, 'and I've been teasing him about it and telling him to sit up straight. I didn't know, Mum. How could I be so mean?'

'And what was his response?' Dad asked gently, taking my hand and passing me a tissue.

'He said, "Don't want to." Oh Dad, I feel so awful! Why did he never tell me he couldn't?'

'That's Tommy's way, Daisy,' said Mum.

'But he must have known there was something wrong even before he went for his check-up? And then he had to have another appointment a week later. The specialist would have told him, wouldn't he?'

'Yes, he did,' Mum said. 'But, Daisy, Tommy thinks of you as being his little sister and he loves you a lot. He didn't want you to be told anything until we absolutely had to, he knew it would upset you. He's so protective of you and so for his sake, you've got to put on a brave face now. Can you do that?'

'Yes,' I said, blinking away the tears that had crept into my eyes. 'But what are they going to do this time? Can't they just leave him?'

Dad answered this time: 'No, Daisy, I really wish they could, but they can't. There's no question of him not having the operation. If his spine curls in too far, and it's already beginning to press on his organs, he will get a lot worse.'

'What's it pressing on?' I persisted.

'His lungs and heart,' Mum replied so quietly it was as if she couldn't face speaking the words aloud.

'Yes, Daisy, it's his heart,' Dad repeated before I threw any more questions at him, 'that's why they're going to operate.'

I felt my breath almost leave my body at the thought of what that could mean. I might not have known much about lungs, but I did know it was our hearts that kept us alive.

'You mean his spine could crush it?' I exclaimed, feeling even more panicky as I noticed those words had drained what little colour was left in Mum's face.

'That's why they're doing the operation – so it doesn't happen, Daisy,' Dad said calmly.

'Will he be all right then?' I wanted to know. I noticed their eyes meeting for a split second and understood that whatever they said to me, the doctors must have prepared them for the worst. 'So how are they going to do that?' I added, seeing they were struggling to find the right answers to my questions.

Dad took over then. It certainly wasn't an easy operation to explain to a child and they didn't want me having nightmares: 'It does sound worse than it actually is, Daisy. But it's an operation this hospital has done successfully more than once. They're going to help the weakness in his spine by placing steel rods on either side of it, can't get anything stronger than that! Then he'll be able to sit up straight.'

I knew how long a spine was, that it ran all the way from the neck to the part of the body that we sit on.

'You mean they have to open him up all the way down his back?' I asked, sick just at the thought.

'Well yes, but it's not a deep cut, Daisy. Now, put your fingers on the centre of your back.'

I did.

'Now what do you feel when you run them up and down?'

'Little hard bumps.'

'That's right, it's your spine you are feeling. It's only just under the skin and that's as far as the surgeon has to go. I told you, it's not as bad as it sounds.'

It sounded bad enough to me. The thought of a large hand holding a sharp knife as it sliced all the way down my brother's back right down to his bottom put terrible pictures in my mind that made me tremble. I swallowed hard and realising I was not up to hearing any more for the moment, Dad leapt up to go and make more tea. It was not something I often drank, but this time he put a mug of it on the table next to me and told me to sip it. He must have loaded it with sugar because it was so sweet, but it managed to stop me shaking and slowly, my tears dried.

I wanted to ask about his recovery – Tommy had been worse after the first operation, so what were the chances of this one making him better?

Dad must have read my mind for he took a quick slurp of tea and looking straight at me, he continued, 'I know he hoped his first operation would leave him able to walk but Tommy was quite aware that this was only a dream. The doctors had explained everything to him very clearly. He knew that he only stood a small chance of that happening.'

'What would have happened if he hadn't had that operation?'

'He wouldn't be able to walk today and he would be even worse now. The doctors did their absolute best and it's only lately that your mum and I have seen his health beginning to deteriorate.'

Dad then changed the subject swiftly to our education. He explained that neither Mum nor he wanted us to miss out on schooling – 'Tommy will be in hospital for a while.'

Another horrible thought entered my head: being left on my own with Ned, for Mum said she would be spending all her time at the hospital with my brother. I had thought of talking to Dad about my problem with Ned and telling him how he made embarrassing remarks and touched me whenever he could. Mum seemed to think it was a joke whenever he patted my behind but it certainly wasn't funny to me. Only the day before he had grabbed hold of my bottom and squeezed it hard. He couldn't go too far with me, not with Tommy's eagle eyes watching him, but without my brother's presence I shivered at the thought of what he might try and do next. I knew a lot more than I had when Mum first met him, enough to know he wanted more than the odd cuddle from me. That wallpaper had definitely given me a fast track in sex education and I hadn't forgotten how he had looked at me that time I had to change in front of him. Then there were the times he walked into that tin hut when I was bathing or washing. I could feel his gaze wandering all over my body before I snatched up a towel to wrap around me.

'So, Ned will be looking after me then?' I asked nervously, knowing his was not a name Dad liked to hear.

'Oh no, we won't be leaving you on your own out there. We all know you would want to be near your brother,' said Mum.

I wonder now whether she had any suspicions or at least a niggling doubt tucked into her subconscious.

'You'll be staying in a flat that belongs to the Ronald McDonald house next to the hospital. It's a wonderful place, that building,' Dad added. 'Where you and your mum will be staying was specially built so that the families of children having operations can be near them. Now as we don't want you missing out on your schooling, your mum has talked to the school and they will provide you with plenty of work you can do from there. There are even teachers in the block who will help you, so you won't be missing anything and you'll be close to Tommy. So, what do you say?'

'And don't worry about Eddie,' Mum told me, glancing down at my dog, who as if sensing I was upset was already sitting as close to me as he could. 'Ned will look after him, make sure he's fed and exercised. He's already told me that if he goes anywhere, he'll take him with him in the truck. And you know he's good with Eddie.'

That was true – it was one of the few good points he had.

'So neither of us will be at the farm?' I asked, wanting to make sure I had heard correctly.

'No, not until Tommy can come back with us. I know you like the school there but you won't be away for too long,' Mum reassured me.

What she couldn't see was how pleased I was to be getting away from Ned and the farm. I was beginning to hate the way he grabbed hold of me as often as he could. Mum might have seen it as a bit of a teasing game, but I didn't and neither did Tommy.

'He's such an arsehole,' he kept saying when we were alone. 'I just wish Mum could see it, but then she doesn't see the dark side of him that alcohol releases.'

27

Tommy's surgery was to take place in the middle of the week. It was Dad who took us back to the farm as Mum had already gone back with Ned after they had talked to me. When Dad dropped us off, he said, 'Well, I'll be seeing you both in two days.' For Mum had told us that we would all be staying at the Ronald McDonald house in Melbourne the night before so that Tommy could be at the hospital early.

Using sign language so no one could hear him, my brother told me there was something he wanted to show me when we were both back from school. When I asked what it was all I received was a mischievous grin and a 'You'll have to wait, won't you?'

After school, I had returned home with a satchel full of work for me to do while I was away. We went to our room and he reached under the bed and brought out a large notebook.

'It's for you,' he told me, 'I've been pasting loads of pictures in it.'

Opening it, I saw a photo of Nan and Grandad sitting out in their lovely English garden. Memories came flooding back and placing my fingers on it, I imagined myself there. Picture after picture spun round in my head as I recalled all those peaceful times we had spent at Nan's house. I could see myself sitting in the kitchen, with its old pine breakfast table and sunny yellow curtains, looking through the windows at the green hills in the distance. Suddenly I remembered more about Nan's garden, where I had played hide and seek with my cousins. I wished Mum could have turned our garden into one like that – got rid of the long, scorched grass, the prickly bushes and planted more English country flowers, though I couldn't see Ned doing all the work that must have gone into my grandparents' garden. They had brought in professionals to build it in different layers. It had grey stone steps leading past the roses towards the lawn. It was Nan who made sure that there was a wide variety of flowers and shrubs which kept the garden in bloom for most of the year. Even in deepest of winter, it never looked bleak for there were some trees that retained their leaves, the holly was covered in bright red berries and there were heathers of many different shades of pink and purple. It was certainly big enough for me to have fun playing hide and seek with my two cousins.

Thinking of flowers, another memory popped up: Grandad's greenhouse had the most beautiful orchids and other exotic plants that normally grew in different lands. He loved taking me in there and explaining where they had come from. They even had their own heater in winter – that greenhouse was his pride and joy.

Grandad's other hobby was birdwatching. Off we would go together, him with his binoculars, which he put up to my eyes as well. He would take out his bird book and show me how to tick off the ones we had seen. His pen was blue but I had a green one so we had a record of all the birds I had seen for myself. Though most of them were fairly common, some weren't. He told me about the swallows and how they left when winter was approaching. Looking up at the sky, he pointed out a large flock of them.

'How do they know the way?' I kept asking. To which he replied that maybe they were smarter than humans.

Another photo was of Nan with Fred – the cat I had played with – held in her arms. That picture certainly brought back more memories of happy days. As did the ones of my cousins, who had really shot up since I had last seen them. Standing next to them was Uncle David, who with his floppy, light brown hair like Dad's, had hardly changed at all. And then there were some of me with Fred when he was not much more than a kitten and a couple of Tommy and me.

'I wrote to Nan and told her what I was doing and she got all these sent to me,' my brother explained. 'You were so little when we left and we don't want those memories fading, do we?' And then he showed me some typewritten pages describing things I had forgotten, such as when my cousins and I built a snowman after chucking snowballs at everyone. 'You don't want to forget those times,' he repeated and we laughed together as he reminded me of some of the pranks we had all got up to.

Tommy then brought out the second book. That one had not been opened but like the first one, it had a label: *Daisy's Memory Book*. 'I want to see some writing in that before my op,' he told me. 'Otherwise you might forget so much of that time.'

Then he asked me what I could remember about England

and our grandparents. Truth was, not as much as he did so sometimes I wonder if it was Tommy who painted some of those pictures in my head, or did he just light up the ones that were already there?

* * *

Over the next couple of days before we went back to Melbourne I did as my brother asked and using the photos to jog my memories, I jotted down as much as I could about our life together, including details of all Nan's visits. The day before we were due to go to the hospital, he handed me some more photos. These included more recent photos of Dad and all of us before Mum left. There was one of Tommy when he first got his blue wheelchair – he was laughing as he raced around on it – and then finally shots of Dad at a party for his birthday. Then there were others of us with Eddie when he was still a very small puppy and one of Tommy laughing at something that had been said when we were all outside – he looked so happy in that photo.

The question that was in my mind was why had he suddenly put them all together for me?

But I knew, didn't I?

He understood what the doctors had told him.

That he might not survive the operation.

And he didn't want to be forgotten.

It was a long time later that my memory books became my confidant. I could write inside those creamy pages everything I dare not whisper into human ears.

28

I had heard Mum on the phone saying to Dad, 'That would be great, Peter. Thank you. Your car will be so much more comfortable for him. Better than being bounced around in the truck.'

Unfortunately, Ned heard her too.

'What was that I heard, you telling Peter my truck's not comfortable?'

'Oh, it's just that Peter has told me he's taking some time off work so that he can come and collect us.'

Ned's hands balled up into fists. 'Don't you think I'm able to look after you all?' His shouting made my spine go cold.

'Oh please, not another row, not today of all days,' I muttered under my breath.

'Let's face it, Ned, the car really would be more comfortable for Tommy. It's not a short journey, is it? I want him to be as relaxed as possible on the drive, he has such a stressful time ahead of him.'

'He's never complained before. Neither did you when I brought you all here. The truck was good enough then, wasn't it? So, explain to me will you, just why you want your husband to come all this way out when I had planned to take you all. Is it because you want to spend more time with him?'

'No, Ned,' she answered as calmly as she could, 'it's because he's the children's father.'

'Not Tommy's father, is he? Any more than I am and it's me who's looking after him now.'

Enough! I wanted to scream. *How could you start a row when Tommy's got to go to the hospital tomorrow? Don't you know how scary this operation is and how upset we all are?*

I knew Mum was only thinking of my brother but those words I kept inside my head for they would only make him angrier. Over the months we had been at the farm I had learnt that there would be no stopping him from yelling and shouting until as usual Mum gave in. So instead of spitting out my feelings, I just glared at him.

'All right. If it's so important for you to take us, then I suppose ...' and these were the final words I heard Mum say as her voice tailed off before she walked outside to cool down while Tommy and I just looked at each other. He turned his wheelchair round and went into his room.

'Honeymoon over, I guess,' he said to me when I followed him in. 'Ned might be OK when he's sober, but give him a few drinks and he'll rant and rave at any little thing he can think of. Wouldn't think Mum's happy at having to keep giving in to him for the sake of peace.'

'Not much else she can do,' I replied.

And no, there wasn't, I suppose, although each time she did, he was all smiles again. But not this time. Good thing in a way that Tommy and I were used to it, otherwise we might have got upset. Certainly, Mum did. My brother and I occupied ourselves as much as we could, him on his computer, me taking Eddie out for a long walk. All we wanted was to escape from the toxic atmosphere in the house. As soon as we had finished our evening meal, we made our excuses and took ourselves off to bed.

Mum came into our room with me and helped Tommy get into bed.

'Don't worry, Mum, I'll be all right in the truck,' he told her and leaning down, she kissed his cheek.

'You are such a special boy.' I could hear the tears in the back of her throat when she said good night to us both.

Thankfully, we didn't hear any more angry shouts coming from the rest of the house and I hoped maybe that meant Ned had apologised for his outburst of jealous temper.

'God, he can be such a childish idiot,' Tommy said before changing the subject and asking me about the memory book: 'Hope you've been writing in it?'

'I have.'

'Good.'

I stayed chatting with my brother until I could see he was growing tired and then with Eddie trotting beside me, I went to let my dog out for his last pee of the night. Dogs don't like rows either, I felt, for Eddie had retreated under the table whenever Ned raised his voice. That night, thinking of the day ahead, I tossed and turned for what seemed like hours before finally falling asleep.

Sunlight filtering under the curtain woke me and the first thought that came into my head was the same as the last one I had before I fell asleep – today was the day that we took

Tommy into Melbourne for his operation. When I looked over to his bed, he appeared to be asleep. I wondered if he too had experienced a restless night.

Mum had told us we were due to set off early, so I went in search of her and found her packing some drinks and snacks so we could have a break on the way. She looked up and smiled, greeting me with 'Morning, sweetheart, you'd better get dressed. I'll go into Tommy in a few minutes. We'll let him sleep until the last minute.'

Ned walked in before I left and I expected him to say something to me as well. Usually after a row, when he had got his own way, he was friendly again, but not this time. His face was as black as thunder when he strode out with our bags to put in the truck – not that we were taking a lot with us.

'I suppose you've packed all your prettiest dresses,' he snarled at Mum when he picked her case up.

'For sitting in a hospital ward? I don't think so,' she muttered tiredly, for whatever the reason, knowing he was still in a foul mood.

This made me nervous: I didn't want him taking it out on the truck and driving too fast. Obviously, they had not made it up after we went to bed. I now think Ned was worried about the fact that she would be seeing a lot of Dad – I have since learnt he was not a completely secure man.

Once I was dressed and Tommy had wheeled his chair into the living room, Ned's good humour returned magically. But then even if the two of them had had their differences, he was genuinely fond of Tommy, I knew. And maybe it had begun to dawn on him that he was way out of order to cause Mum to be even more stressed then she had needed to be. After all, he had understood just how serious this next operation was.

*   *   *

When we were ready to leave, Eddie jumped into the truck. 'He's not going to be left here alone,' Ned said laughingly, before bringing out a water bowl for him. Then he lifted Tommy gently into the truck and placed a cushion behind his back.

'You comfortable enough?' he asked solicitously.

'Yes, I'm fine.'

'Good, but in case you get thirsty, you'd better have this ...' An ice-cold bottle of water was placed next to Tommy, who already had his headphones on, listening to music. 'You'll be all right for the journey, won't you?' Ned asked, knowing my brother wouldn't hear him.

And that was the nice side of Ned: when that side of him showed, it made us forget the other side of him. Tommy smiled up at him then, raising his thumb to say he was fine and then turned his music up. Not that Ned being nice and good-humoured because he had got his own way made the journey any better in that creaky old truck.

Even at that age I understood why Mum had given in to him because the last thing she wanted was for my brother to get stressed out from their arguing. After a while, we stopped for a break, where I was able to stretch my legs and give Eddie a quick run. Then it was back on what seemed to be an endless road.

When we got to the outskirts of Melbourne, I could hardly

wait to get out of the truck, my backside ached so much. Even though the road was a smooth drive in Dad's car, the truck had bumped and rattled along and I had seen the odd grimace on Tommy's face when it was particularly hard an impact. Mum gave Ned the directions and finally we pulled up at the residential unit at the hospital. Ned helped unload everything and carried it all in, while Mum and I guided the wheelchair – even though the chair was motorised, it made us three feel united.

The moment we went through the automatic doors, I felt a little of my worry drain away. The place had such an air of calm about it. From the outside it looked like an ultra-modern block of flats, but inside there was a very special feel to it, which was made even better by the friendliness of the staff when they greeted us. I felt that they understood the reason for us being there was far from a happy one and they were going to make sure we were well looked after.

When they took us to our flat, I gasped with pleasure. Talk about luxurious! Comfortable chairs in warm colours, two bedrooms and to my satisfaction, a decent-sized bathroom with a deep bath and a walk-in shower.

Tommy was to be collected by the ward a little later on so he could start the pre-operation routine and have a restful night, but first, he could see where he would be recuperating. I felt a slight relief when I saw his face lighting up when Mum walked around the flat with him.

'We could have a party here,' joked Tommy, giving us one of his cheeky grins.

'A "Get Well" one?'

'No, Daisy, you mutt! An I'm-a-heap-better-now one.'

Ned managed to mutter that the flat looked comfortable and gave Tommy a quick hug before turning to me: 'Can't leave your dog roasting in the truck, now can I?' Then he hugged Mum and after telling her that he would be thinking about us all, he left.

Dad turned up fairly soon afterwards. This made me wonder if he had waited until he saw the truck drive off and I couldn't blame him if he had. Mum made some tea and I saw that my brother was more relaxed now we were all together. About an hour later, Mum received a call informing her that the ambulance was coming over to collect Tommy.

It had already been explained to us that the surgeon wanted Tommy to have a quiet night and that he needed rest as they were operating in the morning.

'We'll go over there with him, but we won't be long. The staff are downstairs if you need anything, Daisy,' Mum told me.

What she meant was that Tommy needed to rest not talk, which is why she would come back as soon as he was in bed. At least I could watch the television, I decided, feeling the emptiness of the room.

Mum and Dad returned with the wheelchair – 'He won't be needing it for a while,' Dad told me. Seeing it sitting there without Tommy in it caused the reality of what was happening to kick in and my stomach lurched. Dad stayed for a short time before telling us both that he would be coming over in the morning and Mum was to ring him if there was any problem or anything she needed.

* * *

In the morning Mum wanted to pop into the ward and see Tommy before he went into surgery. She told me to stay in the flat and she would fetch me a little later. But no, I insisted, I didn't want to be left alone: 'I want to wish him luck and tell him I love him. I can't think of anything worse than the surgery he's having, it's so scary. Imagine having rods of steel put into your back, Mum.'

Just the thought of it planted those treacherous tears in my eyes.

'Oh love, nor can I!' and Mum pulled me close. 'We've got to be strong, Daisy, haven't we? You can come, of course you can, but he'll probably be asleep by now though with the pre-op injection.'

She was almost right, Tommy was certainly very drowsy. But he still managed to smile at us. We'd only been there a few minutes when two men in green scrubs turned up to wheel him into the theatre. It would be well over two hours before he was back in the ward.

'Come on, Daisy, let's walk around a little,' Mum told me and I could tell she was too on edge to want to go back to the flat and wait for the phone call telling her he was out and in the recovery room. So we wandered around a little, found the café and she said we could get something to eat.

'Before we go in, I want to get him a present for when he comes round,' I told her.

'There's plenty of shops in the hospital. Why, the ground floor looks more like a shopping centre than part of a hospital,' she smiled.

She was right, there were shops full of things for visitors to buy for the patients and there was even a grocery store if you didn't have time to go to the supermarket. I chose the shop I wanted to go into – I had just seen the cutest little teddy bear and thought it would be company for Tommy when he was resting. After all, he wouldn't have his computer to play on.

After that, Mum took me to the café. Not that I can remember what it was I ate, I just recall that I found swallowing difficult – I was so anxious that Tommy would not survive this time. I could tell by the amount of times Mum kept glancing at her watch that she was feeling the same. She had also just pushed her breakfast around her plate and gave the waitress an apologetic look when it was cleared – 'Don't worry, Ma'am, no one feels hungry at these times,' said the woman with a supportive smile.

We must have been away from the ward for well over an hour when Mum said she wanted to go back there. I under-stood why: every minute Tommy was still in the theatre told her he was still alive. And again, she suggested she took me back to the flat.

'No, I want to be there too, Mum,' I told her.

Seeing I was determined, she gave my shoulders a squeeze. 'Your dad's coming over a bit later, no point him being here yet. I'll phone him as soon as I have news.'

I was clutching the small paper carrier bag when we reached the ward only to be told, as Mum expected, that Tommy was still in the theatre. I could see that relieved her a little: if he was still there, wasn't that good news?

Without mentioning to the ward sister where we were going, Mum took my hand and together we walked to the doors lead-ing to where the operating rooms were.

'At least we'll see him when he's wheeled out,' Mum said.

I'm pretty sure we shouldn't have been there and I have wished ever since that we hadn't been, for as I perched on the window, I heard the most chilling, almost inhuman screams emanating from the operating theatre. They were so full of anguish and pain, ricocheting around the corridor. A couple of nurses came rushing out into the corridor but then they realised the screams had not come from the side wards. They both took hold of our arms and gently led us back to Tommy's ward. I heard them saying to Mum that Tommy wouldn't remember what had happened.

But we would.

There are nights even now when those screams enter my nightmares.

29

I don't recall anything more about that day, nor even the following one. My brother's haunting screams drove away all my memories of life in the Ronald McDonald house in Melbourne. I have some hazy recollections of doing some schoolwork with one of my teachers helping me. There were also cookery lessons designed to focus our minds on following the recipe – don't ask me about anything I cooked during that time. But I can still almost feel the warmth of Dad's arms around me when he arrived at the hospital straight from work and heard about the screams coming from the operating theatre.

I do have a mental image of Tommy in bed, pale and drowsy from all the painkillers that he was on. My next memory must have been a week or so later when I was able to do some lessons as well as visit my brother, who was by then more aware of my presence. He wasn't able to say more than hello, although he did manage to smile a whispered thanks when I presented him with the little bear. Later, when he was able to use his wheelchair again, he tied it securely onto the front of it: 'My racing mascot,' he quipped.

Eventually, after what seemed ages to me, Tommy was able to join us in the flat, where he was collected for various sessions with doctors and physiotherapists. When he was free of that terrible pain and was more his old self, he got his schoolwork out and settled down with one of the teachers: 'Don't want to get any further behind or I'll never be top of the class again,' he told us.

I still can't recall just how many weeks we were residents in the Ronald McDonald house. To my mind, it seems like months, but when I asked Mum she told me that it wasn't anything like that long. But I'm sure it had to have been quite a few weeks. I can remember Ned visiting us a couple of times, bringing with him pictures of Eddie romping in the fields. He also brought Tommy some new computer games and presented Mum with some flowers – 'Usually they're for the patient,' he told Mum, 'but somehow I think he prefers computer games.'

'He misses you,' Ned told me when he saw me looking at Eddie's pictures again.

'I miss him too,' I replied, leaving out that I didn't miss the farm one little bit. I just wished we could stay in Melbourne – even if our parents would not get back together, we would see a lot more of Dad.

And I would feel safe again.

30

It was Dad who finally collected us from the hospital and took us back to the farm. There was no question of us going in the truck so soon after Tommy's operation. And whereas he could sit in the wheelchair and move it around, we all had to be more than careful when he went outside. Any bump or jolt could be very serious at that stage and Mum and Dad had made it clear that we all had to make sure there was nothing left accidentally lying around.

When we arrived at the farm, I jumped out and opened the gates so that Dad could drive us right up to the house. Ned must have heard the car, for he came rushing out with a big smile on his face. As did Eddie, who with tail wagging so fast it was a blur, made a beeline for me. Ned shook Dad's hand and asked if he would like a beer or something cool to drink after that drive. I heard Dad say he would have a soft drink before he got the wheelchair out of the car and gently helped Tommy into it.

Ned came out carrying a tray with a big jug of lemonade and several glasses: 'Joyce made loads of it for us as a welcome home gift,' he told us as he plonked it down. It was the first time I had seen the two men together. There was Ned, with his long dark hair, wearing a tight T-shirt that showed off both his muscles and his tattoos, a scruffy pair of shorts and muddy work boots and then there was Dad, his neatly ironed shirt tucked into a pair of chinos and freshly barbered sandy hair all neat and tidy. Talk about complete opposites! On the face of it they appeared friendly enough, though Dad had always been good at hiding his emotions.

I need not have worried that Eddie might have forgotten us – the way he ran up first to me and then Tommy was enough to tell me he had missed us too. The funny thing about dogs is that they sense who they can jump up to greet. With Tommy, he just gently nuzzled his hand and licked him in greeting whereas I had got such excited high jumps as he couldn't contain himself, trying to reach up to lick my face.

Dad excused himself fairly quickly using the long drive back and meeting some friends later that evening as his excuse. He hugged Tommy and me, told us he would be seeing us in a couple of weeks, said goodbye to Mum and Ned then got in the car and waved as he drove off.

There was a lump in my throat. I had become used to seeing him every day and hated the thought that I would have to wait a whole two weeks before I saw him again. And I knew by the expression on Tommy's face that he felt the same.

*   *   *

The first few weeks at the farm passed unusually smoothly. Ned's good mood remained – he was clearly pleased to have us all back in residence – and Mum looked happier than she had done in months: her son had survived the operation and her partner was back to being the charming man she had fallen for when they first met.

Ned kept telling us how much we had been missed before adding, 'Still, the one good thing about you all being away is that it gave me more time to work on the house. I got a couple of old caravans up here as well, they're at the back. Going to do them up for guests.' He seemed enormously pleased with himself. And the house did look better – the walls were now painted a soft blue and he had turned Tommy's and my big bedroom into two smaller ones. The wall between us would hardly have been soundproofed, but at least we now had our own space. 'I know it needs decorating still,' he told me, 'and a bit more furniture, but it's a start.'

Mum was also pleased by the changes and delighted to find that the fridge was full of food. Ned had stocked up for us so that she could concentrate on helping Tommy with his exercises.

The first couple of times when my brother and I came back from visiting Dad, Ned asked us what we had got up to. When we told him about the good times we'd had meeting up with our old friends, he seemed genuinely pleased for us. I hoped that seeing what life would be like without us had made him turn over a new leaf. Tommy was more sceptical and told me he didn't think Ned was capable of continuing as he was: 'Give it a few more weeks and he'll change back,' was his opinion.

And my brother was right. As the months progressed and Tommy slowly turned into his former lively self, Ned gradually began to change and not for the better although he put on a good show when his brothers and some old friends began visiting. Parties would commence on a Saturday morning and last all over the weekend.

So, this was why he had got the caravans, Tommy and I suspected.

Trucks would drive up the rugged track that Ned had made easier for cars, perhaps with Tommy in mind. Loud music would blare out, cases of drink would be taken out and the parties would commence. Tommy and I enjoyed the early part of them when the women helped Mum with the food and drinks were passed out – well, soft ones and cans of cola for everyone under sixteen, I'm happy to say. Ned's young nephews were good fun as well, as were the friends Tommy and I had made, who we invited to join us. Come evening, Ned and Mum were called on to sing and loud applause along with plenty of friendly banter would come in their direction once they took a final bow.

Ned had installed a chemical toilet at the back of the house as well, otherwise I could never have faced going to the tin hut if a whole troop of visitors was using it. Luckily for us, some of the more adult parties were held when Tommy and I visited Dad. At his house, we could sit peacefully with our homework before meeting up with friends.

It must have been towards the end of that year when Tommy told me that he had a girlfriend. I guessed he meant Sharon, who we had met at Joyce's house. Her dad had come over and picked him up a few times, though I had just thought they had computer games and music in common.

Not that I was surprised. I liked Sharon and like my brother, she had just turned fourteen and gave me the nickname 'Little Sis'. Mum and I already knew Tommy had an eye for the girls. Only a few weeks before he had told us about Sharon (the one he called his girlfriend), he had run into the glass door of the shopping centre. The reason being he was so busy eyeing up some pretty girls who were gathered near the entrance. They were teenagers too but they had touches of make-up and were dressed in shorts or very tight skirts. It took only a few months for Tommy to be back to his old self and him getting into trouble at school also pleased me as it really meant he was much better.

Not that my brother ever allowed his disabilities to stop him from looking at girls. Something I learnt a few weeks after we had returned to the farm:

'Hey, Daisy, did I tell you that I asked the doctors if I would be able to have sex after the operation?' he told me.

'No, you didn't!' I laughed. 'Anyhow, what did they say?'

'When they stopped laughing, you mean? They said I would, but that I should wait until I was a little older.'

'Mmm,' was all I could manage to say until the thought of him looking up at the doctors from his hospital bed and asking that question caused me to burst out laughing.

31

Maybe everything would have stayed all right for us if Ned's drinking only took place at the parties but we could all see he was consuming more and more, which was making his behaviour really erratic.

'I think that last honeymoon is coming to an end. Wonder how long it will be before the next big row,' Tommy mused.

The answer to that was a very short time indeed. It was after Ned's stepfather Rory turned up and one of those rare days when Ned had picked both Tommy and me up from school. He had been doing, what he said was 'a bit of business' in town and Mum had asked him to get a few groceries and to pick us both up. When we arrived at the farm, it was to see another big truck already parked at the front of the house.

'Who does that belong to?' Tommy asked.

'Dunno,' was Ned's response, but from the rather unhappy look on his face, I thought he knew exactly who had arrived. As soon as Tommy was in his wheelchair, Ned strolled into the house saying, 'Where is he then?'

Mum was looking a bit shaky as she replied with a shrug, 'Outside somewhere.'

'Are you all right, love? Has he upset you?' Ned wanted to know.

'No, not really, but he's been nosing around since he got here and asked, or should I say demanded, that I got him something to eat. And he smokes like a chimney, doesn't he? Just about blew it in my face. He has no idea of personal space. I could smell his breath and that wasn't pleasant.'

'What! Do you know what he wants?'

'Said he was looking for something he had left here.'

'What time did he come?'

'Soon after you left and I hadn't even bothered getting dressed. You know me, nothing like getting an all-over tan. So there I was, at the back of the house – stark naked apart from my boots, that is – pegging sheets on the line when he turned up. Talk about embarrassing! I never heard his truck, he parked it at the front so I really jumped when I heard him.'

'And what did he say?'

'Boo!'

Ned burst out laughing at that and Mum joined in after a second.

'And then what happened?'

'He was staring at my body while I was trying to hide myself with a wet sheet. Eventually he turned his back and said I'd better get in and he'd like some coffee once I was decent.'

Tommy and I almost split our sides laughing when Mum had told that part of the story.

'What was he looking for?' Mum asked again and before

Ned could answer, a shadow fell across the doorway as a large, florid face man came in.

'So, you're back now?' he said to Ned. No friendly greeting, I noticed, just a scowl. 'Where are my guns? I need them,' he added.

'Where you put them, out in that old shed at the back. Remember? You buried them out there so no one could find them. Anyhow, what do you want them for now?'

'*My* business,' he responded firmly. 'You just come and help me get them. And bring a spade.'

Ned opened his mouth to protest only to be prodded hard in the chest.

'Now is what I meant, boy.'

Their eyes met and for the first time ever, I saw that Ned could be intimidated. Without saying another word, he went outside with the other man – his stepfather.

32

For several days after that curious visit from his stepfather, Ned was in a foul mood. He announced that he had a gig and needed to meet up with a few people.

It was in the early hours of the following morning that their shouting, which was loud enough to carry all over the house, woke me. I hated rows, hated them screaming at each other and hated seeing Mum's tear-stained face. I had never witnessed that sort of behaviour before. There might have been a chilly atmosphere in the house at the end of Mum and Dad's marriage, but nothing even vaguely like this.

Before we left England, our home had always been a happy one, with friends of Dad's visiting, me playing with their children in the garden and Mum telling me all those stories. Then there were the wonderful weekends and holidays at Nan's, where I never heard a row or even a minor disagreement. All I wanted when I heard those raised voices was to bury my head under my pillow until it stopped. I just knew this wasn't going to be a one-off, but the start of those violent arguments made my whole body shake; I expected there to be some intervals between them when there would be embarrassing honeymoon periods when Mum would look radiant again and behave in a girlish flirtatious way, though they would only last until he went off again for a day and most of the night.

Oh, he always had reasons why he disappeared for hours. Either he was singing in one of those bars, or he had met up with friends who were going to help him with the farm. Neither Tommy nor I believed a word he said, nor I think did Mum— she just wanted to so much.

The next episode did not take long to occur, only this time both my brother and I were dragged into it. Usually we made our escape when it started but this time we left it too late. He called her a possessive bitch in front of us, she told him he was a lying bastard.

Time to go, said Tommy's expression. That was until Ned called Mum something else – a very bad word, Tommy told me later. When he heard it, it was enough to make his face go red with anger. He pushed his wheelchair towards Ned, shouting through his voice machine, 'Don't you talk to my mum like that,' and his fist waved in the air as he tried to lash out.

Ned laughed at him at first and responded by imitating Tommy's flailing fist.

'You're such an arsehole, Ned, you bully Mum and keep touching my little sister, think I don't notice?' I'd never heard my brother express himself so fiercely, nor use the arsehole word. Maybe it was that which stopped Ned in his tracks. Instead he drew back his hand and slapped Tommy across the face.

Tommy's head reeled with the force of it, while Mum leapt out of her chair, shouting, 'You bastard! Don't you dare hit

my son,' at Ned and I rushed over to my brother. I had never seen anyone hit him before, not even at school when he
had upset someone. They just wouldn't have raised a fist to
someone as fragile as my brother. The idea was unthinkable,
especially since the rods had been put in either side of his spine.
And striking him across his face, where I could already see the
stain of Ned's fingers, caused the anger to curl up inside me.
Every impulse made me want to do nothing more than lash out
and kick the drunken man standing in the middle of the room
without a hint of shame in his expression. Instead what I saw
was more anger – I felt a tingle of dread at the thought of him
hitting Tommy again.

'You show a little respect,' Ned practically snarled as he
stood swaying and glaring at Tommy, who just looked back at
him with contempt.

'It's all right,' he said to both Mum and me. 'Just shows what
I called him hit a nerve, doesn't it?'

'How could you hit him?' I yelled at Ned, my whole body
trembling with rage. 'Hitting a boy who can't hit you back!
What does that say about you?'

'That you better watch your manners as well,' he replied.
'And you, just sit down,' he snapped at Mum, pushing her back
onto her chair. 'This is my home and I'm not going to be insult-
ed in it. Do you understand?' I saw his clenched fist raised to
just above her head. It didn't land on Mum, thank goodness. Instead he forced it down, but I noticed it was trembling as he did
so – which told me it had taken all his willpower to not do it.

Why doesn't Mum say something? I asked myself as I looked
over at her, only to see that she was pale-faced with shock, her

gaze fixed on the man she no longer knew. That was the first time I began to understand that Mum was scared of Ned when he had been drinking. She might still love the sober man, the one who could be charming and fun, the one who bought her flowers and told her she was beautiful. But that other man who appeared when he was drunk, the one who was full of rage and bitterness, was the one she must have wanted to disappear.

Ned just glared at us all, poured some more brandy defiantly into his glass and tossed it back before striding out of the room.

Did he feel guilty in the morning about what he had done?

Maybe he did, just a little. From what I learnt about him, he too did not like the person that drink turned him into. Not that I could blame drink for everything. After all, it didn't leap from the bottle and trickle down his throat, now did it?

33

I can't however blame alcohol for how Ned acted when he picked me up from school a few days later. He thought nothing of driving that truck when he was drunk, I knew, but that day he was completely sober.

Occasionally if he had to go into town, he would collect me from school. Sometimes, unless Tommy was already on his coach, he picked us both up. That day he had timed it well enough to make sure it was only me. To begin with, I was pleased at not having to sit on the bus for ages, but it didn't take long for me to wish I was on it instead of being in the truck. When I climbed in, I had noticed a few small parcels on the back seat. I didn't have a clue where they came from but being a child, I was a little curious about them – I suppose I was hoping there might be something for me in them. If there wasn't, why was there one sitting between us? In a way I got that right for inside was something he wanted to show me.

For the first few minutes of that drive he chatted away. 'So, what did you do at school today?' he asked, which was a normal adult question unlike the ones that followed.

'Oh, mainly arithmetic and English,' I replied.

'Not got any boys chasing you then?'

'No,' I told him, squirming a little. Boys were just boys. Some were annoying and some I could play with. At nine, I hadn't reached the age yet when I saw them as anything else.

'What? You mean you haven't played the game "I'll show you mine if you show me yours"?' he laughed.

I just about stammered that I didn't know what he was talking about.

'You will soon enough, a pretty little thing like you,' he told me and a hand rested a little too high above my knee, making me want to brush it off.

My heart fluttered as all of a sudden, Ned turned off the main road onto a country one that seemed free of any traffic. *Was he going to start touching me?* But no, he gave me that mocking smile of his and passed me the package.

'You're nine now, soon you'll be a teenager,' he told me. 'Time for you to stop believing that you're still a little girl. Now take a look and see what teenagers really get up to when they're a bit older.' Picking up the package, he tipped the contents into my lap – there were lots of photographs of young people.

'Now pick them up and have a good look.'

I didn't want to, but I knew that he would laugh at me if I said so and call me a prude, whatever that meant. And for some reason when Ned's eyes were fixed on me, I found it difficult not to do as he asked so I turned several over. The first one was not too bad, just a scantily-clad, large-busted blonde. Then there were a couple more similar ones with the girls smiling into the cameras.

'Go on, there's some really good ones a bit further down,' he urged.

It was then that I came to the ones he meant and touching them was as if I had burnt my fingers. Girls wearing nothing but studded leather collars and kneeling on their knees, a naked man with a huge penis standing just behind them. I didn't know what an erection was then, so luckily I just thought for a moment that he must be deformed.

'They're just having fun,' Ned said airily as I looked at the next picture of the same man lying on top of the girl. With fingers that had gone numb, I dropped them onto the floor as bile rose in my throat. I remembered then what Ned had said when we were scraping the porn off the walls: that he had much better pictures than the ones his dad had put up.

He must have been joking then, I had thought, though he clearly wasn't.

34

There are days so special that we want to store our memories of them in our minds and never let them go. Then there are the bad days, when we are too lost for words to describe them. The ones we try to erase from our memories, but they dig their claws into our subconscious and visit us when they are least wanted.

I was between ten and eleven when the bleakest day of all entered my life. It waited until Tommy and I had been enjoying each other's company in the sun to strike.

Not that there hadn't been any warning in the weeks running up to it.

I had been looking forward to the holidays and Friday was to be our last day at school for a couple of weeks. The day before the holidays began had been like any other, with me catching the bus to school, hanging round with my friends during our breaks and then catching the bus back to the farm to find Mum waiting by the gate for me, which was not so usual.

'Jump in,' she told me, opening the door, 'thought I'd save you walking up the track.'

In I got, really pleased to see her. She had turned the ignition off and seemed in no hurry to turn it on again. It was not often that we were on our own together and I was happy to have her to myself, even if it wasn't going to be for long.

As much as I loved my brother, there were times when I had to push jealous thoughts aside. It was just that he always got more attention than me. Of course I knew it was because he needed a lot more help, but that didn't always stop the little green monster from whispering, 'What about you, Daisy?' And to be honest, I was also just a little resentful about his transport to and from school. His ride in the minibus got him there and back in thirty minutes. So there he was, smiling away, with a plate of food in front of him when I returned well over an hour later. I mean, the minibus was only half full, so why couldn't I go on it as well?

'It's the rules, Daisy,' Mum explained when I brought it up.

That was the beginning of me being none too keen on rules. If the driver had allowed me to go home with my brother, then Ned would not have been able to turn up and offer me lifts.

And it was those times in his truck that were bothering me.

As though sensing that there was something niggling away in my head, Mum still didn't start the car. Instead she turned to me and asked if everything was all right: 'You've been a bit quiet lately, anything bothering you? You know you can tell me anything, don't you?'

Just for a moment I wanted to spill everything out. Tell her that I hated the rows she and Ned had, that I still hadn't got over the anger I felt about him slapping Tommy. But even worse would be telling her how uncomfortable Ned made me feel. Just the way he looked me up and down was bad enough, but I really couldn't stand how often he used excuses to touch me. And if she didn't agree with me over all of that, I knew she would be horrified at him showing me those revolting pictures that made me feel sick.

That was my one chance and I didn't take it. But then how was I to know that I wouldn't get another opportunity for a long time? It was just that at that moment I didn't want to spoil us being together by upsetting Mum. I simply said, 'I'm fine.'

'So you're happy with everything?'

'Yes' was the only answer I felt I could give it then. On hearing this, she turned on the ignition and began telling me about some more improvements she and Ned had in mind for the house – a conversation that came to an abrupt halt when she spotted something just off the side of the truck.

'What's that?!' she exclaimed and peering through the screen I could see there was something half-hidden in the long grass at the side of the track.

'Oh my goodness, it's Tommy!' she gasped, throwing the car door open.

Both of us ran to where we could see his wheelchair lying on its side with him underneath. We pulled it off him, thinking for a second that he would be badly injured, but much to our relief he wasn't. He must have been badly shaken up, but Tommy being Tommy, he did his best to hide that and attempted to sit up.

'That's the second time you've done that!' I exclaimed as the relief made me burst out laughing.

'What were you thinking, trying to get down here?' Mum asked.

'I wanted to check the mailbox to see if my new computer game had arrived,' he explained.

At this I turned my head a little – for a few seconds I had seen such a lost expression on Tommy's face that I felt so sorry for him and I didn't want him to know.

My brother hated not being independent. He just wanted to be a typical boy and in many ways he was. But not enough to get himself down a track that I could have sprinted down in a couple of minutes.

'Anyhow, where's Ned?' Mum asked.

'Up in the fields.'

Mum spoke very gently as she simply said, 'Come on, let's get you home. We won't bother waiting for Ned. You know this track needs to be sorted out a bit more, it's still not that great for cars either.'

Between us, Mum and I managed to get the wheelchair in the truck and then lift Tommy in.

I felt so much sympathy for him once we got him back to the house. He had tried to laugh it off, but I sensed it was not really the accident that was upsetting him, it was more the lack of freedom. There was so little he could do without help and he had thought he could go and pick up his own post at least.

Still, for the first few days of the holiday we had a great time. Meanwhile Ned was doing his best to get back in Tommy's good books – I don't think he understood that he had never really been in them in the first place! He had told us to invite over the friends we had made locally and he would sort out the food and soft drinks. Tommy looked a little amused as he watched Ned setting up the barbecue while he sorted out the music he wanted played. The moment our friends arrived, Tommy's favourite music blasted out.

I noticed with a bit of a grin that Sharon made sure it was Tommy she sat next to – that day my brother looked so contented as a girl he really liked was paying him attention. And our friends, despite the fact that they sometimes had difficulty understanding his speech, showed they enjoyed his company too.

How I wish that photos of that day had been taken. I would have placed them in my memory book and whenever I wished, I could have looked at them. But even now if I close my eyes then I can still picture that day clearly – that afternoon is one of my happiest memories.

It must have been three or four days later when Ned took himself off again – 'It's business,' was all he told us.

'Most probably trying to sell one of the cows for enough money to help buy us a decent kitchen,' I heard Mum say for the inadequate kitchen was a constant frustration to her. There was no doubt we needed one so I hoped that's what he was up to, though judging from the rows I had heard going on between them, I had my doubts.

So, it was just the three of us at home, which, even if Mum didn't, both Tommy and I preferred. Let's just say it was a lot more peaceful when Ned wasn't there, especially as it being the school holidays, we didn't have to get up. I crept into the room, saw he was awake, he patted the bed and I got in so we could snuggle up and tell each other stories that made us giggle away. Some of them were about Ned and his ways, others about different things that had happened at school.

Hearing us, Eddie came into the room, his tail wagging and wanting a stroke, which he received from both of us. Tommy loved him almost as much as I did and didn't say a word when Eddie – ignoring the fact that he was no longer a small puppy but quite a heavy dog – climbed onto the bed. It actually spins me out when I think of that time, like the universe knew we needed that special time together.

Unusually for her, Mum left us alone that morning – I wonder if she somehow sensed how important that time was for us. She finally came in, smiling away at us.

'Well, you two, the sun's up, which is more than I can say for you,' and she chucked over my shorts. 'Off you go and get dressed while I sort Tommy out,' she told me.

I knew Tommy wouldn't want me to stay while Mum helped him get dressed and into his wheelchair, so I took myself off to the tin shed, had a wash and then pulled on my clothes and stayed outside, basking in the sun until Mum called me in for breakfast.

As soon as we had finished and I had helped her clear up a bit, I picked up Eddie's ball, which made him jump up and down in excitement, and we went outside. I wished we could have gone to the beach, dived into that blue sea and walked on smooth sand, but taking Tommy anywhere on her own had become too much for Mum to handle. It would be a long drive and she would have to help him get in and out of the truck.

That evening when Ned returned, he was back into one of his good moods. He gave me a kiss on the cheek, handed Mum a large bunch of flowers wrapped in pale pink paper and told us he had done the deal with a farmer and 'got a good price for her', meaning one of the plump cows in the field who had produced a couple of calves over the time we had lived there – 'She's being collected in a couple of days, so Liza, now you can get that new kitchen.'

That certainly put a big smile on Mum's face, which meant both she and Ned were in good spirits, which stayed with them for the rest of the afternoon.

'I'd better get supper ready,' Mum said, looking up at the sky where the huge yellow globe beginning to sink from our sight was painting the sky with sweeps of crimson and gold. 'You and Tommy can go and watch television, if you like.'

I could tell from the smells wafting in from the stove that supper was not going to be too long, when my brother made sure he got my attention by clicking his fingers. Turning to him, I felt a little impatient for I already knew what he wanted. And I was right, he was rubbing his stomach and grimacing to tell me he was hungry. I called out to Mum that Tommy was asking for something to eat before I resumed watching the television.

'Biscuit?'

'Yes please, Mum,' I answered, seeing Tommy nodding his head. Within a couple of minutes, she had walked in with it on a plate.

'There you go, love, it's only one because I want you to enjoy your supper,' she told him before going back to her cooking.

To be honest, her giving him food whenever he asked, even if a meal was almost ready, irritated me. If I asked for anything, I was told that I could wait until supper was ready but that evening, I kept my thoughts to myself. Now, I'm able to understand the reasons she always gave him something to eat whenever he asked: his appetite was not good and if he went past being hungry, then it disappeared altogether and he would only pick at his food. Always underweight, since his operation, he had lost a few more kilos – which, as Mum kept saying, he couldn't afford to.

It's just one of those terrible acts of fate, wasn't it, that he asked for food that night and was given it? I forgot to be irritated with him and didn't tell him dinner was nearly ready and he only had a few minutes to wait. Instead, I gave in and called out to Mum.

His face lit up when Mum brought it in. 'Tastes good,' he said and took another large chunk. I turned again to try and watch the cartoons on the television, then I heard him making choking sounds, something he did nearly every time he ate, so I didn't think of it as being any big deal at first. Not until those sounds grew worse, making me jump out of my chair and pat him hard on the back. This was something I had done so many times before, though this time for some reason I felt scared and called out to Mum that Tommy was having one of his attacks.

Suddenly I saw, for the first time, real panic in his eyes. He reached for his throat with his good hand and I could hear those sounds turning into rattling gasps and watched his face turn red. This time I screamed for Mum and she came flying in. She did what I had watched her doing before, grabbed hold of his chest and squeezed as hard as she could. I expected to hear a big cough and see a large lump of food shooting out of his mouth, but this time nothing happened. If I had seen panic in Tommy's eyes I could hear absolute desperation in her voice when she called out to Ned to come quickly.

'Let me take over,' he told her and after one look at Tommy, he pulled him up frantically from the chair, wrapped his arms around him and squeezed as hard as he could. Tommy might have had his disagreements with Ned, but whenever Mum needed him to help with my brother, Ned was there, I have to give him that.

It was when all the red left Tommy's face that I heard Mum scream: 'His lips are turning blue, do something, Ned!' He tried to stick his finger down Tommy's throat but Tommy kept biting, which Ned knew was an automatic reaction and not a good sign. For the smallest fraction of a second, Tommy's gaze met mine – it was as though he was looking straight into my soul – then his body went limp and his eyes closed. By then, Mum was so panicked she was just screaming at Ned to try harder to help him.

They turned Tommy round so I could no longer see his face as Ned pumped under his ribs so hard, I thought they would break. But still nothing came out of his mouth. Ned shouted that we needed an ambulance and Mum screamed the number at me: 'Three noughts, Daisy, make the call and tell them to hurry!' My whole body was shaking as I ran to where the phone was and dialled the number. I tried my best not to sob down the receiver when asked if it was police, fire or ambulance I needed. I spluttered out that my brother was choking to death, that his lips had tuned blue and that he had Rett syndrome. The operator tried to calm me a little as she asked for my address.

'Right,' she said, 'got it, it's on its way.'

By the time I hung up, Tommy was on the floor with Mum and Ned and they were still working on him. Mum looked up at me and I saw the utter sadness in her eyes as she told me it would be better if I went outside now and not watched any more. She must have known then that what I had already seen was to stay in my head for years. For a moment I stood where I was, too numb to take in what she was saying.

It was Ned who spoke then, giving me clear instructions: 'Daisy, I need you to go to the gate and wait for the ambulance. Just go onto the road when you hear them and wave your arms so they'll know where we are. The quicker they can get to Tommy, the quicker they can help him breathe. And take a torch with you as well. Turn it on only when you need to on the path and save the battery for when you hear the ambulance.'

His words penetrated the fog in my mind and I took off as fast as I could. Eddie, sensing my fear, lolled along beside me, which made me feel I was not totally alone. I found that comforting because once darkness fell, the outside was a dark and scary place. That rutted track and the high grass on either side was pitch-dark and eerie. Not knowing what might be hidden in that grass out there, dangerous creatures and poisonous snakes made me petrified of venturing down that track at night. It was my love for my brother that made me do it. I wanted him to be saved so much. It was scary just opening the gate, for on the other side of it was more darkness, but I knew I had to.

I stood there for about forty minutes in the pitch-dark. Eddie must have sensed my panic and pressed himself against my leg. A lorry came past, the only vehicle I had seen in that time, and for a moment, I thought it was the ambulance. As its tail lights vanished, I became just about hysterical, screaming and sobbing as I called out my brother's name. Then I heard the siren and knew the right one was coming. Switching on my torch, I ran out into the road, waving it. The driver pulled over and drove straight through the gate I had left wide open, siren and flashing lights full on. That sound pounded through my body, making me shake even more. Even now the sound of sirens freaks me out as it takes me straight back to that terrible night at the farm.

I ran back up to the house with Eddie at my heels and saw that they had placed something down Tommy's throat. While I stood there watching, a huge piece of biscuit came out. Ned, I saw, looked devastated and noticing that, the medics told him that it was so firmly lodged that there was no way he could have managed to get it out. They kept assuring Mum and Ned that they had done their best, then started pressing on Tommy's chest. I heard them say there was a slight pulse and I felt a wave of hope. Hope that began to disappear when they brought out a machine to try and shock his heart into beating. Two paddles were wired up to a machine and as electricity surged through Tommy's body, he jerked into life. They checked him again and I saw by the shake of the medics' heads that it had not succeeded. They tried again and then again but each time they looked more and more worried and they stopped trying to shock his broken body. I looked on in horror. My mouth was open in a silent scream and tears were rolling down my cheeks as Mum was whimpering and saying his name over and over again, like a mantra.

The medics did not stop working and Tommy was placed on a stretcher with some sort of breathing tube in his mouth. I stood there numbly as I watched my brother being carried out to the ambulance and heard the sirens slowly fade as he was taken away at high speed. We were to follow in the truck and as we were leaving, Ned told me to lock Eddie in the house and pick up some cans of coke from the fridge. Mum said afterwards how could he even think of getting cokes at such a terrible time, but I suppose it was just his coping mechanism – sometimes being practical helps you deal with a situation better.

The journey to the hospital was almost unbearable. Mum was crying the whole time except when she paused to blame herself. I sat beside her quietly, my hand on her shoulder, just praying for a miracle.

When we arrived at the hospital and rushed in, Tommy was already hooked up to a life support system. Mum asked if there was a heartbeat, but from the look on the doctors' faces, the answer was no. Maybe the specialist didn't know how he could talk to Mum on her own, maybe he thought I was in such a state of shock and would probably not understand what was being said – but I did.

Tommy had been unconscious for too long and his brain would have been starved of oxygen, which meant that even if he came back, which the specialist doubted, my brother would have such severe brain damage that he would be in a vegetative state – one that he would never recover from.

Mum stood up as straight as she could, for what she had to say next would take all her courage.

'Let him go,' she said, 'he's suffered enough. I want him to be free now.'

I said not a word, for I already knew he died in that nanosecond when our eyes had met.

Mum suddenly turned to Ned. 'Someone has to tell Peter, he's been a father to Tommy from the day we moved in with him. He's going to be heartbroken,' and then her voice broke, 'I just can't make that phone call. Please, Ned, could you do it for me?'

His hands gripped her shoulders, as he said reassuringly, 'Of course I'll make that call and break the news to him. After all, he's the one who raised Tommy. And you're right, he needs to be told straight away. Now don't worry, I know Peter will understand why it's me and not you making that call. But first, I'll ring those friends of yours who live nearby – you need all the support you can get.'

He gave me a concerned look then. 'Are you all right staying with your mum for a little while, Daisy?'

'Yes,' I murmured as I slipped my hand in hers.

Those friends of Mum's must have jumped in their car immediately and raced along the road as soon as they received Ned's phone call. They were so fast and got to the hospital in what seemed like minutes. There were hugs and 'I'm so sorry love' and Mum collapsed into their care with heart-breaking sobs. I don't think I cried, all I remember is a feeling of complete emptiness inside of me.

They were, I knew, both kind and very religious. Not that I can remember much of that time, I was just so numb with shock. I hadn't had time to assimilate all that happened that evening. Those pictures in my head which refused to disappear for a long time were of Tommy's body lying in that hospital bed. He didn't look as though he was asleep or even like the brother I knew. I felt as though I was just seeing a pale, motionless being, which was an impersonation of him.

The ward sister guided us all into 'a quiet room', as she called it when Mum told her we all wanted to pray together.

'I'll take Daisy for a walk round the ground floor,' Ned told Mum, 'I'm going to ring Peter now that your friends are here.' I think he could see that everything was becoming too much for me. 'Come on,' he said, stretching out his hand, and I took hold of it gratefully and he pulled me up.

Although the hospital was small, compared to the one in Melbourne, it had a coffee shop on the ground floor. The thought of food just made me feel sick and I shook my head when Ned asked if I was hungry. I was beginning to find talking difficult as well. All I could manage was a coke, which he brought over to me. I moved the ice about the glass with the straw and took a few sips while he went to phone Dad.

I felt even sadder, if that were possible, as I thought of Dad answering the phone, expecting it to be a friend and then hearing Ned's voice at the other end, telling him that his son had died. How would he react? I just wished he had been at the hospital with us.

Later, I realised that there was more than one subject that Ned wanted to speak to Dad about, the second one being me. The contents of that exchange he tried his best to explain once he returned from talking to Dad.

'He's on his way, Daisy,' he said and hearing those words I felt something like a spark of relief. Dad was so down-to-earth and calm – and calmness was what I needed then. Once Ned sat down beside me, he explained as gently as he could that Dad was going to take me back with him. He and Ned had agreed that would be for the best – 'He felt you would need him and Daisy, I really think you do. You can see your mum's not in a good place, but I promise I'll look after her. Losing a child is just about the worst thing that can happen to a mother. It will be better for you to be with him until everything gets a little calmer.'

What he didn't say was that going back to the farm and seeing all the mess where he and the medics had worked on Tommy's body would have been just too painful for me.

'Of course I'm here for you, but you need someone who has known you all your life and only has you to care for at this time. And that's your dad, isn't it?' he added.

'But what about Mum? I shouldn't leave her, should I?' I said, because I believed then that my mother was so grief-stricken, she might just kill herself.

'Your mum's stronger than you think,' he told me when I blurted out my fears. 'She's had a terrible shock – you both have – but you mustn't think for one moment she would do that. She loves you, Daisy, she would never leave you.'

'She loved Tommy more, though.'

'No, Daisy, trust me, she loved you both the same. It was just that Tommy needed her more. And I know how much you loved him as well. You showed that when you bravely went up that track and waited there for the ambulance, when you're frightened by the dark. You need a break from the farm now, which is why your dad is coming. I'll look after your mum, get her home and make her rest. The doctors here will give a shot to calm her down and make her sleep. You trust me to take care of her, don't you?'

The truth was that after seeing the tears forming in his eyes when he shouted for me to call an ambulance, I did. I had realised then that despite his anger, his drinking and the way he was with me, Ned had loved Tommy, which made me feel a rush of faith in him. All those negative and uneasy thoughts I had about him disappeared as new positive ones overtook them and I even let myself snuggle up to him for comfort. And this time I didn't mind having his arms around me or recoil as I felt his hand stroking my back as it was comforting. As were the words he said then, 'I know what you had to see today was terrible for you but when Tommy had that accident and wet himself, he wouldn't have known anything about it. I think he had already left us then.'

'Thank you,' I mumbled.

I don't know how to explain it, but I couldn't bear the thought that my brother would have left the world carrying that memory. He had such limited control of his body but he prided himself that unlike many others with his condition who had to wear nappies, he was in control of his body fluids. However, it appeared that Ned understood all this as he squeezed his arms about me a little tighter.

'The last thing he saw was you, Daisy. That's the memory he took with him.'

That was when I felt that there was a bond growing between me and Ned. For the next three hours as we waited for Dad to get to the hospital, he was all I had to lean on. You might ask yourself how a man who seemed to think nothing of his touching and watching me could be so kind. Well, that's the dichotomy I had to live with for several more years. And I did what so many children have done in the past and most probably are still doing today – saw my abuser as being two different people.

There's the nice one who we are fond of and then there's the nasty one we want to escape from. But then I had not turned eleven and was numb with grief and shock for many months after Tommy's death.

I had no idea that during the time I spent with Dad, Ned was busy making his own plans. Ones he would not be able to put in place straight away, but then underneath both his charm and temper was a very patient man.

*   *   *

Dad arrived at about midnight; I must have clung to him like a limpet when he picked me up and held me tightly. He had already gone to see Mum and together, they had visited Tommy to say their goodbyes. It was on that drive back to Melbourne that I saw the streak of gold that turned into a shooting star and as I watched, it went higher and higher until it disappeared from view.

'Let him be free,' Mum had said and now my darling brother was free of all the mortal things that had stopped his freedom – that was him telling me that as he bade me farewell.

'Goodbye,' I whispered.

It was only then that I accepted I would never see him again.

I was so emotionally exhausted and every part of me so drained and traumatised that I fell into a deep sleep. Dad must have carried me into the house and not wanting me to wake up alone, tucked me into bed and then lay down beside me. When I woke, he asked if I remembered what had happened the previous night.

All I could say was, 'Yes, Tommy.' He cuddled me and let me sob my grief out, something I had not been able to do at the hospital. It was he who held me together then. Of course Dad must have been grieving as well. I'm sure the sight of his son lying in that bed would have distressed him as much as it had all of us. But for my sake, and I think for Mum's as well, he tucked away his feelings so that he could be there for me.

There was no sign of Dad's girlfriend Julie that he had told me about a couple of months earlier – they had met at a dinner party arranged by one of his friends – so I felt I just had him to myself and that Ned was right, it was exactly what I needed. Dad didn't mention Julie, who I had only met once, for a couple of days. Then he told me that she had said that she wanted to give us time to be together so she was staying in her own place for a while, which meant that she must be a more important part of his life than I had thought.

And that was when I began to feel that I was losing him as well.

Part Five

Alone

35

So much of that time is a blank. I had friends, but I felt alone. I had a dad, but now I was aware that he had other commitments. Mum, I could see when I did return to the farm, was still in a state of shock and I felt that Eddie was my only companion. Over the time I spent with Dad it dawned on me that not only had I lost my brother, my best friend, the one who made me laugh, but also my protector. Though then I hadn't given a thought to what Ned had really wanted to do with me – he couldn't, not under Tommy's sharp gaze.

Ned must have been aware of that before I was. He must have spent time pondering how to manipulate me before he developed his strategy – he needed to get me to feel sorry for him for this he knew would be my weak point. But first, he needed the house to himself for a short while to get me under his control. This was not something he could do in just a few days, Gran had to leave first. And he knew how much Mum would miss her support. Once that was gone, she would agree to anything he suggested.

I was of course unaware of any of this when I returned home

after being at Dad's for six weeks. Was I naïve to still trust a man who remained sober and thoughtful, and in my vulnerability, let me see only his nice side? Not then perhaps, but now I realise that of course, I was.

36

It was when Dad's compassionate leave from work came to an end that I returned to the farm. Already I had missed some of my schooling and he didn't want me to miss any more. Not that that was the reason for me going, it was more that I wanted to be with Mum – I felt she needed me.

'Are you sure you're going to be all right there?' he asked, no doubt thinking of all the memories that were bound to resurface. But then he had no idea what I had been desperate to tell him about Ned just a few weeks earlier.

I can picture my younger self oh so clearly now on the day when I was trying to pluck up courage to unload all my worries onto him. There I was, perched beside him on the settee with my inner voice saying, *Tell him now, tell him how Ned keeps touching you, the disgusting photos he dumped on your lap and all the rows between him and Mum* – and the worst part of all – him hitting Tommy across the face when he was standing up for Mum. Unfortunately for me, just as a morsel of my courage was beginning to appear, Dad said he had something to tell me so I waited for him to speak first. I was a bit stunned when he said that Julie wanted to meet me – in fact, she was coming over to cook us all dinner. My second-last chance to confide in one of my parents went out the window then, just as it had with Mum. But then I was unaware of two things that would have been important: I would not get another chance and my life would have been completely different, had I told Dad everything then.

And now my life had turned into a sad place, where I had watched how hard Ned had tried to save my brother. I'd been told how well he was caring for Mum and remembered how he had looked after me at the hospital. All of which combined to make me feel it was too late to confide in Dad and ask to stay with him – he was walking into a new life with Julie, wasn't he?

Julie arrived after I had been with Dad for several days. It was clear that I was wrong about him not being serious about her. Now I'm not saying she wasn't nice to me – she was – but the point is that I no longer had my father to myself.

Another anchor of my life was gone.

So, when he asked me if I would be all right back at the farm, 'Yes, I'll be OK and I'll have Eddie, won't I?' was the answer I gave him as I tried my best to appear together. The truth was as I climbed into his car, I didn't have a clue how I was going to cope. It was not just going back to the farm that bothered me, it was returning to school as well – that I was really dreading. How would everyone react to me was the question that kept popping up in my mind. Would they want to talk about Tommy and how he had died? Because I wouldn't.

With all those thoughts running around in my head I felt pretty nervous on the drive from Dad's to the farm. Mum had told me on the phone that her parents had driven down from Byron Bay to stay with them. The journey had taken twenty hours, which was just as well because she and Ned had to do a bit of a transformation on one of the old buses on the land – 'Had to make it look cosy and clean,' she told me.

'Now that would have been a pretty big challenge,' was the remark that popped into my head though I managed not to let it escape my mouth.

At least having my grandparents already there made me feel a little better. I just wished that Dad's parents had been able to come as well. He had told me how upset they were when he told them about Tommy. And Nan had sent me a lovely letter in which she told me that they were planning to visit Dad in the next few months and how much she was looking forward to seeing me again. I had put it in my duffle bag so I could keep reading it over and over.

When we arrived at the farm, my grandparents, Ned and Mum all looking as cheerful as they could, came out to greet us. But there was just one face missing and the absence of it made me want to grab hold of Dad and ask him to take me back. Instead, I held it together and hugged Mum.

Dad was made really welcome by Mum's parents and Ned. And to my surprise he walked over to Mum and placing his hands on her shoulders, spoke quietly to her. I couldn't hear what he was saying, but I did see a small smile appear on Mum's face. For once Ned did not seem at all put out by him standing close to her. In fact, a few minutes later I saw the two men talking and from the odd glance that came my way, I guessed I might have been the main subject.

It was Gran who came over and taking hold of my arm said there was something she wanted to show me – 'A little surprise,' she explained as she opened my bedroom door. 'We all had a hand in doing it up for you.' On seeing the room, I tried my hardest to smile happily at her but I just couldn't – I still felt numb.

Talk about a makeover, but then both Gran and Mum were artistic. Mum, she told me, was the one who had come up with the idea of turning walls into painted gardens. And the walls did look amazing: they were covered in flowers of all different pastel shades. Mum must have spent ages getting them to look so beautiful, but I still struggled to feel anything.

I knew Mum would be upset if I didn't rush out to thank her so I asked Gran if I could just stay there for a few minutes. I'm sure she understood why I wanted to do that. The moment she left me there, I opened the door to Tommy's bedroom and there was the bed we had snuggled up in on the day he died.

I lay on it, trying to imagine him next to me. In my head I could hear his voice telling me those stories that always used to make me laugh such a short time ago. Just wanting to feel his presence, I sniffed the sheets and the pillows – I was certain that the smell on his bedding was still scented with the smell of him. Mum must have felt it too, otherwise why hadn't the bed been stripped and packed away?

Somehow, I felt he was still with me.

I don't know how long I had been in there when Gran appeared. She sat down beside me and took my hand.

'Come on, Daisy, let's go back outside. Your mum's so pleased to have you back and your dad's got to leave soon. We can talk later, can't we?'

And a soft kiss landed on my head.

As we walked outside, Gran told me that the friends Tommy and I had made were all coming over the next day – 'They have begun to make a garden in his memory,' she explained. 'And that's where his ashes will be scattered.'

There must have been a funeral but I couldn't bring myself to ask – I had only thought about his death, not what happened to his body, while at Dad's. He must have told me, but so much of that time was just a blur.

'Seems it wasn't only his family who loved Tommy,' she murmured, giving my hand a little squeeze. And she was right: everyone did, and just those words made my treacherous tears run down my face and dribble onto my chin. I blurted out in a sob that rose from the bottom of my chest, 'Gran, I can still feel him here.'

A box of tissues appeared and my tears were wiped away as Gran tried to soothe me: 'That's because you and he loved each other so much,' she said.

And I found I was able to smile again after all.

Mum I knew was waiting for me to rush over and tell her how lovely the bedroom looked, but I couldn't even do that – I was still so numb and in a dreamlike state of detachment. Somehow my feet moved forward, but my mind stayed in my brother's bedroom.

Before Mum had a chance to ask me, Gran butted in: 'She really loved the flowers,' she said and then whispered in Mum's ear. What she said I didn't hear for some time. Mum repeated it eventually, explaining that Gran had told her that I was finding it difficult to show my feelings and she had to give me time.

'I'm going to show Daisy how the garden's coming on,' she told Mum.

When she took me round to the back of the house to see what Tommy's friends had done, I stood there, dumbfounded. They must have worked so hard to change what was almost a barren piece of land full of spiky grass and stones into this. Hours had been spent digging and paving sections of it. They had even built a fish pond and right in the centre of the garden was a plaque with my brother's name on it.

'It's beautiful, isn't it, Daisy?'

As I read the plaque, a lump rose in my throat.

'It is,' I whispered hoarsely. 'So this is where his ashes are going to be scattered?'

'Yes, love, they wanted to wait until you came back before the garden was finished. They're coming over tomorrow to add a few last touches it. And his friends have written little things that they want to remember him by.'

It was certainly a beautiful oasis and tomorrow, Gran explained, 'They are planting a mulberry tree. It won't be ready to bear fruit yet, but in time it will be covered in purple berries – they told us purple was his favourite colour.'

This would be one part of the farm that Mum and I definitely would make sure did not get overrun by a tangle of weeds and wild grasses. Unlike all the sheds and outhouses, it would never become a mess. They were full of junk, weeds were growing through the floor, rusted machinery and even old cars and trucks that would never run on a road again, not to mention the piles of old seats that had been removed from the two old buses Ned had bought. And let's not even think of the huge spider webs and a few dead rodents. To me, they were places that made my skin crawl – that's the only way I can describe them.

'Good for campers,' Ned told us, though the buses were only used by his friends when they stayed over after a party. When I had explored one it was full of porn magazines, old pillows and green leafy marijuana plants growing under a special light. The one Ned had restored was decked out like a small house and had a big fold-down bed at one end and a small lounge with a TV and there was a chemical loo just outside. He must have worked flat out on it when he heard that Mum's parents were on their way. I could imagine the scrubbing and chucking out all the old rubbish that had been piled up in it, while Mum put together some pretty curtains and bedding – another makeover had occurred while I was away.

Gran looked rather amused when she showed it to me. Guess she had worked out that it had been cleared out at the last minute. Good thing she hadn't wandered into the second caravan that was also at the back of the house as well. I think she was pretty broad-minded but porn and cannabis might have been a step too far, especially with me there – it was most probably locked before my grandparents arrived.

* * *

The following day, Tommy's and my friends arrived, bringing with them the mulberry tree, which they then proceeded to plant. Saddest of all was Sharon, the girl Tommy had considered to be his girlfriend. Although four years older than me, she was the one I felt the closest to.

'Have a look at this,' she said, showing me a pressed red rose. 'He gave me that on Valentine's Day.'

Seeing the rose in her hand made me feel a little happier. The day when we had all been together flashed into my mind, making me remember how contented Tommy had been when he was with her. The fact he was in a wheelchair and could only talk using his machine, or communicate with signs, never seemed to bother her. I felt that she really adored him. She must have been distraught when told he had died, though everyone looked quite sad as they toiled in his memory, as did Joyce when she brought her two children over.

The planting of the tree meant the garden was finished and the Memorial Tribute for Tommy could begin. Gran was right: his friends had all written little notes with some amusing reminiscences and these were read out before his ashes were scattered. Tears rolled and hugs were the order of the day. Mum was beside herself and I saw her sobbing in her father's arms while Gran busied herself trying to comfort me.

Sharon then put on his favourite music and the sounds blasted out – I noticed that the lyrics made my grandparents wince a bit. They were spiritual and perhaps they had expected pan pipes or whale music to be played as we all stood and remembered him.

Ned, determined that they would feel that he had everyone's best interests at heart, changed the music to something a little quieter as soon as he could before busying himself organising all the food being carried out, along with large jugs of soft drinks. We all sat outside eating and chatting more informally about Tommy – we were waiting for the sunset for he had always loved watching it.

The sunset that evening was the most dramatic one I had seen. First, red streaks that looked almost like flames coloured the sky and then shades of blues and purple came through, making the sky look as though it was on fire. Yes, that was a really special day. I felt the embracing warmth of those who had loved Tommy envelop me and that night I drifted off to sleep for the first time since his death without tears.

37

For those first couple of weeks back at the farm, I just didn't give much thought to how Ned had behaved towards me before Tommy died. Since he had comforted me in the hospital those memories had been pushed aside. I never for one moment considered that without Tommy, I had lost my protection.

Now don't get me wrong, that was certainly not something that even entered Ned's head when my brother died for he had tried as hard as he could to save my brother's life. And I knew then and still do now that the grief he showed when he saw that there was nothing more that could be done was real. But that doesn't mean that once I returned from Dad's, he wasn't aware that I was vulnerable.

I have no reason to believe that his actions were spur-of-the-moment ones – he must have spent some time planning how to manipulate me sufficiently for me to give in and allow him to control me. The fact that he learnt through Mum that Dad's girlfriend Julie was pregnant must have been a really helpful tool in his armament. Making me aware that I was no longer the only daughter who would always come first in

Dad's life was the first step he took, while the second was to make me feel sorry for him. That was a plan that certainly hit the nail on the head, especially after he had made me feel even sorrier for myself.

He persuaded Mum to tell me that I was going to have a half-sister or brother in a few months. I can't work out just how he planted the belief that now Dad had replaced Mum and a baby was on its way, I would no longer be of any importance in his life, but he did.

Although Mum treated telling me about the new baby that was on its way quite casually, I could see that underneath she was upset. Did she feel as I did that it would make Dad forget about Tommy or even me? Of course I was too young to feel happy for Dad because now he wouldn't be lonely, though in later years, I was so grateful he had met someone as nice as Julie.

One thing I have learnt over the years is how one person can take control over another; take away their willpower until they become so dependent on the person who they have come to believe holds all the strings. Control can also be achieved by fear, a method I learnt that Ned's father used. Another way is to show kindness and affection while at the same time stripping away all the confidence and independence of the person the abuser wants to control.

Done properly, a vulnerable person will begin to believe that they would be lost without that control, which has so skilfully been put in place. And when it has, fear arrives and mingles with kindness until it becomes the most powerful of the two. The result is that it takes time and immense courage to be able to walk away from the one who has shown both sides of their character for far too long.

*   *   *

For Ned to turn me into his little puppet, he needed to spend time alone with me so he made his plans as to how he could manage to have the house to himself, with only me to keep him company. He knew Gran and Grandad were leaving soon so they were not a problem. In fact, he got Gran to back him up on one of the ideas he had for Mum.

It was after we had eaten a meal Gran had made, one of her famous fish stews with plenty of homemade crusty bread to dip into the sauce, that Grandad made an excuse that he was going to bed – 'Got a book I really want to finish,' he said, but I think he was just tired. It was more or less when he made his exit that Ned began with the suggestion that when she felt up to it, Mum might like to go back to work.

'There are so many things that you're good at,' he told her. 'Music, for instance. Just think of all the different instruments you can play and your artwork, now that's really creative as well. You must have got all that talent from your mother.' Adding that last bit in, he turned and gave Gran a beguiling smile. 'So, I'm sure you could find something really interesting.'

A suggestion that Gran promptly agreed with: 'I think Ned's right, Liza,' she said. 'It would be good for you to get out of the house and meet other people – I know you like that feeling of independence. It's good for a woman to earn her own money and have her own interests.'

As I had heard her opinion more than once on the benefits of being a working mum, I was hardly surprised at my gran being so keen on Ned's suggestions – 'No need to rush, dear, just start looking around for something suitable when you're ready,' she added.

Mum looked over at them both before turning her gaze onto me: 'So what do you think, Daisy?'

'I think it would be good too. You liked your job with the estate agent when we were in Melbourne, didn't you?'

'I did,' she said as if it was just dawning on her and to every-ones surprise, Mum's face lit up a little.

38

When I returned to school, I felt that although the teachers and older pupils were sympathetic towards me, other people seemed to act a bit weirdly. They had all heard of Tommy's death, but not exactly how it had happened. And that was not something I wanted to share with them. Those memories were locked away and I really didn't want to unlock them to satisfy their curiosity. All sorts of rumours had gone around, ones I did my best to ignore, like some of the sideways looks I used to get.

Just sitting in a school room trying to take part in lessons was hard enough without listening to gossip. There were times when I kept having flashbacks of that terrible evening which made everything the teacher was saying go right over my head and I would find myself looking out of the window, making the teacher think I was daydreaming. For a long time I found it really difficult to concentrate. To begin with, the teachers were patient with me for they could see I was far from over the death of my brother. Later, when I had other things to bother me, they began to get less tolerant.

My classmates seemed not to know what to do, but then they were not very old. Few of them knew anyone who had experienced death – maybe the family pet, but certainly not a sibling or a parent. It was the older ones who came up to me and said how sorry they were. But nothing they said made me feel any better and in fact as soon as anyone did say kind words of sympathy, my eyes filled with tears. In one way I just wanted to get out and go home but as soon as I got off the bus, I had to open that gate, which also brought back memories and walk up to the house, only to hear Tommy's favourite music blaring away.

The first time it happened, I froze: had he come back to us? Sometimes Mum was writing poetry about him, which she wanted to share with me. I must say these poems were quite wonderful. Other times, her creative side took over and she would be painting more murals on the walls – they certainly made the rooms look bigger and brighter and I think it helped her cope. She talked about him all the time with me – about the weird dreams she had, how the doctors managed to save him and how one day we would hear the bus and he would be back from school as usual. She said that when Christmas came she would still have cards with his name on them because she didn't want him to be forgotten.

Not that there was much chance of that. His room stayed as he had left it and outside in the garden was the plaque with his name on it.

*   *   *

Seeing as Mum was not really recovering from her loss, Ned decided to work on getting her to agree to go to Byron Bay for a break – she would be with her family there and away from the house, where there were both good and disturbing memories.

'It's the good ones you want in your head,' he told her patiently.

It took just two weeks for him to persuade her to agree to a stay with her family. He pointed out that before she went job hunting, she needed some time out. Wanting to resume work was good, but she needed a complete break first: 'So, I've already bought you a ticket and I've let your mother know you're coming,' he told her.

Mum just said, 'If you think that's for the best, then what can I say? Thank you, Ned.' She was so numb with grief, she would have done anything he asked.

He would look after me, he told her. I wouldn't have to go on that bus to school, he would take me and collect me.

'Will you be all right, Daisy?' Mum asked, looking worried.

Ned had been so kind on my return that I answered yes without hesitation for I too felt that Mum needed a break. So the three of us went to the airport and Ned and I waved her goodbye. And now he had what he had wanted ever since I returned home: just him and me in the house.

*　*　*

So, how did he get me to pity him? I have to say it was no problem for him at all. By then I was only ten and pretty gullible. Over the next couple of days, he made sure I only saw the nice side of him while he cooked meals. We took Eddie out for walks and he told me about his childhood. 'I grew up looking at that wallpaper that you and Tommy thought so disgusting, those were the first pictures I saw. They were all I had to look at when I was small.'

'And your father, he was the one who liked them?'

'Yes, he was the one who put them up and my mum never dared to take them down. He was a silent man, violent too. I can still hear my mother's screams when he beat her. My younger brothers were really afraid of him as well, we used to hide from him if we could.'

'What about your sister, you never talk about her?'

'When Mum left him my sister was only a baby, so she had to go with Mum when she left and then me and my brothers had to manage on our own. But Mum's great, she was able to work so she got some money saved, bought a house, did it up and then sold it and bought another one. She's not badly off now. But she just had to escape, my father was just so violent. It was me who received the most punishment, but my brothers did as well. And they're really screwed up.'

He took my arm then and walked me over to the cupboard door.

'Oh, it's clean now, nothing in it, but it was a dark horrid place when I was little. Had spiders and mice in there and it was really dark – well, it still is,' and he opened the door.

'Imagine being locked in there for two days with no food. That cupboard stank when he let me out and before I could even get a drink of water or something to eat he made me scrub it clean so that it wouldn't smell when he had to put me back in it the next time. And can you guess what he said every time he opened that door and I blinked at the light as I crawled out?

'"Clean up your piss and shit," so was clean the next time I was put in there.'

I shuddered at the thought of any child being locked in a cupboard, let alone for days at a time.

He then told me how he was the one who had to hunt for food: 'I could shoot a gun when I was younger than you, Daisy,' and he took me outside to show me where he had learnt to shoot.

I glanced at one of the walls of an outhouse and they were peppered with bullet holes.

'So that's how I grew up. Lovely, isn't it, Daisy?'

Then Ned told me all about those exercises he made himself do every day when he was young to strengthen his muscles. I asked him why, for surely working on the farm would have made him strong anyway. That's when he told me about the man in the woods and what he had done to him.

'I wanted to make sure that no one hurt me again,' he said.

That was more or less the last story he told me. Mind you, he only told me stories aimed at arousing my sympathy. There was a lot he left out, as I was to discover later. Such as all his escapades and the women he had seduced.

When he was satisfied that he had gained my understanding of his terrible experiences growing up, he described the nightmares that tortured him while he slept, the ones he had experienced ever since the first time he had been locked in the cupboard. And how they had become even worse after he met the man in the woods.

'See your memory books where you write everything down? You don't have to look at them every day, do you?'

'No,' I told him, but I did – there was so much about Tommy in there.

'I bet you only look at the happy ones.'

'Yes,' I said for that was true.

'I have them as well,' he confessed, 'I wrote my thoughts in them.'

And he handed me a couple of well-worn notebooks.

'Some of them I wrote when I was your age and a few when I was even younger, although the last one I wrote not that long ago. I'll let you read what's in there, you can keep them. As long as you promise to keep them safe and not let anyone else see them,' he told me.

'Not even Mum?'

'Especially not your mother. She knows a lot, but we don't want to upset her, do we?'

'No,' I said as he placed the books in my hands and left me sitting on a chair as I started to open them. It took me an hour to get through them and then I came to the one that he told me he had recently written:

Other people store their memories behind the trap door of the attic in their minds.

Why can't I?

Instead I built a room out of red bricks to put mine in, a box without windows or doors.

It was not until I laid the last brick that I realised I was still inside.

Every day, slowly and carefully I try and take that room down. Once I thought I had succeeded and went to sleep with a smile on my face, only to find when I awoke that some silent force had crept up during the night and built it up again, leaving me trapped inside with my memories.

Seven years ago I changed my name to Ned, but it made no difference – I'm still the same person trying to escape the prison of my past.

I felt the tears forming in my eyes when I read the last sentence and thought about my early years and how happy they had been. In England, I was surrounded by people who loved both my brother and me. Then when we all came to Australia, there was another family who showered us with affection and kindness that made me feel part of theirs.

'Did you understand that?' he asked, as holding the notebook in my hand, I walked over to him.

Now my eyes were full of tears for I did not see a man who showed his dark side when he was drunk, but a broken one. Which in a way I still do, although I no longer allow that to excuse what he did to me. But at just ten years of age I felt so sorry for him and when I threw my arms around him and told him so, I gave no thought then to how once I had hated him touching and looking at me – I only thought of the nice part of him when I wrapped my arms around his waist to comfort him. That was the first major step to him living out his fantasies of doing exactly what he had dreamt of doing with me from the very first day we met.

We talked for a little, while I leant against his shoulder and his arm was around me. I told him about my fear of ghosts.

'Don't be afraid,' he told me.

And how I hated having to go outside – I hadn't got over my fear of the dark.

He told me that he would rig up a light outside so that I would be able to see there was nothing there.

'I'm here for you,' he told me and I believed him.

And he, realising that, picked me up and carried me to my room, where he lay down beside me. For a few moments I rested my head innocently on his shoulder for I too needed comfort. Just feeling the warmth of his body gave it to me. And as my eyes closed, for the first time in weeks, I felt myself relax.

It was then that I felt his hands moving gently up and down my body.

Why didn't I jump up, tell him to stop, tell him that I would tell my father if he didn't?

I couldn't – it was as though he had hypnotised me and I was powerless. Grief had snatched away my strength, as he had worked out.

'You know how upset your mum gets,' he whispered softly as his fingers circled around that part of me that was still only a chest. 'You wouldn't want to upset her any more, would you?'

Of course I wouldn't, I told him.

'Good girl,' he said and his hands moved in another direction as he slid my shorts off and pulled my T-shirt up. 'So beautiful!' he murmured.

And that was the start of Ned getting what he had wanted for so long.

*   *   *

Over the time we spent together alone in the house, Ned was careful not to go too far with me. He knew better than to hurt or shock me too much. After all, I was going to school every day and so I could have gone to a teacher for help. Or just fled and run through the gate and gone to Joyce's house. So, he had to take care. Although my eleventh birthday was fast approaching, I hadn't got even the beginnings of looking like a teenager. If anything, I looked a couple of years younger than I was, which would have made the right person even more protective of me. What he had planned had to be a gradual progress.

The first few days were more about his hands sliding up and down my body and fondling me, which didn't seem too bad. Nor did it enter my head then that what he was doing was very wrong. For I hadn't heard of the word 'abuse', so I had no understanding of it. The school had not talked about the matter and as far as I recall, they never did. If they had, I would have spoken out. I'd like to think so but in reality, I was traumatised by Tommy's death. But then my brain was also still so fuzzy and it still felt as though it was full of cotton wool. I could sit through a lesson and have no idea what the subject was, let alone the details. And without Tommy in the room next to mine, or in the house whizzing around in his chair, I was terribly lonely.

It took him a couple more days, while he did some nice things for me, to feel he could go a stage further. When he picked me up from school, he told me that a new pizza place had opened and would I like to go, for he knew how much I liked that particular food? So, it was a question I didn't have to give much thought to before I said, 'Yes, please.'

'Great, a little treat will do you good and save me having to cook as well,' was said with one of his crinkly smiles.

Pizza, an all-gooey cheese base with lots of spicy sausage, was ordered. I tried not to think of the last time I had eaten one with Dad and Tommy on one of our last weekends together at Dad's and tucked in hungrily. As I did with the rich chocolate dessert that Ned ordered for me. I felt sleepy after eating so much and nearly fell asleep on the way back in the truck.

'Think we'd better take Eddie out for a stroll,' Ned said once we got back and walked into the house. No sooner had he said that than we heard the bellowing of a cow that was clearly in some distress. Ned rushed out to the back of the house where the sounds were coming from with me following him.

As we got there I saw why the animal was so distressed. She had somehow managed to escape from the field, which seldom happened, though when it did, Ned and the outside dogs would chase the cow back into the field. Ned's dogs were friendly enough and they often trotted along beside us when we took Eddie out. He would pat them and give them treats and receive adoring glances in return. Now they just looked bewildered – they knew there was nothing they could do to help the cow that was trapped and frantic.

The poor creature had her horns stuck in a large piece of rusty machinery that must have been redundant years ago and was piled up with all the other junk. The whites of her eyes were showing and I could see just how terrified she was. Ned did his best to move the machinery and free her, but nothing worked – the bellows grew feebler as she became even more stressed and I was just hoping and praying that he would be able to release her. Suddenly the cow's body convulsed into shudders until finally, white froth appeared out of her mouth and her body sank to the ground.

'She's not dead, is she?' I asked, feeling sick at having to watch an animal in so much pain.

'She is, there was no saving her – I was just about to get my gun and put her out of her misery,' he told me.

I was so upset that no sooner was I back in the house than I had to rush outside again to be sick. I didn't even make it to the tin hut before I found myself throwing up all that I had eaten earlier.

Ned came over and wiped my face with a damp cloth and then brought me back inside. He sat me down on the settee and began explaining a little about farm life. Not that it made me feel much better to learn that animals don't live very long compared to humans: 'The wild ones,' he told me, 'take themselves deep into the bush to die. The farm ones, chickens, cows even dogs that die on the farm, have to be disposed of.' He would arrange for the cow to be collected the next day.

'So don't go out there until after that truck has gone. But, Daisy, it's the reality of living on a farm,' he said, providing yet another reason why I would rather have stayed in a town.

All he did that night was lie down beside me. I was still so upset about watching that poor creature die in agony and in a way, I think he was too. He understood that to push me any further might just result in my breaking down, so he waited for another couple of days before persuading me to act out one of his fantasies. Each evening we went on our usual walk with Eddie, Ned with his arm around my shoulder and me carrying a bag of carrots for the horses. When we returned, he chattered away, trying to get some laughter or at least a grin out of me. But however hard he tried, little penetrated the fog in my head.

Mum rang regularly to check that all was well and all I told her was everything was fine and that Ned was looking after me very well, wanting her to not have any worries. Maybe I should have told her that I was missing her, for she decided to stay a little longer after that, though no doubt Ned persuaded her too. It was after I had gone to bed that the sound of music blaring through the house told me he was drunk again. That was enough to bring back the memories that made me quake with fear. I put my head under my pillow trying to block the sounds. Not that it worked, and neither did it stop me hearing his staggering footsteps coming in the direction of my room. I felt my bed sag with his weight and heard him say 'I know you're awake', before his hands crept up under my pyjama bottoms. I was just frozen with fear at what he might do next. My silence seemed to quell his interest a little, or the excessive amount of alcohol he had drunk did as, to my relief, I heard his breath (which stunk of brandy) grow louder and knew he was asleep. I pulled myself out of the bed, grabbed a blanket and spent the rest of the night on the settee.

In the morning he was back to being the nice Ned, and nothing was mentioned. Ned had also told my mum that of course he would still take me to school and pick me up; that I was doing well but he didn't think I was ready to go on the bus – it was a long journey and it made me feel better to know he would be waiting for me.

He was right about that: I didn't want to be on that bus in case someone asked questions about Tommy, or rather a barrage of questions about how he had died. Seeing Ned, I was just relieved as I walked towards him, ignoring all the other children I had played with only a few weeks earlier. And there he was, a warm smile on his face, and it made me feel grateful that he understood why I didn't want to face my usual journey.

I had even made an excuse not to go to Dad's. Ned had offered to take me out for a drive instead to show me more of the local area, which meant I would not have to listen to endless chatter about the new baby that was on its way. Of course, I understand now, that he was worried I might tell my dad what he was doing.

*   *   *

It was over that weekend that Ned finally got to act out one of his fantasies. I'm not saying he was rough, he wasn't, but what he asked for was not something I wanted to do – I just didn't have the willpower to turn away from him. Maybe I was scared of him reverting back to the man I did not trust, for then at that vulnerable time, I was alone with him.

Looking back, I can understand that when I was only ten, I could not appreciate exactly why my mother's grief made her need her family so much rather than being with me. Or that just because Dad had found someone who stopped his life from feeling empty did not mean he cared any less for me.

I just felt that all I had left was Eddie.

It was over that weekend that he brought up the subject of taking some pictures of me. He just wanted some really beautiful pictures that he could look at when I was away. I had no understanding of why he wanted them then, nor did I know about the hidden camera in my room that had already recorded me in the nude. Though I did squirm with embarrassment when I eventually sat with him as he watched them on his computer.

I hate to think now just how many of them ended up on the dark Web, being watched by perverts and paedophiles from all over the world. Still, I'm no longer that naïve child so that's a thought I can force myself to push firmly to the back of my mind. Oh, I suppose the early ones were not too extreme, that came a little later when he believed that I was hardly going to refuse him much. The first time it was just me, wearing hardly anything.

That was the beginning of my taking part in something I did not want to do.

* * *

The pictures progressed to what anyone else would have described as shocking. He told me that it made him feel good and he was sure I wanted him to be happy.

His demands did grow a little more perverse as the days went on, though not as deviant as they became when I was another year older and those little buds of mine were beginning to sprout on my chest. The furthest he went happened before Mum returned. He thanked me after, said I had made him happy and lay down beside me. Throughout, the secret movie camera was running and there was the constant click of the stills camera on its tripod.

By the time Mum returned I had accepted that when Ned had me on my own, there were things he was going to make me do.

39

A very welcome phone call told us that Mum was on her way home.

'She sounded as though she's back to being her old self,' Ned told me. 'Her father's a lot better so she's already booked her plane ticket.'

'When's she coming?' I asked, even though I was a bit miffed that she hadn't asked to speak to me.

'Tomorrow – she wants me to bring you with me when I go to the airport, says she can't wait to see you so she's caching the afternoon plane. Which means I'll be able to pick you up from school and we'll both be there as she comes through. That suits you?'

'Yes,' and I could feel a smile spreading across my face.

'Thought so, I know you'll be pleased to see her.'

I was so excited at the thought of meeting her from the plane that I could hardly get the words out to agree with him. I had really missed her, or missed the mum I knew before Tommy died. The one who was good fun and easy to be with. The one whose funny stories I listened to before she in turn encouraged me to tell her all about what I did at school and the friends I had made there.

The second thought that came into my head was that with Mum back in the house, my evenings with Ned would change, wouldn't they? He would no longer be able to come into my room and get me to play those games, as he called them. Or take those pictures of me that made me cringe. Though I knew from the roguish glint in his eye that he meant to spend our last night alone doing just that, which he did. Afterwards, I asked him to let me sleep alone. As he only occasionally spent the whole night with me it was not a problem in getting him to leave. Though it was a problem for me to sleep. I just hoped that was going to be the last time he had his way with me, but deep down, I knew it wasn't.

Since that terrible night, which still invaded my dreams, I had felt myself drawing closer to Ned. Since leaving the house to being in the hospital, not once had I seen a flash of temper. Nor had I for the first weeks when I came home. Not only had he seemed kind to both Mum and I, but to Eddie and his dogs as well. Though, to be fair, even drunk I had never seen him taking his temper out on them. It was later, after Mum had been gone for a while, that everything changed. When he took my photos and made me partake in doing things where, dutiful as a robot my hands went round that part of his body I disliked, I managed to disconnect my brain. It was when I was on my own and those images came into my head that I was unable to dissolve fast enough that I felt grubby. Even so, I still believed that in his own way he did genuinely care for me. He cooked me nice meals, took me to school and there were things I enjoyed doing with him, like our walks when we took the dogs out. I loved the feel of the horses' soft mouths when they took the carrots delicately from my hands and seeing the odd wild creature, rabbits and occasionally a fox scattering into the undergrowth.

So, how did I cope with those other times? I tried to block them out of my head. Told myself nothing had happened and made an effort to fill my thoughts with something nice. Not that it always worked. In my darkest moments I compared myself to Eddie, learning tricks that weren't really ones that dogs normally did or even wished to. It was Eddie's need to be cared for by his owner that he did what was asked of him. Just a pat on the head was a big enough reward, though the odd biscuit made us receive more wagging of tail and licked hands.

Ned might have told me more than once that acts he persuaded me to do were the same ones as teenagers got up to, which only resulted in me not wanting to be one; soon if I was a normal one then I would grow to like it, he said. Comments that made me feel I didn't want to be one. Though it was the word 'normal' that stuck in my head.

Not that I stood much choice about entering those double figures. My eleventh birthday had come and gone a few weeks after Tommy left us. I told Mum that I didn't want a birthday cake or a party or anything else, no cards and no presents. It was not a day I wished to celebrate. I still felt so sad and I knew that I would only feel the loss of my brother when I had to accept all over again that he was no longer with me.

'If that's what you want, darling,' was all Mum said, which had made me feel that she really understood me then.

'I'm sure I'll be all right next year,' I told her.

Though when the day arrived, I could hardly stop myself from crying. Presents or not, I just missed Tommy so much. It was Ned who, seeing that apart from cuddling me, Mum did not know what else to do, stepped in. He must have made a quick phone call for he came back into the room saying that I'd been invited to one of my friends' houses, where there was a swimming pool, and he was going to take me there.

'And they know not to sing happy birthday,' he told me with a grin. I almost found myself giggling though my tears. Another act of kindness. As I said earlier, it was those acts that created the dichotomy which I found so confusing.

Breaking into those thoughts running through my head, Ned took hold of my arm – 'You look as though you're daydreaming again, Daisy' – but I think he might have had a good idea of what thoughts were chasing around in my head then.

Which he confirmed when he said, 'Have to make sure your mum's happy to be back, don't we? We don't want her going back to her mum and dad again for a while, do we?'

'Yes,' I answered, knowing deep down exactly what he meant. Not that he needed to think I would talk. Had I not been left behind with him then nothing would have happened so it wasn't all his fault, was it? I had already concluded that I had no choice but to take part in whatever he asked of me. However difficult he was going to find getting me alone once Mum was back, he would certainly find a way.

That was when the first seed of anger took root inside me and began to have its own voice, a voice that planted negative thoughts in my mind.

40

'Right, let's get you off to school. I'll spend some time in the town, make sure I get all the shopping sorted, have a bite to eat and then pick you up. How does that sound?'

'Great.'

'And don't worry about Eddie being left, he'll be fine. I've found an old mattress in one of the sheds and put that out for him to lie on.'

Another small act to make me feel grateful.

* * *

That day, I could hardly wait for school to end. I even managed to concentrate on my lessons more as well as chatting to classmates on our breaks, something I had avoided for so long. The moment I was free to go, I rushed out to where Ned was waiting for me and jumped in the truck.

'Can see you're excited,' he told me.

And I found myself grinning happily at him.

I just about ran to the part of the airport where the arrivals came through. 'Slow down,' Ned told me as we reached the barrier, 'her plane's not due in for five minutes.' It seemed the longest five minutes of my life until I saw her, a wide smile on her suntanned face, walking towards us, looking happy and relaxed. I, barely able to wait, rushed towards her and was enveloped in her arms as she hugged and hugged me.

She certainly appeared a lot better, there was no doubting by the way she hugged and hugged me how pleased she was to be back.

'I missed you so much, darling,' she said, 'I thought of you every minute I was away.'

'Missed you too,' I told her, for every day that she was gone I had woken just wishing she would come home.

'How has everything been at the farm?' she asked, to which I managed to answer, 'Oh, it's been good. Been having loads of walks and yes, Mum, everything's been OK.'

What she couldn't tell from my remarks was what was going through my mind when I answered her. I was thinking then that with Mum back, everything would be better. Ned would have to leave me alone – no more walking into my bedroom, no more filming me. He could hardly get up to anything when she was in the house, now could he? He wouldn't want to arouse any suspicions that would expose his weird feelings about me. Which meant that he would have to go back to giving my shoulder the odd squeeze and a few sideways glances, which I could now cope with.

Remembering how I had felt when I returned from Dad's just a few months earlier, I wondered how Mum would cope when we returned to the farm. I was sure like me, she would feel Tommy's absence in every corner of the house – I know I still did. Everywhere I looked in the house, I could see him and sometimes I was sure for a split second that I heard the squeak of his wheelchair. I still found it difficult to walk on that part of the room where I had watched him die.

Mum was full of stories about her time at Byron Bay. How everyone sent their love and was looking forward to seeing me soon, though she didn't say when that would be. She asked me what else I had been doing and I told her about feeding the horses.

'And what about you and Ned?'

She asked Ned the same thing, though I'm sure she must have filled him in on her phone calls. His reply was simply, 'Cooking, cleaning and walking the dog.' And then with a grin, he added, 'Looking forward to eating something I've not had to make.'

'Well, you'll have to wait until tomorrow,' was her answer to that.

*   *   *

I was right about Mum feeling nervous about going into the house – I could see her tense the moment Ned sprang out of the truck to open the gate.

'I'll bring in your luggage,' he told her before he parked outside the house, 'you just sit down.'

I noticed her hovering slightly before she took a deep breath, set her shoulders as straight as she could and walked in.

'Supper's all ready,' he said as he carried her case to their bedroom. 'A big salad with some roast chicken – Daisy helped with that,' and a friendly smile came in my direction. 'There's a nice bottle of wine – got your favourite white for you, chilling in the fridge.'

That put him in her good books, as did the fresh flowers he had bought and arranged in a vase.

It was when we had finished eating and Ned had insisted on clearing up that she told us about a job interview she had – 'I've already made the appointment for an interview and you'll never guess where it is?' And just hoping it was not too far away, I waited for her to tell us.

'It's in the school, working in the section where children have learning difficulties and other special needs.'

'Like Tommy had?'

'Yes, so I would be meeting some of his friends. And that would be really good, wouldn't it?'

'Yes,' I said, thinking that Mum and I might be travelling in and out together every day.

*　　*　　*

I must say that everything went smoothly for a while. Mum remained cheerful though there were times that I saw tears forming in her eyes when Tommy's name was mentioned. They formed in mine too, sometimes completely unexpectedly when I suddenly felt his absence acutely. And then came the news that Julie had given birth to a baby boy. That grain of anger which had taken root in me had succeeded in placing some really un-pleasant thoughts in my head. It made me wonder if she would get pregnant again and have a baby girl. Then Dad's replacement family would be complete, wouldn't it?

Apart from that, I was happy that, as Ned had said, Mum seemed to be back to 'her old self'. Her dad had recovered from the tiredness we had seen when he came to the farm and made his excuses to go to bed to read: 'It was just a warning,' she told us, 'he was a bit grumpy about being told that for him twenty-hour drives are over.' She added with a light laugh, 'But your gran didn't take any notice of his nonsense, just told him that he'd better listen to his doctor.'

I could see the following morning that all Mum's energy had returned. After she had told us about the job interview she had, Ned asked if I would feel OK travelling on the bus to school and I told him I was cool about that – after all, he couldn't act as my chauffeur forever. Which meant my alarm was set at six thirty, which gave me less than an hour to get ready and walk to the end of that rutted lane. When I pulled myself out of bed and hurriedly rushed to the tin shed for a quick wash there, Mum was already out pulling up all the weeds on what she called 'Tommy's Garden'.

'Heard you get up,' she said, 'I'll get you some breakfast while you get ready.'

Yes, I thought happily, *the old Mum is back with us and full of loads of energy.*

*   *   *

It was several days after she returned that Mum drove me into town and dropped me off at school.

'My interview's not for another hour,' she told me, 'so I'm going to have a coffee first. Afterwards I'll do some shopping – we need a few things in the house – and then I'll pick you up at the end of school. Thought we could have a little time together. I'd like that, wouldn't you?'

'Me too, Mum, I've missed you so much,' I told her, feeling a warm glow inside me.

It was so good to run up to her when I walked out of the school gates.

'Found a great little café,' she told eagerly, 'and they have some wonderful ice cream, I think you'll like that.'

I would have been happy with anything at all, just so I could spend time with Mum, but ice cream was definitely a real bonus in my books. The café was as good as she had told me, pastel decor, cream tables and comfy chairs with brightly co-loured cushions.

'So how did the interview go?' I asked once Mum had or-dered coffee for herself and my usual cola, as well as a dish of strawberry flavoured ice cream. I was dying to know and be-fore she could reply, I was inundating her with questions.

'Hush, Daisy, just stop! I got the job,' she told me with a beaming smile. 'I'm really looking forward to starting work at the beginning of the new term. That's only a couple of months away.'

'So that means I can travel with you each morning?'

'Yes, Ned will take us both in, but we won't be travelling back together – I'll still have work to do after you've finished.'

My heart sank a little then as I realised that meant I was going to be alone with Ned sooner than I thought. Mum then asked me some very searching questions about him – she clearly wanted to know if he'd been drinking when she was away and she certainly appeared relieved when I told her that he had hardly touched a drop of alcohol. She also asked about how we had got on together and I told her we had been OK and that he had looked after me and cooked every evening.

Why on earth did I not blurt out the truth then? It would have been the perfect opportunity. I think it was because I thought it would only cause trouble and anyhow, she seemed so happy in Ned's company, she might not believe me. Maybe she would think that I was trying to cause trouble and that I was jealous of the time they spent together.

Those were the beliefs I had as a child, which I've learnt are sadly not unusual ones. My adult self knows full well that she would have believed every word, had I told her what he was making me do then. Instead I asked her more about her role at the school and what she would be teaching.

'Music and Art,' she told me, 'two subjects which are good ways of relaxing and expressing ourselves, don't you think?'

As I had not inherited her particular talents in those disciplines, I could only nod in agreement.

She then brought up the subject of Dad, although she didn't ask me why I'd been making excuses not to visit him so often.

'He wants you to meet the new baby,' she told me.

I noticed that she did not say either 'brother' or 'son'.

'Thought you might like to go there this weekend.'

So, I agreed.

*   *   *

This time, when I had arranged to spend the weekend with Dad, Ned offered to drive me part of the way. He mentioned a small town where he sometimes stopped to fill up the truck and told me that was where I would meet Dad, which would make his journey a little shorter.

'I think his new baby's keeping him rather busy,' Ned said when he came off the phone. 'Your dad sounded worried about leaving Julie. I thought for a moment he was going to cancel, that's why I offered to drive you about fifty kilometres. Didn't want you being disappointed.'

'Dad's never cancelled anything, he's not like that,' I protested.

'No, but his life's changed now, hasn't it? So it's to be expected that he wants to help with the baby. Anyhow, not to worry. I'm happy to take you halfway,' he quickly countered as he saw me beginning to look annoyed. 'Saves your dad being in a car for three or four hours, doesn't it?'

I tried not to take too much notice of Ned's remarks, but his words had sunk in, which made me wonder if he was telling the truth. Already I had been told by Mum that Dad had asked me to leave Eddie behind this time – 'It's just for now, while the baby's so small,' she told me tactfully. A request that made me feel really annoyed. Julie was clearly laying down the law and Dad was going along with it, I decided. I was just about grinding my teeth with irritation.

'Have you packed your case? Not that you need to take much, apart from a change of clothes and a toothbrush and comb. And you've put the baby's present in it, haven't you?'

'Yes, Mum,' I said, even more annoyance rising up in me.

Seeing this, Ned grinned at me when I got in the truck. 'Let's go,' he said, turning on the ignition. 'We really don't want to stop your dad spending less time with the baby and Julie, do we?'

Naturally, this made me send him an angry glare.

'Just a joke, Daisy.'

'Well, I don't think you're being very funny.'

And for the first twenty minutes of the drive, I sat in a bad-tempered silence.

*   *   *

Whatever thoughts Ned might have tried to place in my head failed to stop a huge smile spreading across my face when I saw Dad stepping out of his car the moment we pulled up. Without waiting a second, I opened the door to the truck, swung myself down and rushed towards him. He beamed at me as he wrapped his arms around my body and gave me a huge hug. All my doubts about him not caring for me slid away, I was just so happy to see him and he appeared to feel the same.

He and Ned shook hands, Dad thanked him for cutting the time of the journey and then we were on our way to Melbourne. To begin with, I was a little worried that Dad might ask me about some of the excuses I had made not to visit him. Ones like 'I was invited to a party,' which I wasn't, by the way or, 'I'm having friends round,' which I wasn't either and others with little basis of truth that seemed to roll off the tip of my tongue. Not that those excuses had stopped him chatting to me on the phone regularly. He always asked how I was, plus other questions about school; he always said he expected I was missing Mum too. I said yes to the last bit, before telling him I was fine.

To my relief he made no comments about all those delaying tactics of mine, instead he just chattered about some of the work that had been done on the new house he and Julie had moved into.

'You'll see for yourself when we get there,' he said before apologising for asking me not to bring Eddie this time. 'It's just that Julie is still tired. All those feeds she has to give every few hours don't help. Anyhow, the house is looking a lot better than when you last saw it.'

I remembered how it had looked when they took me to see it. A large, rather rundown place that they told me they had plans to renovate.

'Just as well I'm a very good carpenter and my plumbing is pretty good too,' Dad had said with a grin as he and Julie showed me round, 'I can do a lot in the evenings and weekends, which will save us a lot of money.'

'Yes and your dad's got some really good friends who have offered to come and help as well,' Julie added. 'Now this is the room I thought could be yours ...' Opening a door, I saw a large airy room with the windows facing what she explained was to be their garden. 'You can choose the colours you would like in here,' she told me. And without giving it a second thought, I told her that I really liked cream and white. As we drove, I wondered if my room had progressed at all since my last visit.

When Dad and I reached the house I could see straight away that there were already some changes. All those filthy windows with peeling paint were now sparkling clean, the paintwork around them was fresh and curtains had been hung. The front door looked a lot more welcoming too, with its shiny brass fittings, and the entrance hall decorated in subtle shades of yellow and peach appeared warm and glowing.

'Your house already looks nice,' I told him, 'you have been busy.'

'Well, Julie and I both have,' he said and I understood from the firmness in his voice that he was telling me not to refer to it as his house because it belonged to them both. It was time that I accepted Julie as his partner. He had told me the last time he had seen me that he was going to marry her once the divorce went through so there was my choice: give in to his wishes or upset him before I had even stayed a night.

'So, where's Julie and the baby?' I asked. 'I can't wait to see him!'

Immediately I could see that that remark went down well and he gave me a hug. 'It's feeding time,' he answered proudly, glancing down at his watch. 'She'll be upstairs, so let's go and find them.' And I could tell by the way he squeezed my shoulder that my question had really pleased him.

At the top of the stairs he put a finger to his lips to tell me to walk as quietly as I could so as not to disturb the baby and led the way to their bedroom. There, he signalled for me to stay in the doorway. I saw Julie sitting on a low chair, her hands supporting the tiny baby nestling at her exposed breast. She was completely engrossed in helping him feed as she hummed a lullaby just for his tiny ears.

I could tell she was blissfully unaware of our presence. The baby's tiny, clenched fist rested on her shoulder and moved slightly as his little mouth sucked. I had never before seen something so special and moved by it, I smiled up at Dad. I could tell from where I was standing that the baby's small head had grown heavy in her hands and as his eyelids flickered then closed, it was as if he was telling her that he had taken his fill.

It was not until then that she looked up at us and smiled. 'I'll just wind him then put him down in a couple of minutes,' she told us as she placed him higher on her shoulder and patted his back. A soft burp fluttered against her cheek and a dribble of milk dampened her shoulder, which had a small white muslin strategically placed for exactly that event. His milky breath whispered in her ear, while his eyes remained tightly closed.

'He's sound asleep,' she said as she kissed him one more time before laying him in the cot beneath the gently swinging mobile with its tingling silvery notes and covering his small frame with a blue crocheted blanket. 'He won't wake up for a while now so you can come over and have a peek at him, Daisy.'

I tiptoed over to the cot and gazed down at the baby who was my half-brother and despite all the jealous thoughts that had been running round in my head, it was love at first sight.

'The baby monitor's on, so I can leave him. Go and have a look at your room, Daisy, I hope you like it! When you're ready, come downstairs. I'll be in the kitchen,' she added.

'He's really beautiful,' I told her, still gazing down at their son. I saw her face light up – she too must have been wondering what my reaction would be.

'He is.'

'Come on,' Dad said, placing a hand on my shoulder, 'let's put your bag in your bedroom then we'll join Julie downstairs. I expect you're hungry.'

He was right, I was.

As soon as he opened the door to my room I could see straight away that it had been done up to please me. It certainly looked very different to when I had first been shown around. The walls were a rich cream, the furniture was a light oak, a thick cream and white rug lay on freshly polished floorboards and my bed was covered with a cream and white striped duvet. Floaty white curtains moved gently in the breeze.

'You like it, Daisy?'

'I love it, it's so cool-looking.'

'Julie chose the curtains, bedding and the rug.'

'I love them too. I'll thank her as soon as we're all downstairs.'

For the first time I began to feel real warmth towards Julie. She must have known me a little better than I thought to understand how much I would like that clean, fresh look.

41

I was able to hold my baby brother Matt several times over that weekend. When nappy changing time came along, Julie asked if I would like to come upstairs with her.

'Something tells me you want to hold him. Am I right?' she said with an amused smile once the clean nappy was firmly in place.

'Oh yes, please,' I said for the truth was I was dying to.

'You sit in my chair,' she told me before she picked him up from his changing table and placed him in my waiting arms. I stroked those soft little rolls around his neck as I inhaled that newborn scent of baby powder and special soap. My fingers moved to touched the top of his head, feeling the silky almost white light down on it, which would later turn a dark blonde.

The more I looked at those almost translucent lids where feathery lashes hid his blue eyes, the more I thought Matt was absolutely perfect. There was nothing about him that reminded me of Tommy – but then I was the younger sibling and so had never met him when he was as tiny as my new half-brother. The problem that I had believed I had with Julie completely vanished that weekend. Nothing like a new baby in the family to bind us all together a little.

Mind you, now I have children of my own, I can understand why she had been a little snappy with me on earlier occasions. Mainly because when she moved in with Dad, I still looked on the house as being his. Which meant I could do whatever I wanted to in it, like going to the fridge without asking and helping myself to whatever took my fancy. She did try and explain as tactfully as she could why she didn't want me to do that after I had helped myself to a chunk of chicken breast: 'Well, how was I to know you planned to make a salad with it?' had been my snappy response. 'Dad always says we can have anything we want from the fridge.'

But good behaviour won, I realised, when we all had a really good weekend and I simply loved my little baby brother. Even so, it still took a long time before I could really feel I was part of their family. Looking back, I regret that for as I found it impossible to tell my parents about Ned, I could perhaps have confided in Julie and by the time I felt I could trust her, it was too late. But that doesn't stop me feeling happy that we have become friends over the years. Now when we meet, we laugh about that time when I was so unbelievably resentful and difficult.

42

While Mum was waiting to begin her new job, my parents' divorce went through fairly amicably. As Dad had owned the house in the UK, I was told he was as generous as he could be with Mum. Not that I had any idea what the amount was, but I guess by his later actions that Ned did.

Right up to Mum beginning work, Ned's good behaviour appeared to be lasting, though I was a bit wary of him when I saw him beginning to drink again. I was scared his dark side that made Mum and I so miserable would return. Mum, I was absolutely certain, felt the same. She certainly watched him like a hawk when he appeared with a glass of dark spirits and she kept checking to see how much he was pouring out of the bottle.

His belief, he told us, was that he had been able to knock drink on the head while he was looking after me. So, didn't that prove that he was the one in control, not the alcohol? A question that Mum really did not want to answer, although I don't think she had much understanding of alcoholics at that stage, or maybe she just refused to accept he was one.

Ned, who had more than once driven when well under the influence, did his best to show us what a careful driver he could be. When he took us to the shops or out for a meal he would restrict himself to only ordering two small beers. Nor did he show any signs of bad temper when Mum told him that he was driving too fast on the way home. In fact, there were no arguments between them for some time. That was Ned without drink or maybe it was him doing his best to make a good impression. In the evenings when we had finished eating a meal Mum had cooked, up he would jump from the table, telling her to relax while he cleared up.

I could go on and on comparing those two sides of him, but that was the nice one he showed us both for some time. Now when I remember those times I have to remind myself that he was sober when he abused me.

There was the odd night when the three of us went off to one of his gigs, which I really enjoyed. One of the good things about them was they did not bring back any memories of Tommy to either Mum or me. When she got up on the stage with Ned, I stayed put with the same couple I had sat with at the first gig I had ever been taken to: Jenny and Mick. Nothing much had changed about them, they were friendly and pretty good fun and genuinely appeared pleased to see us all.

As both Mum and I were aware that his drinking had often got out of hand at those gigs, it was a relief when Ned kept to his two-beers rule. Mum, who had been watching him carefully, looked relieved when he said no to another round when his friends offered: 'Not when I'm driving my girls,' he told them and I nearly fell off my chair with surprise. Had he really turned over a new leaf, got rid of that side of him which alcohol so easily released? I could see that Mum appeared to think so, although something made me more sceptical and I wasn't so sure about his motivations.

I was only too aware of those looks that came my way and also the times when he went to the part of the house he called his study to spend time on his computer. But then Mum did not know what I did: that there were pictures of me on it. Not that I knew everything then, but there was a lot more on his computer than just me for him to look at. Later, I found that out when he and I were left alone in the house.

It was a couple of months after the divorce that Mum broke the news to me that she and Ned were getting married. I must say it was a bit of a shock, although I suppose I was not too surprised. As Mum was due to begin her new job within a couple of weeks, they decided to have the wedding beforehand.

Invitations were sent out, Ned's two brothers and his mum were coming, as were Mum's two sisters and her parents, who had all arranged to book into a hotel. After the wedding they were making their way to Melbourne to have a bit of a break. Ned's mother had also told him that she had booked herself into another hotel and would be leaving the day after the wedding. So apart from Ned's brothers who were staying in the old buses and bringing their own bedding, the wedding was not going to cause that much work.

Mum had said she wanted a country wedding and not a registry office. They wanted a beautiful rural place and had heard of a mountain resort where there were both cows and horses in the nearby fields.

'That's what I want,' she stated firmly and that's what she got. Though when she took me there fairly early in the morning to see it, with its deep green manicured lawns it was not that rural compared to the farm where we lived. We walked into the covered area where the wedding feast was going to be and Mum explained how it would look: long white tablecloths with bowls of roses as the centrepieces and the garden would be decorated with hanging lights.

'When they are turned on, all the trees and shrubs will be lit up – it will be so magical. Don't you think so, Daisy?'

'I think it will look wonderful, Mum,' I told her.

'Then we'd better go shopping – I need a new dress and so do you.'

So, off we went and it was clear she knew exactly where she wanted to go for these items as we went straight to the right shop, no window shopping up and down the town for us. Mum must have phoned ahead for they had an assortment of dresses hanging in the dressing room for us both to try on. One of them was a pretty delicate pale pink, which when she tried it on, I told her was perfect.

'You look so lovely, Mum,' I told her, for I did think it was perfect on her.

Mum picked out a light blue dress for me, with a round neck and a full skirt. It was a perfect fit and I loved it. And then after a quick half-hour at a café for celebratory coffee, coke and cakes, it was back to the farm.

43

Mum didn't stay at the hotel the night before as tradition might have demanded but not wanting to be alone with Ned, this break with convention was for me a huge relief. Instead she and I took off early in the morning to their hotel so that she could get ready there.

'Can't have the bridegroom seeing me before the wedding,' was the reason she gave. Though I think it was more to do with us having to bathe in that awful tin hut. 'Hardly luxurious,' she had told us, 'and besides, we're paying for the room from early on, why not make use of it?'

Determined to continue the country theme for her wedding, she arrived at the ceremony on the back of a farm trailer wearing her pale pink dress and holding a pink and silver bouquet of pale pink roses. She did look stunning with her glossy hair hanging to her shoulders and the merest touches of make-up. There was no question about Ned's attire: with his black hat and new white shirt, not only was he looking really handsome, he was certainly at his dashing best.

I wish I could remember more of that day, I know there

was dancing and everyone looked happy. And my close friends who had been invited kept saying how pretty Mum looked. Maybe much has been wiped from my memory because only a short time after they had been pronounced man and wife, everything changed once again. The belief that Mum had that she had fixed Ned and now had this happy beautiful family life on the farm she would soon realise was sadly never going to happen.

Two weeks later, when she began her new job, Ned's plan went into action and he had me to himself for the time between school finishing and Mum getting home. And what about Ned and me? How did that turn out once Mum was working?

Not as well as I hoped.

Having her at home during those weeks between her arriving back from Byron Bay and beginning work had given me a false sense of security: Ned had only acted that way towards me because Mum was away, I had kept telling myself.

Well, I certainly got that wrong.

It had stopped because she was in the house and he knew if she had discovered it, there would be more than a row: she would pack up and take me with her straight away.

So, who was I kidding? Only myself, it seemed.

44

It didn't take me long to realise why Ned had been so encouraging to Mum about finding work. There I was, naïvely thinking it was because he believed it would be good for her – get her away from all the memories of Tommy for several hours a day and she would get to meet other people and have her own pay cheque. Let's just say I was pretty disillusioned when I finally understood what his real reasons were: that he would have me all to himself for at least two hours a day, sometimes even longer if he did his 'good deed' and picked me up from school while making an excuse that he had to do some shopping. This happened at least once a week but Mum just thought he was being kind and giving me extra time in which to do my homework.

All those hopes I had about the reasons he had stopped those humiliating and horrible actions that made me want to curl up with shame were quickly dashed to smithereens. I had to face up to the fact that he hadn't stopped wanting to take my picture and was still making me hold the parts of his body that repelled me – he had just put his desires on temporary hold. He was fully aware of just what Mum's reaction would have been, had she caught him or seen any of those pictures of me on his computer. While the idea that she wouldn't believe me had been firmly fixed in my mind, he knew differently: she would have bundled as much of our belongings as she could into suitcases and left him, taking me with her. No doubt she would have stopped at a police station on the way or even phoned Dad to ask for help in reporting Ned's crimes. Of course as an adult, I know that is what she would have done but as a child, I didn't feel confident in her reaction. At eleven, I believed it might be me she would get rid of – a belief that stayed with me for far too long.

Looking back, I can see just how clever Ned was at pulling the wool over people's eyes. He also knew that it took a lot for someone who loved him to stop believing what they wanted to. And Mum wanted to believe that the man she had got to know during the time he wrote her email after email was still the man she had fallen in love with.

For example, Ned had been smart enough to get all the ingredients for our supper ready earlier. Oh, he would leave the odd thing for me to do so that when Mum walked in she saw two people busy preparing everything for dinner.

'You've done your homework?' she would ask me nearly every time and I would lie on almost every occasion saying, 'Nearly, just a bit to finish off, Mum.' She was not to know that between the time I caught the bus home and she arrived at least two or three hours later, Ned continued to get me to do things, such as posing in ways I hated so much: he wanted me to give sultry pouts, to bend forward slightly and then there were other poses that I can't bring myself to describe here. He seemed obsessed with photographing me and worst of all were the ones of me playing with those parts of his body that he found exciting.

That must have been around the time that my teachers began to lose patience with me. We were not given much homework to take home but unlike my classmates, who after eating a snack got theirs done at the kitchen table, Ned had other ideas for me. He took no notice at all when I told him that I would get into trouble.

'I never bothered with mine,' he told me repeatedly, 'and I did all right, didn't I?'

'Depends what you thought was all right,' was the retort that came to mind but I did not have the courage to utter it. I tried to do just the small amount we had to complete, but because it was rushed, the quality of what I handed in was shoddy, even in my books. Not only that, but because I was hardly paying much attention in class, some of the homework didn't make much sense to me.

Another thing I have learnt is that a fairly placid child who is disturbed can turn into an aggressive one. I became verbally rude at school and my homework, if it was done at all, was described as sloppy and littered with careless mistakes by my teachers. While they had indulged me in the months after Tommy's death, their patience was clearly running out now.

Early on, the requests to pose for photographs and execute acts had been asked for by Ned with some degree of affection, but as the months slipped by and my body began changing shape, his requirements became more deviant. By then I could hardly call them requests either, they had become more like demands that I had lost the willpower to say no to. In my mind I said, 'I won't do it,' or even better, 'I'll tell Mum.' I could have asked him, 'What do you think Dad would say if I told him?' But however much I rehearsed those words in my head, none of them ever left my lips.

45

How long did it take for the honeymoon period to end? I'm not completely sure, but I do know it wasn't long, maybe twelve months or so. The air of romance that seemed to surround the pair of them wherever they were in the house or out with friends did not disappear overnight, it just began to fade slowly.

I can remember vividly the first time Ned picked up a full bottle of bourbon and had downed it all by the end of the evening. I knew then that it was the beginning of a downward spiral and that his feet were fixed firmly on that path. Whatever excuses he made, such as it was just a one-off binge, might have convinced Mum, but the facts were becoming more evident. She never objected to the odd glass of wine or two; she enjoyed a drink when she came back from work and maybe a glass of wine with a meal, but she had never been a heavy drinker. But then she had not really come to terms with the fact that she had married an alcoholic.

One who had managed to stay sober until he achieved what he wanted: a wedding and a family who were now tied to him.

Ned, I began to understand over the next few years, had,

as did his father, little respect for women. He might have told himself that he loved them and the sober Ned did in his own way, but the man who alcohol produced was convinced that he owned them. I also came to realise however often he attempted to control his drinking, the desire for that liquid that changed him always won over any remnants of common sense.

A year in a detox place might have worked but I think he was one of those people who could never be saved from his addiction and over time, I had doubts about him wanting to do so. He once told me when I was a couple of years older that he was far happier when sober.

'So, why drink then?' I wanted to know.

'Because I do,' came the answer.

Didn't he know that with every mouthful he swallowed, he was releasing the obnoxious bully who tormented both Mum and me? I think he did and like us, Ned hated that side of himself. He had told me how terrible his childhood had been with his drunken bully of a father, so why was he following so sure-footedly in his footsteps?

It was after his drinking resumed that I suspect Mum, like me, lay in bed worrying over what mood he would be in when he returned from one of his gigs. To begin with, he was not too bad, though I could often hear him stumbling about the house and then the sound of another drink being poured. After that, it didn't take long for him to begin staying out all night. It was the gig, he told her, it went on late – well, the gig part was most probably true but he wasn't singing all night.

'Got a bit pissed ...'

OK, that was believable.

'So, I bedded down at a friend's house ...'

Female one was what I thought and so did Mum so the old arguments that made my whole body shake began again.

I had seen Mum going through his pockets, looking for proof of something that was only going to hurt her if she found it – luckily, she never did. After one enormous row where screams and shouts kept me awake all night, Ned decided to come back every night – at least for a while anyhow.

Not that him returning at night improved my life. Having to do some of my homework in bed by torchlight cut time off my sleep – it seemed no sooner were my eyes closed then back he came. Evidently, by the way he shouted for Mum to get him something to eat, he was the worse for wear. There were other evenings when he returned early enough to eat with us. No sooner had he consumed his food than a joint was lit up. Of course I knew by then what the smell was.

Weed is supposed to make people friendly and peaceful, helps them enjoy music and makes them want to dance to it. That would have been great, had it been true in Ned's case. And it might have been, had he not mixed it with the best part of a bottle of bourbon. The lulling effects of the dope fast vanished into thin air as alcohol-fuelled aggression overcame them. There were the odd days when there was some respite and the charming Ned appeared for a while but by then Mum wasn't able to drop her guard. And the more he saw of that, the more often he would begin to drink again. Knowing another row was simmering, I would make my way to bed, where I lay trembling, imagining the outcome. I hated those rows so much. It was on one of those nights when I had tossed and turned until I finally drifted off to a restless sleep that I felt Tommy's presence in the room near my bed.

Did I dream it or was it a memory of an earlier conversation? I really don't have the answer, but I can remember every word I heard him say.

In that stage when I was semi-conscious but not sound asleep, I knew there was something my brother wanted me to know, but I had to keep my eyes shut – opening them would make him disappear.

'You mustn't be fooled by Ned being nice sometimes,' he told me. 'Mum might be, because she wants to believe that. I always knew how his eyes followed you, how he touched you when he thought no one could see him, but I did. I knew all about him and what he got up to before he met Mum. I heard about it at the camp when she first met him and all the kids at school knew his history. His reputation stank and now I see him and know who he is. He's got no respect for women, that I know. Goodness knows how many he screwed once he began his singing career. His dad was the same, chased women constantly, even the ones who didn't want to know – everyone knew about him and his drug dealing.

'That's why Ned had no friends at school, the kids were told to stay away from him. His dad wasn't a man anyone wanted to mess with. Though once he found out that a great body and a good voice went a long way, he discovered that all he had to do was crook his finger to get loads of females running after him.'

'What else have you heard about him, Tommy?' my mind asked.

'He saw picking up women in bars as a bonus on top of his performance fee. He felt it was something he was entitled to. He never had much of a problem when word got out about the next gig he had lined up, there's a type of female who went there just hoping to get lucky with him.'

My eyes almost opened wide at that – I'd never thought of women chasing men.

'Trust me, Daisy, he didn't swagger over to them because he wanted a nice chat about the weather. When he selected the one he wanted to shag, he just got what he wanted. I heard there were loads of times when they only got as far as the car park. Then he'd go back in, looking for the next – he's not someone who wants to spend the night with just the one woman. But you know what else I heard?'

'No,' I said while asking myself if I really wanted to hear any more.

'He's still doing it – that's why he doesn't take Mum along to all his gigs. And not only that, there's always one woman that he sees more than once.'

I wanted to ask more but when my eyes fluttered open, there was no one in my room.

46

I could see that Ned's actions were causing Mum to have bad periods of anxiety which made me feel angry towards him and protective of her. How, I kept asking myself, could he act like this? Why had he married her? Hadn't she gone through enough?

The other part of my mind kept asking why she didn't leave him. I think for a long time she believed he would sort himself out with her help and there were days when it seemed as though he had. But that never lasted for very long. Even when his good behaviour returned for a while, it didn't stop her from having trust issues which still caused arguments. Ones he used as an excuse to again pour out endless drinks before turning on his music to full volume so that it blared out all around the house. I would bury my head under the pillow trying to block it out, but it was impossible for me to get a good night's sleep when he was in that aggressive mood.

On the days when Mum had the morning off work and she was not going to drive me in and drop me at school before she went to work, I had to set my alarm clock for six thirty.

To catch the bus, I had to leave by seven. I tried to look at my homework on that journey, only to find my eyes closing with tiredness. Not only was my homework a bit of a mess, I had dark circles under my eyes too.

'Looks like you had a late night again, Daisy,' my teacher observed unsympathetically. From the expression in her voice she clearly believed I'd been up to no good, which was confirmed by her second remark which made my blood boil: 'You might get better marks if you put your efforts into doing your homework.'

Halfway through the next lesson she caught me looking out of the window and ticked me off again for my lack of concentration. I could hardly tell her I had so little sleep, not because I had stayed up late, but because my stepfather was determined that no one in the house would have any sleep at all. That was around the time I had begun dreading the sound of his truck returning at night. I'm sure Mum could tell by the noise of its engine as he parked and whether he slammed the door to his truck or not just how drunk he was. If I was still up, I would see her tensing up.

When he came back much later and we were both in bed, she would have been even more nervous as to which Ned was coming through the door. As soon as I heard his heavy footsteps staggering around the house I would lie there waiting for what was going to happen next. Usually it was his loud aggressive voice yelling at Mum to wake up and get him some food. That's when the screaming and shouting episodes began – the ones that made me put my head under the pillow and beg silently for them to stop.

* * *

What was always confusing to Mum and me were Ned's mood swings. Oh, he could be nice and there were times when I caught flashes of the Ned who had looked after us so thoughtfully at the time of Tommy's death, the one who had cared for me when Mum was away, the one who could be good company; the one who could make us laugh and was charming to be with. But that Ned was fast disappearing day by day. I could see he was, but I believe Mum couldn't – she still believed that she was his lifeline and that she could fix him, but the only person who can help an alcoholic is themselves.

Nor do I think then she knew just how depressed I was becoming. That was something I tried to hide. Not being able to sneak into the bedroom next to mine, where Tommy would have comforted me, made it so much worse. More than anything, it was that black cloud hanging over me that affected my schooling. And the teachers didn't recognise my problem instead seeing me as being lazy and having little interest in my lessons. Not that I can blame them for I was the popular girl, full of flippant comments that hid the real me.

What no one knew was how I cried into my pillow almost every night. I desperately missed the life we had when Mum and Dad were together: orderly, calm, clean and safe. But now he was no longer just my dad – he was going to marry Julie and soon his baby son would be calling him Daddy.

47

Mum must have found the lies Ned told confusing, but I didn't. I just knew that when he disappeared for hours on end, or made an excuse why he had stayed out all night, that it was because he was cheating on her.

He would tell her that he had a gig, but that he'd been asked to come alone. And I would see the disbelief on her face. It made me want to scream 'Liar!' at him, but common sense told me not to.

'There are other ways of dealing with him,' I told Mum. 'Just tell him we want to come. Be firm, you're married now and you have the right.'

I could have clapped when she finally took my advice and stood up for herself.

'Got another gig on Saturday night,' Ned told us nonchalantly when we were having supper on the Thursday beforehand. 'They've only asked for me, but it means I can bring some good money back – that will come in useful.'

'Ned, I like listening to the music as well as singing,' Mum replied. 'Even though I know people like it when I do sing.

So, I could get up for a couple of numbers even if the management doesn't want to pay extra. And Daisy can come with us so there's no problem with leaving her without a babysitter. Do us all good to have a family night out, won't it? And besides, Daisy really enjoys listening to you too, don't you, darling?'

'I do, I really do,' I answered, giving him a wide smile that he really did not deserve. 'It's always a treat for me to watch you and you look so great up on that stage,' I managed to add, putting the most innocent expression on my face that I could possibly manage.

'You like to earn money, don't you, Ned? Well, you won't have to pay for our drinks if Daisy and I are with you. The last time we were at a gig we were sent over more than we could manage, weren't we?' added Mum.

Meaning no doubt that he wouldn't be free to buy drinks for whichever female caught his eye.

'All right, you can come,' he said tersely but I could see he was pretty angry at being trapped into agreeing.

What none of us knew was that there was certainly another woman lurking in Ned's background, who he then had to contact and tell her not to turn up. A request that she decided to take no notice of, as we all found out towards the end of the gig.

I spotted her before Mum did: a raven-haired woman with an unpleasant sneer on her face was staring at us as soon as we came in and grabbed our table.

So, that's one of the women he's screwing, was the thought that came straight into my head. I just hoped that Mum didn't notice, though from the expression I saw fleetingly cross Ned's face, I knew her presence there was bothering him. I had hoped that the couple I had sat with at other gigs were there, but there was no sign of them. There were heaps of other people, mainly men, who Mum and I had never met, who came up to him and slapped him on the back – 'Good to see you, Ned,' they all said before waiting in vain to be introduced to us.

'Are you going to get us some drinks then?' Mum asked and my stepfather reluctantly made his way to the bar. I saw the woman grab hold of his arm and him shaking it off angrily. Good thing Mum was looking at the stage, where a couple of female singers were belting out some Dolly Parton songs. Not that their voices sounded anything like hers – and their bosoms couldn't compete either. I imagined Tommy chipping in for to-wards the end of his life he had started to pass comments on such things.

Once they had finished to a loud round of applause, up came the red-jacketed MC to announce not only was Ned going to sing, but it was a lucky night for everyone because he had brought his beautiful partner with him. *So not everyone knew Mum was Ned's wife*, I thought, and I doubted the raven-haired woman knew she was either.

Mum looked worried then – there was no one she could leave me with and although I was nearly thirteen by then, I still looked very young.

'I'll ask Mike,' Ned told her, 'he's a decent guy,' and I saw him gesture to one of his friends, a burly young man with a pleasant smile. 'Would you do me a favour and sit with Daisy when Liza comes up to sing?' he asked.

'My pleasure,' he said, grinning at me.

Ned did his swaggering walk up onto the stage and taking hold of the mic, opened with one of Johnny Cash's songs 'Hurt'. As usual, the crowd went silent so we could hear every note he sang. Two more songs followed – Freddie Mercury's 'The Great Pretender' and of all things a Country and Western number called 'Stand By Your Man', each one gaining more applause and even a few catcalls and yells for more.

All the time Ned was up there on stage, my eyes kept darting in the woman's direction. I could see the scowl on her face when she was talking to another couple of flashy women who looked just as tough and tarty as her. It was pretty clear who they were talking about. Not that I had a clue what they were saying, though I was to get a good idea a bit later.

It was when Ned called Mum up that I could just about feel those dagger looks burning into my back. That was when I sensed trouble was brewing. I half turned my head round when Mum started walking to join Ned on the stage so that I could see them. The three of them were nudging each other and then loud catcalls came from them soon after Mum began singing.

They had underestimated Mum though. She stopped in the middle of her song, and speaking into the mic, she said to the whole audience, 'I'm sorry if you're not enjoying my singing, would you like me to stop now?'

'Yes!' yelled the trio.

'No!' shouted the rest of the audience amid calls to the troublemakers to be quiet.

It was at the next interval between sets that Ned really looked worried. He went over to the manager and I saw from the way his shoulders shrugged that he was not going to help. Mike stayed put by my side but he was most probably thinking that Ned needed backup.

To begin with, Mum appeared calm. She might have guessed why that dark-haired woman had mocked her singing, but the bar was not the place to tackle Ned. As for trouble, she came from a lifestyle where the management sorted that out, not the customers.

It was when Mum's need to go to the loo overtook her that everything suddenly got much worse. The women's lavatories were up a flight of stairs that led to where a few rooms were also rented out. I had gone with her and it was not until we came back down the stairs that we realised that the dark-haired woman was waiting for us at the bottom. We tried to ignore her and just walk past, but that was not something that the woman was going to allow. She pushed me aside and, drunk as she was, managed to get her vicious words out.

She shouted how she was Ned's girlfriend, told us how they always had wonderful sex, especially the last week in one of the upstairs rooms, and Mum should 'just give up and piss off'. Mum made absolutely no comment and ignored her. She just said to me, 'Let's get back to our table, Daisy.' But drunks certainly don't like being ignored and quick as a flash, the woman's arm shot out, grabbing hold of my mother's hair. Mum might have been tiny compared to her blowsy, almost Amazonian attacker, but she moved fast – up went her knee, which hit the woman sharply in the stomach, winding her.

That did it – screams of rage came spewing out of her mouth, mixed with foul swear words and some of her spittle landed on Mum's face. I should think everyone in the bar could hear her and suddenly my stepfather and one of the bouncers came running over. Ned tried first to break them up but the woman caught an even bigger handful of Mum's hair, tugging at it as hard as she could. Mum shouted at Ned, making him draw back his arm and swing a punch, hitting Mum on the side of her head. When she staggered backwards, her rival grabbed at her again and then the bouncer dragged the dark-haired woman off her, forcing her fingers open to make her let go of Mum's hair.

I must have finally started getting some guts as I started yelling too, this time directing it at Ned: 'You leave my mum alone, it's all your fault!' I was so angry, I was shaking from head to toe. It was one thing what he was doing to me, but hitting my mum was far worse.

Taking no notice, he pulled Mum by the arm back up the stairs. 'Mind your own business, Daisy,' he yelled at me when I kept screaming at him to let her go. I could hear them shouting at each other and then it went all quiet.

It was Ned's friend Mike who came over and took me back to the table: 'Best let them sort it out,' was all he said.

At least that woman had been removed from the bar and I didn't have to look at her, but that didn't stop me fretting until Mum returned. A bruise was already coming up on her face and she looked as though she had been crying as traces of mascara were evident on her cheeks.

'Sorry, darling,' she said to me, 'you shouldn't have had to see that.'

And I knew better than to ask questions. All I could see was Ned at the bar with a group of his friends, knocking back drink after drink while Mum sat pale-faced, waiting for him.

That night we didn't leave the bar until goodness knows what time. All I know is that it was gone 3am before we arrived home. Mum didn't say one word to Ned, she just sat in the back of the truck with her arms around me for the whole journey. It was that drive back that has stopped me ever going up in one of those funfair machines that spin people around high up in the air. That journey back home was terrifying: Ned refused to give the keys to Mum and we could both see he was blind drunk. What made it even worse was when the outside air hit him.

Instead of letting Mum drive, he opened the back door and pushed her in then shouted at me to climb in with her. Thank goodness there were no trucks or lorries coming towards us or we would all have been killed. He was swerving from one side of the road to the other as he sped down the country roads as fast as he could.

As soon as we arrived at the house, Mum unlocked the gates as he was in no state to do so. He stormed into the house looking for more drink, while she and I went to my room. We curled up together on my bed waiting for the storm that was Ned to abate.

After that, I wanted nothing more to do with him. I heard all the excuses: that it was the woman he tried to hit, not Mum. Maybe that was true, but I didn't believe a single word of his other excuses. He insisted the woman had been chasing him and no, he hadn't phoned to ask her not to come, why would he have her number anyway? I just hoped that Mum would give up on him now, pack her bags, throw them in her truck and take me and Eddie and leave – we could go to Melbourne or back to her family.

I'm convinced that wish might have been granted if I had spoken up then – but I didn't.

48

Any hope I had that Mum might leave Ned had evaporated by the time I went to school on the Monday. All I could think was that it was like living with Jekyll and Hyde. One moment there's a nice guy – all smiles and charm – and within minutes of him swallowing the magic potion (in his case bourbon), whoosh, quick as a flash, there emerged the unpredictable and violent Mr Hyde.

All I wished for was that this had happened on one of the weekends when I was visiting Dad – anything to get away from the house. I could hardly bring myself to look at Ned. I wanted to put my fingers in my ears so I could block out the sound of him spouting out his apologies to Mum as he followed her around the house like a scolded puppy. He was making every effort to get back in her good books. Out came a monotonous stream of lame excuses which Mum and I both knew had little or no thread of truth in them – that the other woman had caused the row and wrecked what might have been a nice evening. He insisted she had been pestering him at more than one gig and he had told her that he wasn't interested. Everything she said was untrue, it was just a fantasy of hers. And no, he hadn't phoned to tell her to stay away, which was another insult she had hurled at him. He didn't have her phone number anyhow, so he couldn't have. Mum could look at his phone if she wanted. The woman must have mental health problems, he was getting her barred from his gigs so Mum and I could come the next time and finally, he had not meant to hit Mum – it was the other woman his fist was meant to land on. That last bit might have been true, but we both knew that none of the other stuff was – and I could tell by the grim look on Mum's face that he wasn't even close to fooling her.

Mind you, I was pretty pleased to see it was hardly working and tried to keep the smirk off my face. I just wondered how it was that after all he had drunk, he was still able to stand up. Thankfully, seeing as he was not getting anywhere with Mum, he muttered something about getting some work done outside: 'Got a few animal carcasses to get rid of,' he told us, which was hardly an attractive thought.

But at least it was something he had been asked to sort out many times. The cow that I had seen die was taken away the following day, but not all livestock that died on the farm were got rid of that quickly. When chickens that were locked in at night to protect them from foxes reached the end of their lives, they were tossed behind the sheds and left to rot there. I hated walking past and seeing those poor bodies covered with flies. Even worse if it was a bigger animal such as when a calf had been stillborn – Ned would usually drag it round the back of the sheds too. Though they did eventually have to be buried when the smell was overwhelming.

When I think back on it now, I realise Ned was an extremely tough man, although deep inside he was also broken and sad. But in his own way he did try and do what was needed around the place.

I can remember him saying, 'That's farm life, Daisy,' when I'd been upset at seeing the dead calves and hens outside. I wasn't too sure about that, having seen other farmers' immaculate animal sheds. Nor did I see anything that was dead lying around on their land. When I asked Ned why that was, he told me, 'They burn them, big evil-smelling bonfires. Still, it keeps the maggots and flies away, I suppose.'

I didn't really like that idea either. And as was so often the case as I got to know him, I didn't believe him so I asked my friends who lived on livestock farms, who told me he was talking garbage. All dead animals had to be removed by the government's approved carriers so they could be checked for disease such as foot and mouth and bird flu.

'Looks like he's not paying his taxes, Daisy, that's probably why he doesn't want to contact them.'

What I was told seemed very likely and of course I now know it to be true.

*   *   *

As well as other farmers obeying the rules, they probably also secured their fields better than Ned did. Must have been at least once a weekend when one of them was on the phone complaining that yet again some of our livestock were out on the road, causing problems for traffic. Out Ned would go with the dogs and have them herded back. But still, whereas the farmers and their families were friendly to me, they were none too keen on Ned: 'Hasn't got a bloody clue how to run a farm,' I overheard one saying.

The worst complaint was made by the nearby farmer who just about exploded on the phone when our old bull, a massive black creature with enormous horns, escaped. He frightened the farmer when he saw it careering off the road and onto his land. His children were on the farm and they had the dogs with them. They had rushed home when they spotted the bull but Ned's enraged animal could have endangered their lives. The farmer told him that he had no other choice than to inform the police. My stepfather knew what would happen then, especially with an animal as dangerous as that one was; it would have to be shot. He asked him to wait, saying he knew how he could get it back. Now it might be easy to get a wayward cow back with dogs nipping at her heels, but this bull was a very different matter, the farmer told him.

Later, I learnt that the farmer had told him not to be so stupid, saying he was risking his life for what? A bad-tempered bull that was a danger to everyone.

As soon as he put the phone down, Ned muttered that this time he would need more than the dogs to get the bull back. What he didn't say was that the bull would have lowered his head and one by one, speared them with his horns. Just as well he didn't as Mum would have been quite hysterical at the thought of what Ned was going to attempt. She might be furious with him, but she didn't want to become a widow so soon after the wedding.

The warning he had been given didn't stop my stepfather from tearing out of the house and jumping onto his motor bike. Maybe a sober Ned would have agreed with the farmer to let the police kill the bull, but the alcohol was still in his body. I just think that must have wiped out his last few remnants of common sense when he decided he was a one-man band who could control a bull whose head would have weighed almost as much as his body.

By the time he got there, the bull had managed to get through more than one of the farmers' fields. I still don't know what was in Ned's head when he opened the gates and like a maniac drove his bike at full throttle towards it.

Did he think that just the noise of a motorbike would alarm the creature and make him trot home? The bull saw him coming and pawed the ground savagely, letting Ned know that this was not going to end peacefully. Ned told us later that he didn't have time to turn his bike round before the bull charged and threw both him and the bike into the air.

Luckily for Ned, the farmer had called the police and just seconds after the bull lowered his head to finish off what he saw as his attacker, the police fired their guns. Did anyone stop and think to ring a vet and get that bull darted? I don't think so. I don't know what happened to the bull, I never asked, but I assume the police had killed it.

I was outside the house when I saw with some dismay that Ned was returning. He was dragging himself back to the house. It was a mix of lurching and falling and every step he took was clearly causing him immense pain so I shouted for Mum to come quickly. I could hear his moans, which was unlike him as a stoic brave face was something he always thought to be important. Between us, we managed to get him inside and on to the settee. He had been gone for hours and we heard afterwards that he had refused help from the farmer and the police. He had a dislocated shoulder and a broken collarbone that he had to have in a sling for weeks; his ankle twisted as well, a couple of ribs were broken and he was covered in bruises and minor cuts.

He certainly looked a real mess for some weeks.

The farmer might have been the one who saved his life and got the motorbike off him. He had also clicked his shoulder back in. I should think the police shared the farmer's opinion that he had been pretty stupid as well.

Though Ned never explained why it was that he had to practically crawl back. Surely he should have been driven home or been taken off in an ambulance immediately? And what did Mum do? Got her first aid kit out. Cleaned up the grazes, strapped up his ankle and offered to take him to the hospital to assess the shoulder and the ribs. Did he go? I think they both wanted him to get the alcohol out of his blood first.

And me? For a while I forgot why I never wanted to speak to him again. I boiled up the water and then made him strong sweet tea. Mum had to hold his hand when he drank it, it was shaking so much, he could hardly lift the mug to his mouth. Luckily, there were painkillers in the house, which she gave him and then after propping him up with cushions, she let him rest on the settee.

'You could have been killed,' she told him and seeing the tears glistening in her eyes I knew that she was not going to leave him this time.

49

So, there was Ned to my great annoyance back in Mum's good books, or at least back in her affections. There's nothing like seeing an injured man to bring out a woman's caring side. Can't say I didn't feel a little sorry for him, he did look rather pathetic. His shoulder and arm had been strapped up at the hospital, as had his ankle. Nothing much he could do except phone a couple of friends and ask if they could help out a bit. Which they agreed to and they took over one of the buses. Mum made him apologise to the farmer as well after she had phoned to thank him for saving her husband's life.

She did get a bit of a lecture about telling him to secure his fields and driving a motorbike when so drunk. He explained to Mum that Ned shouldn't keep any more bullocks past a year old because they would only grow up to be equally dangerous: 'Farmers are using artificial insemination now,' he told her, 'much safer for everyone.'

Not that Ned seemed particularly interested in that suggestion when she told him. But at least he did what she asked and picked up the phone to add his personal thanks. It sounded as though the farmer was quite good-natured about it too – he even asked if we needed some help around the farm. Ned politely told him that he had already arranged it – doubtless, he was not wanting the farmer seeing how many rules he was in fact breaking.

*   *   *

I felt something had to be done about our life with Ned. Mum might think that the shock of being tossed by the bull would change him, but I didn't. At school I pondered that question of what could be done – I just didn't want him touching me again. It was something that I should have made clear right from the beginning. If I had threatened to tell Dad, then he would have stopped. But how could I admit it had been going on for over three years? I would be blamed as well, wouldn't I? This was what I believed back then, telling myself that I could hardly explain it away by saying I hadn't been able to summon up the courage to tackle it.

At least I knew his body was almost certainly too sore to try anything with me when I got home. He couldn't drive either, so for a while I travelled in with Mum and caught the bus back from school. Neither of us talked about that night at the gig – I had a feeling that the subject was now off limits. Instead, Mum chatted more about her work in the special needs section, especially how much the pupils there enjoyed her music lessons.

For the first few days I was right about Ned not trying to persuade me to do anything I didn't want to. It made me rather complacent and that was a mistake. He might not have had the physical energy, but he had his other interests, which I discovered much sooner than I wanted – one of which he had decided that I was old enough for him to share with me too. Not that he showed me everything straight away, it was a gradual build-up.

'Got a film on my computer,' was one of the first comments he made when I reached home, with a look of glee on his face.

'What is it?'

'Let's go and have a look, shall we? You'll see, it's a nice little film,' and with a sinking feeling, I followed him to the small room where he kept his computer. The one that he told Mum held all his files about the farm.

And that was the first time I was introduced to the ghastliest porn I had ever seen. Girls with studded collars around their throats were linked to chains held in men's fists. As the film went on, I saw those chains being pulled, making their lithe bodies crawl along behind them. My first thought was that they looked too young to be involved willingly in such acts: were they forced into this or were they paid too much to refuse? Or were they like me, trapped in a situation they couldn't get out of? I had seen something similar on one of those pictures Ned's father had pasted onto the walls, but seeing it on video somehow made it appear much worse. Seeing a dog collar around a woman's neck had shocked me, but these visuals actually scared me.

It was the glazed expressions on the girls' faces which told me they had tried their hardest to block out what acts they were taking part in. Later, I wondered if they were drugged. There was no way that I could believe that they were past the age of consent but then that first film did not show any sexual acts – that came about a week later.

Ned was certainly smart enough not to show them all at once. He hardly wanted Mum to arrive and see me pasty-faced and looking shocked.

The next film he got me to watch showed some sexual acts which I turned my head away from. What made it worse for me was seeing that every picture was of women – or rather girls – being degraded – they demonstrated to me that men who got turned on by these images had no respect for women at all.

It was a couple of months later when Ned showed me another film that shocked me even more. It was not even about normal sex, even I knew that: it was about power. Surely no woman would have enjoyed being beaten, having two men having sex with her at the same time and whatever else the film showed? I shut my eyes as it got too much for me to watch but Ned just laughed, telling me, 'Don't be prudish.' Even if there were some who did enjoy what they were doing, not one of these porn 'actresses' as Ned called them, appeared to be enjoying themselves.

Ned went quiet for a while and there were no more films. By now he had got his strength back and could drive again, which meant he could pick me up from school. He began doing that about once a week. For me, that drive back to the house was a horrible one: my hands would be clenched in my lap as silent questions of what he had planned for me this time whirled around my head.

It must have been when I had just turned fourteen that he finally showed me something that I found completely unnerving. I couldn't even move to get away from the screen, I was too numb with shock to move. Instead I could only stare at what was on that screen: a woman having sex with animals. I can't find the words to describe how sick that made me feel. All I can say is that I could feel bile rushing up to my throat when I saw them.

Surely some of those acts would have injured the woman taking part? Or maybe, which I so hoped was true, they were not really doing it and the filmmaker was just using techniques to make them look as though they were. Even so, what sort of person would get turned on by them?

For the first time I felt frightened to be left alone on the farm with Ned. Was he going to try every trick in the book to get me to take part in something like that?

Once I was away from the screen, I relaxed a little. I rationalised that however screwed up Ned was, he would never force me to do something like that, would he? I kept telling myself he wouldn't. But whatever happened, I had to find a way of not being on my own with him.

I asked one of my friends if I could go to her house to do my homework. All right, I found walking back home in the dark frightening, but that had to be less scary than being around Ned and not knowing what plans for me he had up his sleeve.

50

By the time Ned recovered from the incident with the bull, his confidence also returned although he was careful to restrict his drinking. He could hardly afford another near-death experience to win Mum back again. He suggested throwing parties again and at first, Mum seemed a little reluctant – she didn't want anyone encouraging him to drink heavily. Ned got his own way after a couple more weeks, said it would be good for all of us to have some friends over.

Despite feeling annoyed that once again, my stepfather was getting what he wanted, I enjoyed those days when various musicians turned up to record their backing tracks that were used in karaoke nights. Those parties were good fun, mainly because I was also encouraged to invite my friends over. They good-naturedly kept telling Ned and his friends the titles of the latest popular songs: 'You want to mix them with the oldies,' they told them as they listed their favourites.

Having a good time still did not quell the anger that had built up in me since Mum had decided not to leave Ned. In those fairly early teenage years, I never accepted that her staying at the farm was partly my fault. I just didn't believe that if Mum knew what he got up to with me, she would have left. Which was fairly unreasonable thinking as I had watched his fingers typing out his passwords and memorised them. So that would have been enough proof. But then, what teenagers think is justified anger makes them entirely obstinate, something I have learnt since I became the mother of one. But at that time, I was at the age when parents were not meant to make mistakes. When I was older, I acknowledged that like me, parents were mere mortals. It came as a great shock when I found out when I was six that there was no Santa Claus. Still, at least when I faced up to that, my anger disappeared after a short time.

Although I can't remember details of all my birthdays, my fourteenth one is pretty clear. As it fell in the middle of the week, I had two celebrations. One was at Dad's, where friends I had kept in touch with since I had left were invited. My little brother was toddling around by then, looking totally engaging and with his gummy smiles, all my friends kept saying how cute he was. Dad fired up the usual barbecue or as he now called it, 'The Barbie'. Julie waited until we had slowed down on eating all the grilled chicken, chops and sausages before bringing out a huge cake covered in pink icing and with fourteen candles on it.

Yes, that was a really good and memorable day.

*   *   *

Mum organised another party for me the following weekend. The second one had all the friends that both Tommy and I had made since we moved to the farm. A few weeks after that was our half term, which began with Ned inviting his musician friends over again. Not only did they turn up, but his seventeen-year-old nephew, Luke, arrived the evening before. If anything, he looked a bit like a younger version of Ned – all long jean-clad legs and dark hair. Like his uncle, he had a wide smile, but somehow, I felt the resemblance stopped with his looks.

He had told Ned that he had a job lined up in Melbourne in a couple of weeks and fancied a break in the bush. To which my stepfather had told him that he could stay in one of the buses for as long as he wanted.

The good thing about the group that was coming was that they didn't expect Mum to spend the whole day cooking. They brought food for the barbecues, there were loads of salads and once the fire had reached the perfect point, the men stood round it, bottles of beer in their hands, chatting away as the meat sizzled. The women were happy to leave the cooking to them and sat together in shadier parts.

I had invited Jess, my closest friend, over that day – I hadn't got to know Luke then and I wanted someone my own age to have some fun with. They were practising their music outside when we nipped in to get a cool drink. Opening the fridge door, in front of my eyes was a box of white wine. The temptation to try it was just too much to resist – 'Let's have a glass of that,' I said and Jess agreed: 'Just the one though,' she said, 'we don't want to get pissed, do we?'

Don't we? I thought angrily. If Ned could drink, then so too could I. That was the silly decision I made, which caused me to knock back my glass of wine in one. As soon as I'd downed the first one, I poured another and then another and then some more.

So, what do I remember after that? The answer is nothing much, only what I've been told. Evidently, I could hardly see in front of me. Jess did try and stop me pouring out more, but I wasn't in the mood to listen to any reason – I somehow managed to get outside before in front of everyone, I vomited all down myself.

Mum and Jess got me back inside as fast as they could. I have a vague memory of them getting me in the shower but even those gallons of water gushing down on my body did not sober me up enough to return to the party. Instead I was tucked up in my bed with a bucket beside me. Jess stayed with me for a while to make sure I didn't throw up again. And I didn't; instead I slept through the rest of the day and the whole of the night until I woke to a bright sunny morning the following day. My head was thumping, my throat dry and when I pulled myself out of bed, my legs were wobbly. Dull memories came into my head of helping myself to the wine and being sick – little wonder Ned had blackouts when he was drunk. Though in a way not being able to remember much can be a blessing.

I just about squirmed when he laughingly asked how I was coping with my first hangover.

'Urgh! I'm never going to touch a drop of wine again,' I declared, feeling my cheeks burn as everyone who had stayed over joined in the laughter. And true to my word, I never have.

Luke could see I was embarrassed and came over: 'Come on, I fancy a walk – you can show me around a bit. Bring Eddie too, he looks as though he could do with a walk as well. And the fresh air will blow those cobwebs away.'

We walked for a while almost in silence. He was right, the fresh air did make me feel better. Plus, he was nice enough not to mention anything about the day before. He had brought a couple of bottles of cold water with him and when we found a shady place under the trees, he suggested we sat down for a while.

'You can lean against the tree,' he told me, handing a bottle over and I gulped some cold water down gratefully. He was good fun and I was feeling a lot better when we walked back. I began to wish he was staying for longer – there was something about him that made me relax more.

Not that Ned looked that happy when he saw us laughing together on our return. I saw his quick sideways glances but I didn't think that Luke had – I was wrong about that as I was to find out later.

*   *   *

The following morning, Luke was waiting for me.

'Let's go for another walk,' he said and when I looked outside, I noticed that Ned's truck had gone.

'Oh, he had a couple of people to see,' Mum told me. 'They're interested in buying some of those bullocks that are just over a year old.' Though she was careful in not telling me what they wanted them for. Had she done so, I doubt if I would ever had dug into a steak again.

'Have your breakfast first and then go for a walk,' Mum suggested.

I had a peculiar feeling about Luke hanging around, waiting – I felt there was a reason for him wanting to get out of the house with me. He said very little when we went outside, paying more attention to Eddie than me as we set off walking in the same direction as we had the day before.

'What's wrong?' I asked as we sat under the same trees for he was not usually as quiet as he was being. It took him a couple of minutes to manage to tell me that he had seen those photos of me on Ned's computer and if I had blushed earlier, I should think my face turned a bright red when I heard those words.

'Does he know you saw them?' I asked.

'Yes, he caught me deleting them. I think that's why he's gone out. He was really angry with me. Daisy, you looked so young and lost in them. Goodness knows who else has seen them. I've deleted them off his computer, but he's probably uploaded them onto porn sites.'

So, playing for time, I asked what had been said.

'I told him what I thought – that he was a pervert and that he's got to stop. I thought he was going to hit me when I said that.'

'And what did he say then?'

'Tried to brush it off, saying it was only a bit of a game and nothing had really happened. They were just pin-up pictures, and you didn't mind him doing it anyway. Is that truth, Daisy? That he didn't do anything else?'

I felt some relief that Luke had apparently only seen the first images where I wasn't completely naked and just looked as though I was posing for Ned. I knew he was hoping that I would deny anything else had happened – he was too young to cope with thinking what he should do if I told him more. Though there was something else he knew that I didn't: there had been a camera in my room which he had ripped down when I had breakfast.

So, did he believe me, that there was nothing else? I don't think so. He would hardly have deleted those pictures if he had. But he wanted to believe me, so that was enough.

He left the farm before Ned returned, which really confirmed what I thought.

51

Tuesday might not have been a school day, but I had arranged to go to Jess's house to work with her on our homework. We didn't have much to do – it was, after all, meant to be a holiday – just some Maths and English. We both wanted to get our homework out of the way as quickly as we could. She phoned, asking me if I remembered our plan, without saying much about my getting so drunk. Just asked if I was feeling OK and laughed a little when I said I had a headache.

When I told Mum I was spending the day with Jess and we were going to work together, she flashed me a smile and said, 'That's good, but you'll be back for supper?'

'Yes.'

Anything I told her about trying to improve my schoolwork pleased her.

When I set off, I didn't know that this would be the day when I would finally confide in someone. I hadn't any intention of doing so, it was just that Jess had her suspicions that something was going wrong in my life. Evidently when she had come into my room after Mum had got me into bed, I had mumbled something that troubled her. She waited until we had finished our homework before she asked me to go upstairs with her.

'Got something to show you,' was her excuse. Not wanting her mother to overhear anything was the real reason.

'So, what do you want to show me?' I asked once we were in her room.

'Nothing, I just wanted to talk to you without my mother listening. You weren't at all happy on Saturday, were you? I've never seen you like that and I could tell something had upset you. Actually, Daisy, I've been thinking that for a while and when I couldn't stop you pouring the wine down your throat, I just knew something was up. They say a little alcoholic drink helps us to party, but not getting into the state you did. And there's got to be a reason.'

'I didn't know how strong it was,' I said a bit defiantly.

'Come on, Daisy! You mumbled something to me when I was in your room after your mum left.'

Because I couldn't remember her being in my room, far less what I had said to her, I waited for her to tell me.

'You said you didn't want to stay at the farm anymore, you didn't want to be near Ned. So, tell me, what's the problem? I've heard he's got a terrible temper, has he hit you or something?'

'No, he's never done that.'

'So, what's he done? There's been a lot of talk at school about that row at his gig, you know. In fact, I've heard a lot about him, that he's not as nice as he seems. And I'll tell you something else, Daisy, your brother was worried about you – he said he didn't like the way Ned looked at you.'

'How do you know that?'

'He told one of his friends that he had to keep an eye on you, that he didn't trust Ned when you were around. And that's when you were only ten! If he was like that when you were that young, it was bound to worry Tommy.'

'And now my brother can't keep his eye on me and watch out for me,' I said.

'Daisy, tell me what he's done, will you?' she pleaded.

'I don't like the way he touches me,' I blurted out.

As soon as those words left my lips, the tears began to form.

'I can't tell Mum – she'd blame me, wouldn't she?'

'Tell her what?'

'That he takes photos of me when I have hardly anything on. And even worse, Luke, who you met at the party, found them on his computer. Not only that, he found a hidden camera in my bedroom as well. Luke told me he was furious and deleted a lot of them before Ned caught him. He's gone now, but I don't even know if Ned knows that Luke told me about it – he hasn't said a word to me.'

'What happened after Luke told you about the pictures?'

'He left before Ned came back, he didn't want to believe that he had done more than that.'

'Right, so no help from that side of the family then.'

'Don't think he'll tell anyone else, but he told me. He had even noticed that Ned didn't like him being around me, which was another reason he was heading out.'

'So, Ned's jealous of you having friends, is he? Or maybe he's just worried you might talk to them.'

I thought for a moment before saying, 'You know, that

never entered my head, but yes, now you've mentioned it, I think he was.'

'That's even creepier, Daisy.'

'Yes, I suppose it is.'

She managed to wheedle out of me all about the porn he had made me watch. When I described the really ugly stuff, Jess looked completely horrified.

'God, Daisy, if he watches those, I hope he doesn't share yours with anyone! Can't bear to even think about that. So what else has he done to you?'

'Made me wank him off,' and more tears came as she put her arm around me.

'He's got to be stopped,' she told me. 'You've got to stand up for yourself, tell him you won't do anything else with him. Promise me you'll try?'

'Yes,' I said but even though I said the word, I didn't believe it. Nor did she.

'So that's why you never want to go home until your mum's due back, isn't it?'

'Yes, but you know he sometimes comes to the school to pick me up and what choice do I have then?'

'Say no, you like the bus, say anything. Don't be alone with him again.'

Jess gave me another hug, told me that everything would be all right soon and then I left.

*   *   *

Having stayed later than usual, I made my way home down the highway. I think it was having Ned in my life that had put all the fears of men into me. I had visions of being dragged into a car by those men who like young petite female teenagers – there had been enough written about those crimes in various newspapers to make me very wary.

I had discovered a shortcut that made me feel safer. It was the tunnels that Australia placed in many country roads that were designed as underpasses for mammals not just to cross the roads safely but more to prevent road accidents that I used. I had to be careful that there was no wild pig in there trotting back to its home so I would listen for a moment before I entered. One advantage of being small was that I only had to stoop a little as I made me way through them until I reached the tall grass on the other side. Walking through that was frightening as well, I was scared that there would be snakes slithering around.

I managed to get back just in time for supper. Glancing at her watch, Mum said that she would have preferred it if I was going to be late in future to phone ahead.

'Not really happy with you walking back down that road once it's dark,' she told me.

'Oh, there's hardly any traffic on it,' I said, which was true, before adding, 'I feel fine doing it,' which was not.

* * *

It was two days later when Jess arrived at the house. After Mum had greeted her, the pair of us went outside.

'Thought I'd better tell you my mum asked me why you had looked upset when we came down the stairs the other day. I told her you weren't, but she wasn't having it.'

'Well?'

'In the end, I told her.'

'You didn't!'

'I'm afraid I did, Daisy. She asked if there was trouble in your home and had it anything to do with Ned?'

I couldn't really blame Jess, but still I felt sick with nerves all day.

Just what was going to happen next? Mum would be so angry with me was all I could think, telling stories like that to the neighbours. Then all I thought about was what if Jess's mother tried to talk to Mum?

But she didn't – she did something far worse, she told the police.

And round they came that evening, when we were all in.

*   *   *

Although they were wearing plain clothes and driving an ordinary car, there was no mistaking who they were. They showed their ID to Ned when he opened the door to them.

I don't know what he told them, for they talked to him outside. They were clearly telling him that he had been reported because there were suspicions that he had been abusing his stepdaughter.

Not that they were prepared to give the name of who had reported him.

From what I was told, he denied it – which didn't stop them saying they had to interview me and they asked if my mother was inside. When told she was, they insisted on coming into the house and interviewing me. They said I was old enough to speak up, especially as my mother would be there with me.

Ned must have been praying inwardly that I would deny it for he hadn't come up with the usual excuses that men like him habitually make, that I was a compulsive liar and an attention seeker who made up stories.

When they entered the house, I gulped with nerves for I knew what it was about. Mum was just worried that it had something to do with Ned's drink driving or that the neighbour had complained about livestock escaping. When told the real reason, she turned pale and her eyes hardly left my face.

'My colleague will have to ask your daughter some questions while I talk to your husband outside…' said one.

They had obviously brought a policewoman with them so that I might not be so embarrassed by the questions she was planning to ask. First, she reassured me that nothing would happen to me if I told them the truth and that Ned would leave with them if it was true so I needn't be scared.

At this Mum's face turned ashen and all I could hear her saying was, 'This can't be true, it can't,' and then she bit her lip to stop herself saying anything more. And here was my big chance to talk, to get rid of Ned, for they would have taken him straight out of the house. They would also take Mum for they would want to question her as well; they would want to know if she had been aware of the abuse. The thought of my mother being escorted to the station after so much that had gone wrong in her life was not something I could handle.

That was the main reason I said what I did.

'Of course it isn't true,' I told them and turning to Ned, I spoke directly to him: 'No, you never did anything like that, did you?' And I tried to give a light laugh to cement my denial in.

I'm sure the police regretted not bundling us all in their car and taking us to the station, where they could have interviewed us each in separate rooms. By the way, the woman officer handed me her card – I was pretty sure she at least believed I was lying. But there was nothing they could do, except say goodnight and leave. As soon as they had gone, I just got up and walked into my room – there was bound to be an outburst and I did not want to be part of it.

To my surprise it was Ned who knocked at my door and asked if he could speak to me. He had told Mum that he just wanted to know where the story had come from and he had a right to ask me.

I expected fury and had to tell myself that there was nothing more he could do, but instead of looking angry, he appeared grateful.

'So why did you say I hadn't, when we both know it's the truth?' he wanted to know.

'What, you're admitting that you're abusing me?' I said.

'Yes.'

I just cringed at his reply – I wanted him out of my room and the conversation over. Oh, he tried to apologise, said he didn't know that he had upset me.

But I was having none of that: 'You knew I didn't want it so now you'd better leave me alone, hadn't you?'

I saw for the first time that our roles were slightly reversed.

When he opened the door to leave, Mum was just outside and I could tell she had been crying.

'Daisy, tell me the truth now, has Ned been molesting you? Because if it's true, I'll leave him right now.'

Part of me wanted to say yes, but I just couldn't. Maybe I thought she wouldn't leave him and then it would be them against me, or was I just too ashamed to admit it? Or did I not want to break her heart? For looking at her, I suddenly saw her not as my mother but as a vulnerable woman who still had not recovered from losing her son. Or was it a mixture of all that?

'Daisy, I'm asking you one more time, is it true?' she persisted. 'Because I don't want to live with a man and then find out when you're grown up that it was.'

She waited.

'No,' was my answer.

52

People often ask me where I met my husband and how old I was; the truth was that I was at school and it was when I was about ten. He was in a class a couple of years ahead of me – in fact he and Tommy were friends of a sort. Mostly because the pair of them were often in detention together. Brent had, as he recalled, had a reputation of being a bit of a bad boy who was always in trouble.

I used to see him smoking just outside the playground; a habit he told me later that he had begun when he was around ten. Then, when we bumped into each other, I was just Tommy's little sister to him, who was hardly worth talking to. Though I did see a more considerate side to him just after my brother died. He was one of a group of older boys who came over to me to say how sorry they were and I could see Brent really meant it. But after that, we rarely talked, for to me he was just one of the boys my brother had been friendly with.

I must have been somewhere around thirteen when he started paying me some attention. Not that I was interested in boys then. Well, maybe a tiny bit, I suppose, and I can't say it wasn't flattering as all the girls in my class kept saying he was the best-looking boy in our school. That made me smile because I remembered that was exactly what Mum had once said about going out with Dad. With his thick light brown hair and large sparkling eyes of a darker shade, I had certainly noticed that he was attractive. He might not have been very tall, but that didn't stop him from strutting around confidently. And his jokes were amusing, I must say.

I might have been persuaded to have responded a little more to the odd compliment he paid me, if I wasn't engrossed in another interest, dancing, that was taking up a lot of my time. Although that was not the only reason, of course: Ned and my home life stopped me wanting boys as friends. I didn't want anyone wanting to touch me and as you can imagine, my trust in the opposite sex was pretty limited.

It had been one of the teachers who had encouraged me to give dancing a try. She had started a school dance club and she thought it was something I would be good at. Or I suspect she thought it would be good for me. If she had seen that underneath my rather cocky attitude, I was actually depressed and needed something that would interest me, she never said. It had begun when she approached me after a sports lesson: 'You are so nimble with everything you do,' she told me. 'Why, you simply flew over that horse. Just watching you makes me think you would be a natural at dancing.' She then went on to explain she had a group who practised dance after classes and she would like me to come along and take a look at them.

'What sort of dance is it?' I asked, thinking she might have been talking about ballroom or something equally boring.

She mentioned jazz and I almost snorted. As far as I knew that was music for older people, where the men had scraggly beards and the women wore either cord trousers in winter, or baggy cut-offs in summer, with drab coloured sweatshirts.

Seeing my reaction, she almost burst out laughing and I could see the amusement on her face: 'I think you'd better come and see a class before you make up your mind, I'll just say it's a very contemporary version.'

'All right, I'll come and take a look,' I said with little enthusiasm evident in my voice.

What a shock it was the first time I went. My feet could hardly stay still, first the drums started their beat and then wind and brass instruments joined in. My body twitched with the desire to move to it. I was just about wide-eyed with excitement when I watched the dancers. Talk about movement, this music was not just about legs moving, it was about every part of their bodies moving to the rhythm – legs, arms, torsos and heads. As I swayed in time to the music, I was just dying to go over and join them.

'So now what do you think?' asked my teacher, still with that amused expression on her face.

'Oh, I love it! I had no idea dance could be like that.'

'Good, you can start your first class on Monday. We have them twice a week on a Monday and Friday, which means you can catch up at any lost homework over the weekend, doesn't it?'

'Eh, yes,' I managed to get out and saw her smile again – I don't think she thought homework was my main interest.

Having those two classes after school meant that I would be

able to go home with Mum. At least I would not be on my own with Ned for those days. When I told her about the dance class she was really pleased for me: 'Have to get you some leotards at the weekend and another pair of trainers,' was just about the first thing she said before adding, 'We could have some lunch out, just the two of us.' Another invitation that made me happy. So, Saturday was our shopping day and soon I had a bag stuffed with everything I needed for those classes. Over a pizza lunch, she told me again how pleased she was that I had taken such an interest in dance and that I was learning to express myself so well.

*   *   *

On Monday I began to feel really excited about my first class, although slightly apprehensive about what to expect. It was brilliant and by the end I already felt that it had started changing things for me. It was as though I had entered another world where the beat of those drums and the voices of the clarinet, trumpet and saxophone spoke to me as they guided my limbs to do as they wished. I felt such freedom as I allowed my body to express my emotions.

Moving to the beat made me feel stronger, more in control and the worries that came into my mind almost floated away as I danced, though there were times when I felt the loss of Tommy even more acutely. Images of his face, with that roguish grin of his, swam in front of me. That smile, that since his death I had come to realise had hidden the pain he felt at being trapped inside his bent and broken body. I know now that he must have felt that every day of those years when he lived his all-too-short a life. It was when my mind saw him that, as I finished my class, I felt the dampness on my face where my tears had streamed down it.

Dance was certainly far more emotional for me than I had ever thought it would be, but it was also great fun. I just knew I had found something that could help me grow physically and emotionally stronger, more independent and more confident.

Around about then, Brent seemed to give up trying to talk to me – I suppose I just didn't give him any encouragement. When he asked what I did in my spare time, I had just told him dancing: 'At the school club, not anywhere in town,' I said in case he got the wrong idea. I received a white sparkling smile after that comment.

'Oh, there I was, thinking you were sneaking into the local clubs,' he said and we both laughed at that. I was not one of those girls who could, with a little help from make-up, make myself appear older – if anything, I looked younger than I was.

53

If it hadn't been for the gradual freedom dance gave me, Brent might have just remained the bad boy who smoked cigarettes at the back of the school. Not that at the beginning of my classes I gave him much thought.

After a year of those classes which I could hardly wait to go to, my teacher told me that she considered me the best dancer in the group. She pointed out that being so tiny and light, I could be swung up in the air more easily, but it was how I did it so gracefully that most impressed her: 'You really express yourself beautifully,' she added, though she was tactful enough not to ask me about my tears. Maybe she knew that my freedom of movement made me think of my brother, who with the use of only one limb, strived every day to be in charge of his own life.

'I know you're taking your classes seriously,' she had said, before she started telling me about the competitions that were coming up over the next few weekends and she told me that she would like to put my name down if I could take part in them – how did I feel about that?

'Great!' I told her, my face beaming with happiness.

'I think these classes have been good for you, Daisy.'

'They have,' I agreed.

Which was true, for they had made me far more focused. Both Mum and Dad were delighted when I told them about the upcoming competitions. Mum told me that nothing would stop her from being there while Dad told me that he accepted that I would be visiting him less often. I didn't want him to think it was an excuse to see him less. It was not that he or Julie had done anything to make me feel unwelcome and I loved my baby brother, it was just that seeing the three of them looking so happy together made me wish even more that I was still part of a happy family life.

*   *   *

I had been right about dancing building up my confidence in the year between my first lesson and confiding in Jess. I had been learning so many movements, but more than anything it made me want my freedom.

It was some days after that evening when the police had arrived at the farm that I began to plan how I could get away from there. For ages I had felt that my life at the farm was stifling me and that I had to find a way to leave. Waiting until I was eighteen and leaving school was just far too long, I decided.

It had taken several months after the bust-up for Mum to have a life with Ned again. Whereas for him, little had changed. If he had felt either grateful or ashamed about the abuse, he kept that to himself. I did my best to avoid him, but what I really wanted to do was move out completely and have a normal teenage life like all my friends. I was so sick of what he was like when we were alone together. Did he stop trying to abuse me? No, of course he didn't.

'Too late to change your story now,' he said mockingly, more than once.

'Oh, I could and they would believe me,' was my answer and he backed off, but that didn't stop me feeling uncomfortable. I wanted out from this crazy way of living. Mum might have been able to put up with Ned's moods, I no longer could. Losing Eddie, my faithful companion who had hardly left my side since we brought him home, had made me begin to hate the farm. I was heartbroken when Mum broke the news.

After I stopped crying and made her tell me how he had died, I blamed Ned for doing so little work on the upkeep of the barns and fields. Almost everywhere I looked, I was confronted by piles of rubbish and inside the large barn were piles of old machinery. Evidently Eddie had jumped over something in there and his collar had caught on a rusty bit of the tangled mess. He ended up being slowly strangled as he hung there. Another horrible death for me to come to terms with. I must have cried buckets of tears then, for his passing brought back so many sad memories of loss and death. The atmosphere at the farm was hardly relaxing and I could feel Ned's eyes on me far too often; I could also sense that Mum was still suspicious. If only she would leave him, was the thought that ran continuously through my head.

Yes, I did know how I could make her do that, but I wanted it to be her decision. I didn't want it to be only about me.

Part Six

Escape

54

At that time, one of the girls in my class, Jill, told me about her very long journeys back and forth to the school. She lived a long way out as well, but in a different direction to me. It took her even longer to get home, she said.

It was while she was complaining about her journeys that the beginning of an idea came to me: if she stayed with us at the farm, Ned would have to keep out of my way. The other thought was that as she too wanted to live nearer to the school, maybe between us we might be able to persuade our parents to agree to it. When I put the idea to her I succeeded in getting her interest. 'We'll have to do it in stages,' I told her and within a matter of seconds she turned me into her best friend: 'I'll talk about you when I'm at home so my mum knows about you and your dancing,' she told me.

That evening, I put the first part of my idea up to Mum: 'At least my dance classes will mean she doesn't have to catch that bus on those days.' Mum happily agreed – 'Be good for you to have someone your own age living with us,' she said straight away. She told me that my having made plenty of friends made her happy. Even more, she was very pleased with how my dancing had progressed: 'It's something you could consider taking up as a career,' she told me when she heard about the competitions I was due to enter. I had also offered to do something else – teaching the little ones to dance – I was pretty convinced that this could be my major reason to move nearer the school.

I'd given Jill some advice as well. That we did our homework together, and put all our effort in, so that our mothers began to think that us being together was getting the two of us better marks. It took less time than we had thought to get what we both wanted. Jill's mother rang Mum to thank her for having her daughter to stay and it sounded as though they got on well. It was on a later conversation when Jill's mother told mine that it seemed as though her daughter was doing better at school now that she had not got so much travelling to do. She was even considering renting a small flat in the town so that Jill could study more. About a week after that call there was another one in which Jill's mother's Betty told Mum that she and her husband had definitely decided to rent a small flat in town for their daughter. Her suggestion was that I could share it and by the end of that call both mothers had come to an agreement that they would split the costs.

'Just in the week, mind you – you must come back with me on the Friday,' Mum had told me, adding, 'and you had better keep up the studying.'

It was Jill's dad who found the flat, which was within walking distance of the school. Mum took us both to have a look at it and I was pleased to see it was not as small as we had thought. A decent-sized living room with cupboards separating the kitchen from it, a shower room and two bedrooms. Two bedrooms were good for I was a bit of a neat freak and I had seen from the way that Jill tossed her clothes all over her room and covered her chest of drawers with make-up that she was just the opposite.

Once we were in the flat, I made every excuse not to go back to the farm. I used the fact that I was seeing Dad as the obvious one, which I had decided I'd better do. He told me he was really pleased that I had a real interest and I was to let him know when I was performing to an audience.

'Julie and I would love to come,' he suggested, which really pleased me.

I had a dance competition on the first night at the flat, and Jill met me after my dance lesson. 'Let's go out and celebrate that we've got away from our homes', she suggested, with rather a devilish grin. Not that I needed any persuasion. I didn't bother changing out of my shorts, which got me a few whistles as we linked our arms together and trotted down the road to the nearest bar. I remember now that feeling of complete freedom I felt that night. No more being watched by Ned, no more being told what to do. I was in charge of my life now. And, in the bar, I raised my glass to it.

55

It was some time after I had practically moved out that Mum began to accept that I was making my own life. I was now over fifteen and not only was I busying myself with competitions, but also teaching dance to little kids. What she didn't know was that Jill and I were known as the party girls, for my new freedom had gone a bit to my head. Mum and I met up occasionally for an early supper, which we enjoyed, although she was aware that I was going to have more excuses to avoid going to the farm. Occasionally I had to humour her and make an appearance, but she must have sensed I had no interest in being there. Ned always seemed pleased to see me and looked disappointed each time I left.

A few months after I had moved into the flat, Mum took me out for a meal where once our last mouthful was swallowed, she dropped her bombshell. I have to say it was the best news I had heard for a long time, not that I showed just how pleased I was: she and Ned were splitting up and she was moving back to Byron Bay.

'Are you getting divorced?' I asked hopefully.

'No, I just need a break from him to decide what I want to do. Now about you, darling? You must know I would like it if you came with me. Your gran would love it if you did and of course so would your cousins. You could finish your schooling there and the school is almost within walking distance. So, what do you say? I've investigated jazz dance groups there and there's one really good one too. What do you think? I know you love Byron Bay.'

I thought about it for a minute. Can't say it wasn't tempting. What I hadn't told Mum was anything about Brent, who I had finally agreed to see on the evenings when I wasn't dancing. He and I were having fun, meeting up at his friends' houses and swilling back beer. I had mixed feelings about agreeing to that – years with Ned had made me pretty wary around males.

The question that I asked myself was, what kind of person was he really? I knew very little about what he got up to in his free time but I did know he had often got in trouble at school. I tried to think reasonably, there was nothing to suggest he was like Ned.

Once I agreed to go out with him, I became a welcome visitor at his mum's house. Being there was enough to tell me that his childhood had been a happy one for even though his mother was divorced, it was clear that his home had never been one where poisonous seeds had been planted by an abusive father. She had been divorced for a few years but by the sound of it, it had been one of those marriages where they just grew apart from each other and I could also see that she really enjoyed having Brent's friends over.

But while I was being cautious, I didn't want to mention him to Mum – I just felt it was too soon. And then there was my dancing. I was really getting ahead in that, I knew everyone in the group and often some of us would practise together after school even if there was no class. Mum's suggestion that I could make it my profession and teach it as well had germinated and grown into an ambition – one that made me work harder at school because now I really wanted to pass my exams.

So, I turned her offer down and decided to stay, though when she left for Byron Bay, I did feel rather abandoned. When I watched Mum's plane take off and I turned and walked away from the airport, I realised I had no family locally and no support. And I also missed seeing her face, shining with pride, as she sat in the audience when I danced.

Dad might have always been there for me, but it was normally on the other end of the phone unless I was visiting and neither were the same as just popping in, were they? Brent's mother, sensing that, turned up at all my dance performances, where she sat smiling alongside her proud-looking son. She kept telling me the same as Mum had, that dance was a profession I should really consider. My answer was that I had already decided that it was what I wanted to do.

*   *   *

It didn't take long after Mum had left for Ned to try contacting me. My mistake the first time was answering my phone to him. He sounded so sad and lonely then that I couldn't help but feel sorry for him – it made me remember the nice Ned, the one I had once been so fond of.

Don't you dare, Daisy, I told myself, *he abused you.*

But then I thought of his childhood and just how bad it had been. The good memories slipped into my mind, how he had sometimes looked so lost. Which made me begin to understand why Mum had wanted to help him. So, I sent him the odd text message saying, 'keep well,' but was sensible enough not to text, 'thinking of you.'

56

Brent and I were taking things slowly, or rather I was. He was a party guy with a big group of friends, who to begin with didn't seem to want to be tied down. Nor did I, for gradually I was really beginning to enjoy my feelings of independence. I loved being with his friends and staying up til the sun came out.

Jill partied a lot more than either of us, had hangovers in the middle of the week and had begun to skive off school. As for mess, in the flat I was forever tidying up and washing her dishes as well as my own. And as for homework, she had no interest in that either. At least I had peace and quiet when she went out so I could concentrate on my schoolwork.

Brent had by now left school and had managed to get good passes in his exams. He was determined that he would pay for his keep and quickly found a job, though really it was some sort of apprenticeship as he would be training to be an electrician. The downside of that was that it was quite a long distance away so he could only come back at weekends. We spoke on the phone every day and it appeared not only was I missing him, he was missing me more than he had thought he would.

That year was one of changes, it seemed, for it hadn't taken long after Brent began work for his mother to announce that she had a new boyfriend. The first thing we knew about it was when she announced that she was pregnant. Which I have to say she and her new partner seemed overjoyed about.

'And we'll get married before I show too much,' Brent's mum added. 'Just a really quiet wedding.'

Brent was none too happy about sharing a house with the man who would soon be his stepfather – 'It's not that I don't like him, I just feel in the way. The house is not really big enough for me to have my own space.' No sooner had he brought that up than Jill moved out. Not that it was her decision, it was forced on her by her very angry parents. They had arrived unannounced and told her to pack all her possessions up for she was leaving – she had taken advantage of them by persuading them to get her a flat. Those lies she had told about wanting to be nearer school because of the long journeys meant her academic work was suffering. They had found out that she wanted to be in town so she could party every night. All of which the school had made clear when they telephoned her parents so now Mum had to pay the whole rent, which she was not too happy with either.

It was suggested that I found a new flat mate who could help with the bills.

Something that Brent offered to do if he could stay with me at weekends.

Not that he could manage sharing the rent, because he was renting where the job was, but he could help with the bills, so at least that was a start. I said I would think about it, but really, I didn't need very long to say yes.

He told me the first weekend we spent together that one of the reasons he wanted to get a job locally was so that we could set up home together formally. I was a bit unsure of that and I knew both sets of parents would kick up a fuss. I had finally told Mum about him but I don't think that either she or Brent's mum were very happy about us growing so serious about each other – we were still only teenagers with our whole lives in front of us was mentioned more than once. So, both of us told them that the flat had two separate bedrooms so we would be all right sharing it at weekends.

Which might have been the case had we stayed in our separate rooms, but inevitably one thing led to another. And what happens when teenagers don't stay in their own beds happened. I became pregnant. Oh, not straight away. Some months had passed by then. Spending a night in bed with Brent had not happened overnight. I was still nervous as to what it would be like, but I needn't have worried: he was so gentle, so careful of me and afterwards when I lay with my head on his shoulder and with his arms wrapped around me, I finally felt safe and secure.

We were still a pair of kids really, but even so, we should have known a little more about birth control, shouldn't we?

The first time I had rushed out of the classroom, the teacher thought it was just something I had eaten, or was it a bug of some sort, she asked me. But I knew what it was – I hadn't had a period in two months. I just kept hoping that every morning when I went to the lavatory that there would be a stain of some sort that told me there was one coming. But that didn't happen and then I began to feel sick. I kept it hidden from Brent at the weekends and almost breathed a sigh of relief when he phoned to say he had some overtime and couldn't get back.

I don't know how long I thought I could hide it, though I suppose I was hiding it from myself, so really what I mean is how long did it take me to accept the fact that I was probably pregnant? The answer to that was when I had no choice. It was when I had to rush out of the classroom, not just once but for three days running. That's when I was asked if I was pregnant.

My answer was I didn't know.

The Head was quite kind, more concerned that I was on my own than anything else. Because she didn't want to make a call to Byron Bay before she knew if I was pregnant or not, she had someone take me to the doctor. She made sure it was a female one I was to see, she just thought I would be more comfortable being examined by a woman. It didn't take long for the doctor to confirm that I was indeed three months pregnant.

Which meant the Head had to contact my mother and the same day my schooling came to an end: morning sickness in the classroom was just not acceptable. The Head reassured me that I was not being expelled, insisting that I could return to school at a later date.

I think both she and I knew it was not going to happen.

Luckily, my sixteenth birthday had been and gone so I might have been young but not underage. The Head decided to leave that to my mother. She had a pretty good idea who the father was, but I refused to admit it when she asked; she just shrugged when I told her he didn't know that he was about to become a father so I didn't want to talk about it.

So, she wished me good luck – she could hardly have congratulated me – and wished me well as I walked out of the school for the last time.

57

When I said that the first time I met my baby brother Matt, it was love at first sight – it was. But when my daughter was placed in my arms, I felt something far deeper, a wave of such uncontrollable love that tears of joy ran down my cheeks. She was just so beautiful – those tiny pink nails, that soft down covering her head, her eyes fluttering beneath almost translucent lids – there wasn't an inch of her that wasn't perfect.

While I had been waiting for her to enter the world, I had played soft music and talked to her when she was still curled up inside me. I wanted to touch every inch of her, to feel those little feet that my fingers could encircle as they kicked out at me, to see the wrinkles in the black and white scans where she lay all curled up inside me. But here she was in the world now and I just knew that there was nothing I wouldn't do to keep her safe.

Brent managed to arrive later that day – the phone call from Mum that she had made while Ned was carrying everything out to the car and then helping me into it had made him move fast. He had finally got a job locally only a week earlier, but even so, he had persuaded his company to give him a few days off as paternity leave.

I watched as his arms curled round her as he held her to his chest.

'She's ...' and the words failed him.

'... perfect,' I said.

Mum just smiled at us both.

'She is, isn't she?'

*   *   *

Dad and Julie arrived the following day: 'So I'm a grandad now,' said Dad, bending over to give me a hug. To my surprise, they invited me to stay with them until Brent managed to get somewhere for us all to live. I could hardly wait until he and I had a place for ourselves and I so wanted the three of us to be together. There was no hiding the fact that he had looked over the moon when he was holding his tiny daughter. And now he had that job, he was looking a lot more confident as well. Evidently, electricians earned quite good money.

'Not straight away,' he had told me, 'need a few months' experience first, but we'll manage all right.'

And I could see that like me, he could hardly wait for us all to be together in our own place.

'Oh, and of course Brent can come and stay, whenever he's not flat hunting, that is. And I'll put Matt's baby cot in your room. Like I said before, we have all the kit so don't go out shopping for anything yet,' Dad told me.

When I told Mum about Dad's offer she didn't seem concerned or even disappointed that I would take her granddaughter away as soon as we left hospital, which made me wonder what she had hidden up her sleeve. Mum adored Pia and was honoured to be a part of her birth. She tried to support me as much as she could and had a real connection with Pia. She was busy sorting her life out, and went back to Byron Bay after a few weeks.

Julie had brought me what she called a baby sling, so that my tiny baby could rest comfortably on my chest during the journey, while Brent followed us in the car that his mum had helped him buy. She too had turned up at the hospital and told me if I needed any help once we had moved into a flat, all I had to do was call her, which made me feel a little more comfortable – looking after a brand-new baby was more than a little challenging.

'There's a surprise waiting for you when we get home,' Julie told me and smiling away, she refused to elaborate and told me I'd just have to wait and see what it was. But it only took a few seconds, when we reached the house, to discover what it was.

The front door opened as soon as we pulled up and to my utter amazement, Nan and Grandad came out to greet us – I was just about blown away at seeing them.

'Had to come and see my newest great grandchild,' Nan told me when she saw I was just about open-mouthed with amazement. I hadn't seen her for over two years when she had arrived to meet Matt, so I was utterly thrilled.

'When did you get here?' I asked, for I had only been at the hospital for a short time.

'Oh, we came over nearly a week ago, we wanted to be here when you had the baby. Thought it better to meet you here – can't have too many visitors in the maternity ward, can you?'

She shook Brent's hand, congratulating him on being a father – Nan knew all the words to make him feel welcome and part of the family.

It was a day or so later when Brent had disappeared to go and look at a couple of apartments that his mother had shortlisted that Nan told me that Brent and I would be very welcome to stay with her if we ever wished to come to the UK. It was then that I began to notice how frail my grandfather was looking. Distant memories of my childhood came back when he showed me his orchids and taught me the names of birds. In those days he had been so full of life, now the journey had clearly drained him. I wondered then just how many more times they would be able to fly over to Australia – it was such a long journey. Another thought that I tried to push out of my mind came: that we always think that those we love will live forever, but they don't.

It was Grandad's voice that brought me back from the past: 'So many Australians do come over,' he was saying in response to Nan's invitation, 'they like to try and meet up with their relatives, find their roots and see where their great, great grandparents came from. And if you decide to stay, there are good jobs for electricians too.'

I knew then that the invitation was not a casual one – they really wanted us to stay with them and meet up again with the rest of the family I had not seen for so many years. Nan made sure I could see how everyone looked now, passing over photos of my two cousins. She then told Brent a few stories of how we had all played together as children, adding that the family would be so pleased to meet me again and the new members too – 'And we would help with the fares, so you needn't worry about that.'

I was so tempted to say we could go later on in the year but the sensible side of me knew it was too soon. Brent had just begun his new job and had already taken time off, so no long holiday for him. Visiting the UK would just have to wait and was something else to look forward to.

Now I knew why Mum hadn't seemed bothered by my coming to Dad instead of going back to the farm with her. But even so, there had to be another reason why she hadn't tried to get me to go there. Although she hadn't told me anything, I felt that things had once again gone wrong with Ned, which would not be good for either me or the baby.

*   *   *

I stayed with Dad for around ten days – Brent had returned to work after the weekend. I was really grateful to Julie, for she was so good at showing me everything I needed to know about baby care, although I seemed to find it came fairly naturally.

Nan, who could never resist buying things for others, took the baby and me shopping. Julie had given me the cot and pram and lots of baby clothes but Nan had more girlie clothes in mind. But there were enough baby clothes to last Pia until she was walking. She then took us out for tea. Well, Pia slept while I tucked in, although as my daughter's feeding time was almost due, we couldn't indulge in a lengthy break.

It was not long after we returned that Brent phoned to say he had found a flat – 'It's small but cosy,' he told me. It was sparsely furnished and his mum had donated a heap of stuff and he had already bought some extra furniture for it – 'So I'll be able to take you back when I come over at the weekend,' he said with evident excitement in his voice.

Of course I felt excited by the thought of us having our first real home together and I had wanted us to be together for ages, but I still felt a little apprehensive at being on my own with my daughter when Brent was working. I loved the flat as soon as I saw it. To quote Mum, it did need a woman's touch – a few ornaments, the odd picture, some brightly coloured cushions – and as I stood there, the shopping list ran through my mind. To me the best things about it were that it was clean and comfortable and had plenty of cupboard space. Well, I did say I was a bit of a neat freak! The spare bedroom was small, just room for a single bed and a bedside table.

'We'll get a bigger place by the time Pia's walking,' Brent told me, 'but for the moment this room can do for when your mum comes to stay. And I'm sure she'll be up here in the next couple of days.'

* * *

For the first week I felt happy, but it took just a few days for me to feel I had a problem. I was simply exhausted, which I suppose was not unusual as I was having to wake up to feed the baby, but I was young. I began to feel tearful all the time, had little appetite and just wanted to sleep. When we first moved in,

I took Pia out in her pram and we would go for a walk and I'd have a coffee, but now I had to force myself to do that. More for the baby's sake than mine, for the sun gave babies their vitamin D, didn't it?

It took a while before I was diagnosed with postnatal depression. It was when I took Pia to the clinic to be weighed for the first time and burst into tears that I was sat down by a kindly nurse and told to wait for the doctor. It was explained to me that it was not uncommon to feel depressed after having given birth to your first child. I was asked if I was having trouble bonding with my baby, but the way I told him that no, I wasn't and that she was just so precious to me made him smile.

'A lot of this type of depression is caused by tiredness and broken sleep patterns,' he told me, writing out a prescription, 'but if you don't start feeling better soon, then please come back.'

Luckily, I didn't have the type of depression that affects bonding – I had a different one, which made me feel hopeless and suspicious of Brent. I would look at his computer to see if there was any porn on it. That would have made me sick and ended our relationship. If he was late at work, I would phone him in tears, thinking he was seeing someone else. In fact, I could hardly bear letting him out of my sight.

Brent must have got pretty fed up with me and I can hardly blame him. He really couldn't understand what he had done wrong, which was hardly surprising. At least he had the good sense to go to his mother and talk it through with her – that's all it took for her to appear on my doorstep and to talk through everything with me.

'A little therapy would help,' was her advice. 'I think from what you've told me, you've seen your mum with an unfaithful man and it's made you frightened that you're with one too. Now my son understands what type of depression you've got, he will help as much as he can. He loves you, Daisy, and he dotes on Pia, but he's young and there's a limit to how much he can understand. I think a therapist would be the best thing for you and it just so happens I have the phone number of a good one.'

And that was that: she made the call and babysat when I went along to the assessment. I decided there was no point in skipping things and out it all came: my happy English childhood, my brother Tommy, the farm and the porn and Ned's abuse. One session became a weekly one and the therapy helped me a lot. I came to realise that I was one of the lucky ones. Because my early life had been secure, it had given me the strength to put my abuse behind me. I also learnt that some children who have never known a happy childhood suffer the effects of that, sometimes for a lifetime – which made me someone who could be trained to help others who have been abused as a child.

When I asked how, my therapist explained that there were people trained to help others see the future. Therapists were the ones that helped them deal with the past, but a certain type of life coach could help them see how positive their future could be.

She gave me the details of a course I could study at home, and if I worked hard at it, by the time my daughter could go to nursery school, she had no doubt I could begin work. The medication had helped and I studied hard and enthusiastically, learning more about the long-term effects of abuse. By the time my daughter was old enough to go to a nursery school, I was able to begin working part-time at the practice I had attended.

Brent kept asking me to marry him, but I still wanted him to change some of his habits – I just didn't think he was totally committed to being a husband. His single friends were still demanding of his time and he would disappear off for a day's fishing, of all things, leaving me alone in the flat.

58

I felt that Brent and I needed a complete change of lifestyle – I just hadn't worked out what it could be.

I had been right about Mum: she had left Ned and this time was determined to divorce him. He had started drinking and staying out all night again. She stayed with me for a couple of days and then left to go back to Byron Bay – 'Come whenever you want,' she told me, 'I'll always get you and Pia a ticket.'

What I didn't tell her then was about my therapy.

Brent kept suggesting we get married, but it was not something I wanted to do before my own therapy and all my coursework was completed. He also brought up the subject of us going to the UK. He, like many other Australians, wanted to see the country that his grandfathers had been raised in – 'Do a bit of a search and see if I have relatives there.'

Again, that was something I wanted to put off for a while.

'We're young,' he kept saying, 'and it will be a bit of an adventure we can do together.'

Still, I wasn't sure. It wasn't that I didn't want to spend time in England, I just felt it was too soon.

*   *   *

So, what made me eventually decide that I wanted to return? It was Skype. It really must have been the biggest factor for all of a sudden not only could I talk to Nan but to my Uncle David and his sons. Since I had been a child, letters had arrived from England, but by the time I had reached my teens, my life there had become a distant memory. With Skype, it all changed and I was meeting my family all over again. My cousins chattered away to me, as did my uncle and especially Nan.

Once again, she invited Brent and I to visit for as long as we wanted – we could have the flat that had been my Great Gran's, if we so wished. She did say as well that as Brent had British ancestors, he must have family over there in the UK that he had never met and one of the things Australians love is looking up their distant families and seeing where their roots lie. I still had a British passport but he would need to prove his British heritage to get an Ancestral visa to work there.

The other reason that I began to think that going there would be good for us was that we would be away from all Brent's single friends, who thought nothing of knocking on the door in the evening and asking him to join them for a drink. None of them were even dating yet, let alone thinking about marriage and starting a family.

This could be our new start, I was beginning to believe.

Now don't get me wrong, I loved Australia and the thought of cold English winters was something that Mum had constantly moaned about, but our trip was not planned to be forever, just for a while at least...

* * *

I decided then that the next time Brent asked me to marry him, I would say yes. After all, I did love him. He had stuck by me when I was going through all that postnatal depression and really supported me when his mum explained how it affects women; he never got angry about my jealous and unfounded suspicions either. He might have played a bit too hard, but he was diligent at work and had sailed through his probationary period. If I wanted us to feel we were a couple bound for life, then marriage it would have to be.

I talked about the work we had both got qualifications for with David, who Dad had suggested I spoke to. It only took him a week to come back and say there would be no problem. He had spoken to some of his contacts and they had found out that the work I was now qualified for was in high demand. Plus, I could continue studying at the same time and get further levels of qualification. As for Brent, electricians were in demand, so he wouldn't have any problem getting work.

Right, I thought, *we will go.*

Now all I had to do was wait for his next proposal of marriage.

Epilogue

It didn't take Brent very long to once again ask me to marry him – I think he had guessed this time what my answer was going to be. He had arranged for his mum to babysit, telling me it was because he wanted to take me out for dinner. And this time it was not to our usual pizza place – he said he wanted to try somewhere really special.

Then he told me that I should really try to look my best! He had even organised a taxi to take us to where we were going, wherever it was. It was when our cab drove into the sweeping driveway of a luxury hotel set in beautiful grounds that I realised what he had meant. Taking my arm, he led me into the restaurant at the back of the hotel. With its huge windows looking out onto the gardens, it was just about the most glamorous place I had ever been in.

'This would be the perfect place for a wedding, wouldn't it?' he said.

Which told me exactly why he had brought me there.

And yes, it really was a dream place for a wedding – I couldn't have chosen a better place myself.

He then asked me again to marry him and this time I said yes.

The next question was when. My answer was just after Pia turned three, which was only a few months away. I was never one to rush into things – if I was getting married, I wanted everyone there and my wedding day to be as romantic as Mum's had been. Though I had a slightly more conventional dress in mind. Which, with me being so tiny, meant it would have to be made specially for me and that would take a little time. I also wanted my daughter to be able to stroll around: at two she was still unsteady on her feet and then there was still one exam that I needed to take to become a qualified life coach, especially if we were going to the UK.

Brent then asked me if I still wanted to go to the UK and I could see that the idea was even more exciting for him than it was to me.

'We could have our honeymoon there,' I said with a grin.

'What?! Fly for nearly thirty hours on our wedding night?'

'Well, we could spend a night here,' I said, although I had a pretty good idea that was what he had always had in mind.

We agreed on this as a plan and with an immense feeling of happiness almost bursting out of me, we toasted each other with the two glasses of champagne the waiter brought over.

So he knew exactly what Brent had been up to, I thought.

*   *   *

The one thing I decided I had to tell Brent about was Ned. Now that Mum had filed for divorce, neither of us would have any reason to see him. I waited for a couple of days, then told him that I was cooking supper so he'd better not be going out with his mates.

'As if I would,' he said, shooting a cocky grin in my direction.

It was after I had checked that Pia was sound asleep that I said I had something important to tell him. He looked a little worried then, most probably thinking I wanted to postpone the wedding or worse.

'It's about Ned,' I said, a hesitance in my usually confident voice.

But before I could say any more, his hand reached over and took mine: 'I know, Daisy, I heard about the police coming to your door and the reason for it.'

'Why didn't you say anything?'

'Because it was up to you. Must say, it was tough being pleasant to him at the farm. But for you and your mum's sake, I managed. Otherwise I wouldn't have been able to visit you over those months of your pregnancy and that wasn't on.'

That was when I knew with complete certainty that I had made the right decision to marry Brent.

*   *   *

I'm not going to describe every detail of our wedding – I've already told you about Mum's. Just be assured that my dress was gorgeous, a white strapless floor-length creation, my bouquet was pink roses and my bridesmaids wore the palest of green.

Was it as magical as Mum's? Even more so!

And who came? All my family from Byron Bay, Dad and Julie, of course (well, someone had to give me away) and just about all Brent's and my friends. There were speeches, there was Mum and Brent's mother with tears in their eyes and my flower girl of a daughter falling asleep under the table long before the dinner was over. And then there was the party after the sun slid away and all the fairy lights lit up those exquisite gardens while we danced the night away.

Mum took Pia to her room while Brent and I spent the night in the honeymoon suite at the hotel.

'Honeymoon's over for now,' he said over breakfast, which we had in our room.

Being the person I was, I had packed everything we needed to take with us before the wedding. Dad had given us a very generous cheque as a wedding present – 'I want you to enjoy the UK,' he told me.

We had decided between us not to prolong leaving. Enough goodbyes had been said at the wedding, Brent's friends looked more than a little upset.

When we see you next, you will all be married with kids, I thought, *and like Dad, once you settle down, then you won't be thinking of going on pub crawls with your mates.*

So instead of staying for goodness knows how many farewell parties, we had booked the flights for the day after we returned to the flat. A friend of Brent's was taking it over, as he wanted to set up home because he too was now settling down with his pregnant wife-to-be.

Brent had arranged for one of his friends who had a truck big enough for all our luggage and a pushchair to take us to the airport. Mum, Dad, Julie and Brent's mum arrived at the airport to wave us off.

There were hugs, there were good wishes and quite a few tears.

There were promises of us looking after each other and managing to make regular Skype calls despite the time differences.

And then we walked through the barrier, turned once for our last wave and headed for the huge plane that was taking us to where we would begin our new life.

Acknowledgements

The life of a writer is quite an isolated one and when writing the story of a survivor of sexual abuse, it generates a very special relationship between you both. To Daisy, thank you for trusting me with your story and giving me so much of yourself. Your notes were invaluable. I know it is painful to examine the details of your experiences and I hope I did your story justice.

To Caroline Bagley, my Cape Town friend, who read every draft section and corrected my grammar and my spelling. (So dog's bowels became bowls, plus a few other dire examples.) But, more importantly, debates with Caroline over what may need cutting or expanding, which went well into the late evenings over many late nights. Thank goodness for WhatsApp and some Cape Town wine. A couple of glasses helped oil the creative flow!

To my agent, Barbara Levy, who for twenty years has given me advice and guidance.

To Jane, my great copy-editor who challenges me and inundates me with questions as she finetunes my final edit.

And, finally, my immense thanks to Beth of Bonnier Books

UK. In all my years of writing, no editor has motivated me onwards and upwards like you have. Encouraging me every step of the way, and I think helping me become a better writer. You have a vision of this genre that mirrors mine; we need to appreciate the thoughts and consequence on the victim and the perpetrator. I look forward to working with you again and again.

Toni Maguire, January 2022